ROMANCING
THE EAST

JERRY HOPKINS

ROMANCING THE EAST

A Literary Odyssey From the Heart of Darkness to the River Kwai

TUTTLE Publishing

Tokyo | Rutland, Vermont | Singapore

Published by Tuttle Publishing, an imprint of Periplus Editions (HK) Ltd.

www.tuttlepublishing.com

Copyright © 2013 Jerry Hopkins

Library of Congress Cataloging-in-Publication Data
Application in process

ISBN 978-0-8048-4320-1

Distributed by

North America, Latin America & Europe
Tuttle Publishing
364 Innovation Drive, North Clarendon,
VT 05759-9436, USA
Tel: 1 (802) 773 8930
Fax: 1 (802) 773 6993
info@tuttlepublishing.com
www.tuttlepublishing.com

Japan
Tuttle Publishing
Yaekari Building 3rd Floor
5-4-12 Osaki, Shinagawa-ku
Tokyo 1410032, Japan
Tel: (81) 3 5437 0171
Fax: (81) 3 5437 0755
sales@tuttle.co.jp
www.tuttle.co.jp

Asia Pacific
Berkeley Books Pte Ltd
61 Tai Seng Avenue #02-12
Singapore 534167
Tel: (65) 6280 1330
Fax: (65) 6280 6290
inquiries@periplus.com.sg
www.periplus.com

Indonesia
PT Java Books Indonesia
Jl. Rawa Gelam IV No. 9
Kawasan Industri Pulogadung
Jakarta 13930, Indonesia
Tel: 62 (21) 4682 1088
Fax: 62 (21) 461 0206
crm@periplus.co.id
www.periplus.com

First edition
16 15 14 13   5 4 3 2 1   1212MP

Printed in Singapore

Contents

Introduction

Asia. The Far East. The Orient.

Nowhere else do the words "exotic" and "erotic" and "illicit" and "mysterious" and "dangerous" all so comfortably and uncomfortably fit, simultaneously. From the time of Marco Polo's fifteenth century trek from Italy across the empire of the dreaded Kublai Kahn—the epic journey itself called a hoax by some today—no other place on earth, not even the languorous South Pacific or deepest, darkest Africa, has so challenged and enchanted the Western mind.

And still it is today. However soaked in blood its recent history, and disturbing the ongoing human rights abuse, no matter how unsettling the social and cultural homogenization, despite the demand of disease and poverty, Asia has never lost its itchy irresistibleness, staying deeply rooted in the outsider's dreams as a sometimes scary but always enticing fantasy.

As large sailing ships supplanted camel caravans, Western dreams of pleasure and profit blossomed in these exotic lands as fast as the trading companies and navies could negotiate concessions or, using gunboat diplomacy, plant flags and expand empires, whether the locals liked it or not.

For more than a hundred years, Asia was where Western imperialists introduced breakfast baguettes and wedding cake architecture, cricket, railroads, bureaucracy, and Jesus Christ. In exchange, they levied taxes and filled their ships' holds with silk, china, spices, rubber, tin, gems, and other goods, while helping themselves to the "coolie" labor to grow, mine, and process this found largesse, providing opium aimed at enslaving China, and enjoying the lugubrious native female companionship at every plantation, remote posting, and port.

Whatever the big, pale round-eye desired, in Asia it was available and affordable, and in the early days, it was there for the taking. But then came radical change.

In the three decades following World War Two, Japanese sovereignty was restored, South and Southeast Asian nations reclaimed and redefined independence, communist forces gained control of China and the former Indochine, and Korea was divided into two parts. Led by the reconstructed Japan, Asia mounted a counterattack upon the long-unquestioned economic domination of the West, creating a reversal that by the end of the century appeared to be unstoppable.

Not long after Sony conquered the electronic world and curry became the UK's favorite fast food, manga and hentai went international, Macau surpassed Las Vegas in gambling, Toyota took Ford's number two position in US automotive sales, and seers said the travel industry was next, predicting that by 2020 visitors to China alone would leave all European and American destinations behind. China and Japan also gained control of a fearsome percentage of all US government bonds and manufactured and exported so many cheap retail goods a book was written about an American family's impossible struggle to go a year without buying anything "Made in China."

Today, in too much of Asia, political instability, brutal dictatorship, and racial and civil violence are entering their second half-century. Muslims and non-Muslims continue to take lives in India, Thailand, and the Philippines; a military junta kept Burma (Myanmar) under its oppressive thumb; Communist dictatorships are still easily angered in China, Laos, Cambodia, and Vietnam; and corruption is as open across the entire region as it is overlooked.

At the same time, it is no longer necessary to set aside days or weeks for journeys on ocean steamers, trans-continental railways and the China Clipper, now there are jumbo jets and five-star hotels even in once remote locales. Culturally, American movies and TV are still on top, rock and roll is here to stay, McDonalds is everywhere except North Korea and Bhutan, and there are more than seven thousand 7-Elevens in Thailand.

Both despite and because of all this, Asia arguably remains unchallenged as the world's number one destination for adventure and romance. And we have Marco Polo and a shelf of other western authors to thank for much of that. Joseph Conrad, Lafcadio Hearn, Somerset Maugham, E.M. Forster, Pearl Buck, James Hilton, Graham Greene, Anthony Burgess, and George Orwell are among the names who led the way. Followed by a more recent group, some known primarily for a single book—Richard Mason for *The World of Suzie Wong*, William Lederer and Eugene Burdick for *The Ugly American*, Pierre Boulle for *Bridge Over the River Kwai*, Dominique LaPierre for *City of Joy*, Alex Garland for *The Beach*, and Arthur Golden for *Memoirs of a Geisha* among them—along with James Clavell, hailed for his mega-bestsellers, *Tai-Pan, Shogun, Gai-Jin,* and *Noble House.* Some of the authors were appalled or repulsed by what they found and described. All were enchanted, falling under Asia's spell. As you and I, in turn, fell under theirs.

So popular has Asia been as an inspiration for novelists, one database, *steamyeast.com*, lists more than five thousand titles written in English, either set somewhere in greater Asia or involving something "putatively 'Asian' elsewhere on earth or beyond." (Quoting the webpage's somewhat hyperbolic text.) One student of Asian studies called this list "a good start."

Only a hundred or so titles are considered here, some of them only in passing, with my attention directed to the most influential at the time of their greatest popularity—a factor affected variously by the movies, stage dramas and television shows based on them. Clavell's novels were enormous bestsellers, for example, and the television adaptations made them even more popular, as did the Broadway and Hollywood versions of *The World of Suzie Wong* and *The King and I*. Other literary characters to spread wings in the cinema and on television included the evil Dr. Fu Manchu and his opposite, the affable Charlie Chan.

However different the writers and the subjects and places of their work, it came together. Like what happened when blind men examined an elephant and described its various parts, these authors visited or lived in Asia in far different ways and places over a period of a hundred and fifty years, yet their divergent dispatches and stories joined like the parts of an outsized pachyderm, forming a fantastic "one," a weird and wooly place with scary tusks and a tough skin but knowing eyes, a good place for adventure and romance.

This is not the first time the landscapes of an author's work have been used as a window through which to view both the writer and his time and place. Gavin Young, a former war correspondent and one of the finest travel writers of the twentieth century, tracked Joseph Conrad in a superbly crafted and romantically evocative book in 1991, *In Search of Conrad*. Also, Emma Larkin, another English journalist, in 2008 followed in George Orwell's footsteps in Burma, saying in her *Finding George Orwell in Burma* that *Burmese Days* was not the only one of her subject's novels that suited modern Myanmar; so too did *Animal Farm* and *1984*.

More have looked at Hemingway's Africa (and Cuba), Steinbeck's Monterrey, Dashiell Hammet's San Francisco and Raymond Chandler's Los Angeles; the Dublin of Dylan Thomas, Synge, O'Casey, Joyce, and Yeats. Others have been attracted to history's first novelist, Homer, who recorded in *The Odyssey* an earlier siren's call. While an Australian historian, Gavan Daws, examined the lure of Polynesia through the eyes of five nineteenth century figures—Herman Melville and Robert Louis Stevenson among them—calling his book *A Dream of Islands*. Literary geography is not new.

In the pages that follow, I, too, search for what Henry James called the "visitable past," looking at the effect popular novelists have had on an Asia they both damned and praised, but also on the rest of the world's perception of that largest of continents. While searching for whatever might be left of the original literary landmarks where (quoting Paul Theroux now) "imagination and landscape combine to become art."

I drink in the same bars as Maugham did nearly a hundred years ago and visit Conrad's ports of call, the battlefields of Graham Greene's *The Quiet American*, the colonial police postings of Orwell in Burma, the palaces of Anna and "her" King of Siam. I hike the hill country of Shimla in India where Kipling wrote his first stories, seek some lingering scent of Suzie Wong in Hong Kong's Wan Chai district and of the ladyboys in Saint Jack's Bugis Street in Singapore, eat banana pancakes and smoke dope in the backpacker meccas of Thailand in *The Beach*, and encounter a government policy in Bhutan (one of the places favored in the identification of the mythical Shangri-La) that has replaced its GNP with the GNH, the "H" standing for "Happiness."

Thirty years ago, when he began his search for Conrad, upon arriving in Singapore, Gavin Young looked at the skyscrapers and asked, "Have I come ghost-hunting too late?" I had to wonder the same as I began the trek I recount on the following pages. We both learned that the answer was no.

Joseph Conrad

The Myth of the Great White Rajah

Joseph Conrad was one of the twentieth century's great artists and puzzles, a man who said he detested the sea yet spent sixteen years sailing it, then became one of its greatest literary champions, an author who questioned the political and moral worth of writing and today is praised for inventing a new kind of "modernist" novel, in which adventure and intrigue were raised to the level of ethical parable. All this, in what was not even his second language but his third, after Polish and French.

He also was a romantic and an adventurer, well suited for a time when European empires were at their peak and exploration of the remotest places on earth stimulated the late-Victorian reader's appetite for the exotic (already fostered by Kipling and Stevenson). Although his journeys took him to the Caribbean, South America and Africa, and included gun-running off the coast of Spain, it was Asia he put on the world map, introducing in vivid detail much of Southeast Asia in such novels as *Almayer's Folly*, *An Outcast of the Islands*, *Victory*, and *Lord Jim*, as well as in numerous short stories. Even his masterpiece, *Heart of Darkness*, which told of the horror witnessed as captain of a steamboat on the Congo River, is now identified with Asia, thanks to

Francis Ford Coppola's cinematic retelling of the story set in Vietnam, *Apocalypse Now*.

Born Jozef Teodor Konrad Nalecz Korzeniowski in the land-locked Polish Ukraine, he was orphaned at eleven, raised by an uncle in Poland, and went to sea from Marseilles when he was just seventeen. Shifting from the French to the British merchant navy four years later, he acquired both a Master Mariner's certificate and British citizenship, officially changing his name to Joseph Conrad in 1886.

It wasn't until he retired from the sea at thirty-seven, in 1893, that he began to write in earnest and while his early novels are now regarded as classics, twenty years passed before the publication of *Chance*, a lesser work, brought popular and financial success.

He was born December 3, 1857, in Berdychiv, and died August 3, 1924 in Bishopsbourne, England, of a heart attack, survived by his widow and two sons. He is buried at Canterbury, his epitaph from Edmund Spenser's *The Faerie Queen*: "Sleep After Toyle, Port after Stormie Seas, Ease After Warre, Death After Life Does Greatly Please."

Master, Mariner

"And this is how I see the East. I have seen its secret places and have looked into its very soul; but now I see it always from a small boat, a high outline of mountains, blue and afar in the morning; like faint mist at noon; a jagged wall of purple at sunset. I have the feel of the oar in my hand, the vision of a scorching blue sea in my eyes. And I see a bay, a wide bay, smooth as glass and polished like ice, shimmering in the dark. A red light burns far off upon the gloom of the land, and the night is soft and warm. We drag at the oars with aching arms, and suddenly a puff of wind, a puff faint and tepid and laden with strange odors of blossoms, of aromatic wood, comes out of the still night—the first sigh of the East on my face. That I can never forget. It was impalpable and enslaving, like a charm, like a whispered promise of mysterious delight."

Thus, Joseph Conrad—Second Mate Jozef Korzeniowski, called "Polish Joe" by his shipmates—made his first Asian landfall in 1883, rowing ashore after his ship caught fire, blew up, and sank in Indonesia's Sunda Strait, approaching Java Head.

It was not, as they say in the East, an auspicious beginning, nor was it so discouraging that Conrad, twenty-six years of age, didn't soon come to regard the region as a kind of home away from home. For another ten years, including several voyages in these waters as a captain, he sailed to Borneo and the Celebes in the Indonesian archipelago, along the Malayan coastline through the Gulf of Siam from Singapore to Bangkok. Such exotic destinations would appear in his novels and short fiction and in the hundred years since they were written they in turn would act as the lure and promise that drew generations of visitors after him.

It was a message and a pledge that appeared repeatedly in Conrad's works—the flowery promise above from a barely fictionalized account of the sinking of the S.S. *Palestine* on Conrad's first voyage as a sailor in the British Merchant Navy, written in 1898 and simply titled *Youth*.

Similarly, the narrator in one of the Conrad's best and most acclaimed longer works, *Lord Jim*, said of the man for whom the book was named, "He...had the faculty of beholding at a hint the face of his desire and the shape of his dream, without which the earth would know no lover and no adventurer. He captured much honor and an Arcadian happiness (I won't say anything about innocence) in the bush, and it was as good to him as the humor and the Arcadian happiness of the streets to another man. Felicity, felicity—how shall I say it?—is quaffed out of a golden cup in every latitude: the flavor is with you—with you alone, and you can make it as intoxicating as you please."

Jim (he had no surname) was first mate aboard a ship carrying a cargo of some eight hundred religious pilgrims when it collided with an unseen obstacle while crossing the Arabian Sea. He panicked and fled in the only lowered lifeboat with his fellow officers, abandoning the ship and its passengers, believing the vessel went down. It did not and when a French frigate rescued everyone, Jim was taken before a court of inquiry and stripped of his maritime certificate for his dereliction of duty. The rest of the novel told of his long flight to escape his perceived cowardice, eventually taking him into self-enforced exile as a white trader in a remote tropical outpost called Patusan—in reality, the Celebes, a part of Indonesia's famed "Spice Islands." There, he at last found redemption and happiness—not to mention a lovely maiden to bear his child—as the revered leader of a primitive Bugis and Malay settlement, finally shot through the chest by an angry chief.

Fact begat fiction again. Both the abandonment of a shipload of Muslim passengers bound for Mecca in a ship crewed by British sailors and Jim existed in real life. In 1880, the S.S. *Jeddah*, with nearly one thousand aboard, began to sink, its crew fled, and a French ship sailed to the rescue. As for Jim, it's believed that he was inspired by the *Jeddah's* first mate, Augustine Podmore Williams, whose background (a blue-eyed English parson's son, etc.) matched Jim's in the book's first half, and in the second by the more famous James Brooke, an Indian-born British adventurer who in the 1840s became known as the first White Rajah of Sarawak after setting up an independent state on the island of Borneo.

Conrad never admitted to either source, but the premise stands: such adventure and romance were not the fruit of fantasy, but rooted in reality. Hammering the point home, the narrator in *Lord Jim* recalled the early Dutch and English traders who came to the Spice Islands, seeking wealth: "To us, their less tried successors, they appear magnified, not as agents of trade but as instruments of a recorded destiny, pushing out into the unknown in obedience to an inward voice, to an impulse beating in the blood, to a dream of the future."

Conrad himself came to Asia by a most circuitous and unusual route, but on reflection all the pieces of the puzzle fit. His love of literature and adventure he inherited from his father, a revolutionary (seeking Poland's independence from Russia), a poet and dramatist who translated Shakespeare from English and Victor Hugo from French, reading such authors aloud with his son. By 1867, when the boy was eleven, illness had taken both parents and thereafter a maternal uncle cared for him who, reluctantly, permitted him at age seventeen to join the French merchant navy in Marseilles. Three years later, Polish Joe shifted to the British merchant navy and on his first vessel sailed for Asia with a cargo of coal that would soon self-combust and destroy the ship.

As the years passed and Conrad rose from Second to First Mate and in 1886 won his Master Mariner's certificate—and six months later his British citizenship—he became fluent in English, the language he chose for writing when he began his first novel, *Almayer's Folly*, in 1889. He claimed he had been *thinking* in English for many years, but this should not slight the achievement the novel represented. At that time, his choice of an alien tongue was possibly without precedent. Later, Vladimir Nabokov, Arthur Koestler, Isak Dinesen, Samuel Beckett, and Eugene Ionesco won similar literary distinction, but Conrad wrote in the "King's English" without benefit of any formal education. Edward Garnett, one of his editors, later said, "When he read aloud to me some new written manuscript pages of *An Outcast of the Islands* he mispronounced so many words that I followed him with difficulty. I found then that he had never once heard these English words spoken, but had learned them all from books." (He bought a set of Byron during his leave in Singapore following that fateful initial voyage to Asia and a "thick green-covered volume" of Shakespeare with his earnings.)

If his vocabulary came from his reading, his stories and, most vividly, his characters—as in *Lord Jim* and "Youth"—regularly were drawn from life. One of the most important of these was a somewhat seedy Eurasian trader on the Berau River in Borneo, William Charles Olmeijer, a trader in rubber and rattan whose surname Conrad probably never saw in print so naturally spelled Almayer, as it sounded. Conrad later wrote, "If I had not got to know Almayer pretty well it is almost certain there would not have been a line of mine in print." An exaggeration, surely, but it demonstrated the writer's dependence on life models and his frequent willingness to admit it. Conrad also surely heard heroic tales of a famous captain and trader named William Lingard who (as Tom Lingard) appeared as a major character in *Almayer's Folly, An Outcast of the Islands* and *The Rescue*. He may have kept Jim's inspiration cloaked, but, in fact, for many of his characters, Conrad didn't even bother to misspell their names.

This is not to say he was a journalist. A novelist obviously doesn't get recognized as one of the greatest writers in contemporary English (and offered a knighthood that he graciously turned down) by telling no more than who, what, where, when, and how. Conrad was such a skilled and unique craftsman that T.E. Lawrence called him "absolutely the most haunting thing in prose that ever was" and Graham Greene wrote of having to stop reading Conrad for fear of becoming completely enslaved to his style.

H.G. Wells, reviewing *An Outcast of the Islands* (1896), called Conrad "wordy," but more generally praised the novel unreservedly, as did virtually everyone else. (Wells reviewed the book anonymously and Conrad discovered his identity when sending a note of thanks; they became fast friends.) High praise followed for *The Nigger of the Narcissus* (1897), "Heart of Darkness" (1899), *Lord Jim* (1900) and others, taking him to the crest of critical acclaim.

Conrad also was, in his uncle's words, "lucky with people" and once he left the sea and became a literary landlubber, he drew other famous writers to his company as if gathering some of the finest writers of his time for a group photograph. Besides Wells ("to whom I tell all my troubles"), close friends included John Galsworthy, Ford Maddox Ford (a literary collaborator to whom he confessed that he came to detest the sea), André Gide, Norman Douglas, the young Stephen Crane and the giant he called "the old man," Henry James.

Nonetheless, success came to Conrad slowly. It wasn't until 1912 when he published *Chance*, a story that appealed to women and offered one of Conrad's rare happy endings, that, at the age of fifty-five, Conrad finally had a bestseller and he could stop flogging his original manuscripts to collectors to pay the bills.

It was not difficult to understand why. Conrad may have provided his readers with the thrill of a boy's adventure story, but it came wrapped in questioning prose as opaque as the ocean mist to which it was so often compared. His were tales of moral and emotional ambiguities that made the reader work. There were shipwrecks and headhunting Dyaks and tribal wars and pirates and typhoons. No fewer than nine of Conrad's leading or important characters killed themselves (reflecting his own failed suicide attempt at twenty after making a financial and romantic shambles of his young life) and when they didn't top themselves there seemed always someone ready to do the job for them. Yet all that action didn't come without a price: a "choice of nightmares" to be sorted and, always, human psychology to comprehend. In *The Nigger of the Narcissus*, Conrad wrote, "My task which I am trying to achieve is, by the power of the written word to make you hear, to make you feel—it is, before all, to make you see."

As positive as he was about the exotic pleasure and promise of the East, at bottom he was a pessimist. The human race was a disappointment to Conrad: "The intellectual stage of mankind being as yet in its infancy, and States, like most individuals, having but a feeble and imperfect consciousness of the worth and force of the inner life, the need of making their existence manifest to themselves is determined in the direction of physical activity. The idea of ceasing to grow in territory, in strength, in wealth, in influence—in anything but wisdom and self-knowledge is odious to them as the omen of the end. Action, in which is to be found the illusion of a mastered destiny, can alone satisfy our uneasy vanity and lay to rest the haunting fear of the future—a sentiment concealed, indeed, but proving its existence by the force it has, when invoked to stir the passions of a nation. It will be long before we have learned that in the great darkness before us there is nothing that we need fear."

However gloomy his prognosis, it is for the sea tales—and that awful African river journey into the "heart of darkness"—in which Conrad first diagnosed our ills that he forever will be remembered and read. And however much he gave his readers to think about, he also forever will be Asia's drummer boy, leading an army drawn by his ripe and hearty introduction to the equatorial latitudes in prose that rolled with the hypnotic rhythms that he surely learned from the sea.

Besides, it was still possible to be a sort of White Rajah in these climes, was it not? If not in darkest Borneo, then perhaps in a destination somewhat more accessible.

"To Bangkok!" Conrad's young hero cried out in "Youth." "Magic name, blessed name. Mesopotamia wasn't a patch on it. Remember I was twenty," the youth, now not so young any more, told his drinking partners in fond remembrance, "and it was my first second mate's billet, and the East was waiting for me."

This certainly won't match everyone's notion about what a White Rajah should be, but for the twenty-first century it may satisfy quite a few.

When the British war correspondent and travel writer Gavin Young set forth *In Search of Conrad* (the title of his 1991 book) and arrived in Singapore, he wondered how much of Henry James's "visitable past" remained. As he tracked the earlier writer's voyages and sought traces and descendants of Conrad's real life characters, he discovered a surprising number, especially in eastern Borneo, described by Conrad as one of the "lost, forgotten, unknown places of the earth." (Called Sambir in *Almayer's Folly* and *The Outcast of the Islands*, Patusan in *Lord Jim*, and Batu Batu in "The End of the Tether.") No better guide than Young's exists for today's traveler. An earlier, more scholarly guide is Norman Sherry's *Conrad's Eastern World* (for which there is a Western complement).

For those who enjoy sleeping with literary ghosts—Gavin Young and Graham Greene were among them—hotels across Southeast Asia claim Conrad as a former guest, the Raffles in Singapore and the Mandarin Oriental in Bangkok among them. Although Conrad never actually slept at either one, he is reputed to have had a drink in what is now the Oriental's Authors' Lounge, above which there is a suite named for him and nearby a roughly ship-shaped restaurant called Lord Jim. Of course today's prices would make old Polish Joe blanch.

Anna Leonowens
And the King of Siam

It was on Broadway's musical stage and in Hollywood film that Anna Leonowens became famous—in forms of dramatic expression that didn't even exist during her lifetime—and it was her vivid imagination, expressed both in her memoirs and in her own highly fictionalized autobiography, that made her, at least among historians, somewhat infamous.

When her two volumes of memoirs, *The English Governess at the Court of Siam* and *Romance of the Harem*, were published in the United States and Great Britain 1870 and 1873, the exotic stories told were accepted as true accounts of her years as a "governess" and teacher in the court of Siam's revered King Mongkut. In fact, she was employed only to teach "English language, science, and literature" to some of the monarch's numerous children and as later investigation revealed, not only was she not a "governess" or anything approaching an influential confidante to the king, much of what she wrote was judged to be untruth and distortion so serious that even today, all dramatic forms of her story are banned in what is now called Thailand as being defaming to the monarchy.

Anna Edwards was born in India in 1831, three months after the death of her father, an enlisted man in the Bombay infantry (she claimed a later birth in Wales, identifying her father as an army captain killed when she was six), and while still a teenager married Thomas Leon Owens, a clerk (she said army captain). He died of apoplexy in Penang, Malaya (she said sunstroke while on a tiger hunt), leaving her a penniless mother of two, with whom she moved to Singapore where she operated a small school for officers' children, soon to be hired by King Mongkut, in 1862.

After leaving Thailand, she spent several years in America, where she wrote her books, eventually settling in Canada, becoming known as a suffragette and a founder of the Nova Scotia College of Art and Design. She died in Montreal in 1915 at eighty-three.

Although her Siamese memoirs established her as the personification of the eccentric Victorian female traveler, she was well forgotten by 1944 when Margaret Landon wrote a novel based on them, *Anna and the King of Siam*. This bestseller was then adapted for the stage, film, and television as *The King and I*, and with each reworking strayed further from reality, simultaneously reinventing both Anna and Siam and its king, building higher the Asian romantic myth.

The King and Who?

In a sense, Anna Leonowens was the Victorian era's version of a "gonzo" journalist, a predecessor to Hunter Thompson, a writer with imagination and bravado who didn't let the facts get in the way of a good story. Were she born a century later, Anna might have called her memoirs *Fear and Loathing in the Court of Old Siam* for they carried all the requisite ingredients for an exotic literary feast.

For nearly six years (from 1862-1867) she served as a teacher in the fantastic palaces of King Mongkut, absolute monarch of what was then called Siam (now Thailand), a man who had spent twenty-six years as a chaste Buddhist monk before shedding his saffron robes to take twenty-seven wives, by whom he had eighty-one children, the largest number by any in his dynasty. In addition, he had a "harem" of hundreds of concubines.

In many ways, Mongkut, also known as Rama IV, the fourth monarch in the Chakri dynasty, was a progressive. As a monk, he had traveled freely around the country, observing how life was conducted at the simplest and poorest levels. As an abbot in a prominent Bangkok temple, he discouraged the Brahmanist practices and animist spirit worship that had been embraced by Buddhism and accepted the notion that people were not enslaved by fate. He cultivated relationships with western missionaries, who coached him in English and other western languages and introduced him to western science and technology (steam power was just then gaining favor in the west).

When he became king, he issued rulings affecting even the simplest acts, as when he discouraged "the inelegant practice of throwing dead animals into the waterways." Most significant, Mongkut in 1855 signed a diplomatic and commercial treaty with England's John Bowring that opened the country's doors to foreign trade so widely the effect was to reverse the self-sufficient nature of the economy forever. In addition, one of his most valued confidants was an American physician, Dan Beach Bradley, who suffered no recriminations for his open criticism of the king's polygamy, something that might have earned others deportation if they were lucky, more likely imprisonment or death for *lése majesté*, a draconian policy that in the twenty-first century still sent offenders to prison for little more than imagined affronts.

Yet, Mongkut also condoned slavery and extended the rights of upper-class men to treat women as legal property. He did nothing to change the custom of prostration, which meant any inferior—virtually everyone in the kingdom—had to fall to his or her knees and crawl in the presence of royalty. The palace also still held monopolies in gambling and the trade of alcohol and opium. Add the dazzling palaces and temples, elaborate rituals (both religious and royal), frequent public pageantry, and such regal quirks as the collection and care of "white elephants."

In such a setting, the reserved English schoolmarm—someone who was secretly taking notes—surely must have experienced something approaching ecstatic delight. And if in her enthusiasm, she fudged some of the facts and enhanced others, who could be surprised? Shouldn't she also be forgiven for making the sort of mistakes any outsider might when immersed in such an unfamiliar cultural environment?

It was in her outright fiction that offense was found. When she said the king sent troublesome wives into underground dungeons, not only was there no basis in fact—he even permitted those who wished to leave his court to do so without consequence, and twelve did—in swampy Bangkok, much of it below sea level, until the invention of steel rebar and cement much later, such subterranean constructions were impossible. She also claimed to have witnessed the royally ordered public torture and burning of a consort and her lover, a Buddhist monk, a fabrication. Finally, she called the king a "barbarian."

No wonder she still causes palace blood to boil.

Whatever the truth or untruth, Anna and her fanciful memoirs were largely forgotten when an American novelist named Margaret Landon, a former missionary, rediscovered them and further fictionalized the story of the civilizing "governess" and her untamed king, publishing in 1944 the bestselling *Anna and the King of Siam*. The *Atlantic Monthly* critic was "enchanted," saying, "the author wears her scholarship with grace." (The grace may have been present, but certainly not the scholarship.) In the years that followed, Landon's work was adapted again and again, for the stage, film and television, with the characters played by such a heady variety of personalities as to leave the reality of the Siamese court deep in the historical dust.

The very English Rex Harrison played the first cinematic Mongkut in a film based on Landon's book, opposite Irene Dunne in 1946. This was a dramatic adaptation that made a further travesty of facts, with Anna's son Louis dying and the king giving him a royal funeral (not true; he lived a long, fruitful life and a trading company he founded in Bangkok continues under his name today) and Anna being called back to Siam to the king's bedside as he lay dying (in fact, he died of malaria a year after she left Thailand).

It was Anna's next incarnation that gave her story legendary status, when in 1950 Gertrude Lawrence's business manager and attorney was given a copy of Landon's book. He, in turn, suggested a musical adaptation, despite his client's limited vocal skills. Richard Rodgers and Oscar Hammerstein II, already much acclaimed for Broadway's *Oklahoma!*, *Carousel*, and *South Pacific*, were signed to do the music and when Harrison was unavailable, a young actor named Yul Brynner was auditioned for what would be the defining role of his career.

From this point onward, the written word—the source—lost ground in terms of impact to that achieved on the stage and film. By the middle of the twentieth century, stage plays and movies already had been adapted from the works of Joseph Conrad, Somerset Maugham, James Hilton, Rudyard Kipling, and Pearl Buck, among others. But from the time of *The King and I* that balance of influence shifted. Readers of novels about Asia would still point the way, their authors continuing to provide the siren's call, but now it would be "readers" in New York and Hollywood seeking new "properties" for theatrical and cinematic adaptation who with a dazzling cast of actors and actresses would wave the banner most effectively. Where book readers might number in the hundreds of thousands, millions lined up at the box office for *The World of Suzie Wong, Love Is a Many-Splendored Thing, Sayonara*, and *Tai-Pan*.

In *The King and I*'s somewhat flimsy and, really, rather silly plot, Mongkut promised Anna a house outside the palace compound and failed to deliver, so many of the lessons she devised were concerned with longing for a home. The king was nonetheless pleased by her performance in the classroom, even when she showed her students on a world map how small Siam was compared to the rest of the world. There ensued a gentle battle of the wits between the two over her status as a servant or advisor to the king. He asked her to "guess" what he will do when rumors reach Queen Victoria in England that he was a barbarian, allowing her to suggest he entertain the British expatriate community at a banquet.

Meanwhile, Mongkut received a "gift" from the king of Burma, a woman named Tuptim, delivered by a young man called Tum Tha, who had fallen in love with his young charge. She was matter-of-factly dispatched to Mongkut's harem, where she composed a play to be performed at the forthcoming banquet, inspired by the American Civil War era novel *Uncle Tom's Cabin*. The anti-slavery message in a time when slavery was practiced in Siam, was absurd, but the performance was incredulously well received and the king was toasted by his guests.

Now the king had two rebellious women in his court and he was not pleased, having Tuptim brought to him for a whipping. Anna urged him to cool his anger. The king gave in, stalking off the stage. Not long afterwards, when he fell ill and was dying and Anna (once again, fictitiously) was called to his side, she was given a letter in which he expressed his thanks for all she had done. On his deathbed, the king asked his young son and heir, who was one of Anna's prized pupils, what he would do first upon ascending the throne and he said he would abolish the traditional prostration before royalty, an idea ostensibly originating in Anna's classroom.

However preposterous nearly every scene of it was, the show was a great success, thanks to the music—there were several standout songs including "Getting to Know You" and "Hello,

Young Lovers" but nothing that resembled in any way the indig-
enous music of Siam—and, perhaps most important, the colorful costuming and lavish pageantry. There were no elephants, but
the production lacked little else. Brynner's bare-chested, shaven-
headed good looks and imperious manner coupled with an innocence that had him in one scene dictating a letter to Anna to
be sent to President Buchanan in the US, didn't hurt, either.

The musical, which opened in 1951 on Broadway and ran for
nearly four years, was called by Brooks Atkinson in the *New York
Times* "an original and beautiful excursion into the rich splendors
of the Far East."[1] Broadway musicals formed a popular genre at the
time and the soundtrack recording also was an enormous hit and
the inevitable Hollywood film, with Deborah Kerr replacing Lawrence, was nominated for nine Academy Awards and won five,
including best actor for Brynner. The movie also won a Golden
Globe for "Best Film Promoting International Understanding."

In one scene, the British ambassador asked Mongkut, "How
many children do you have?" He replied, "Oh, I have only one-
hundred and six. I am not married very long." The ambassador
looked dumbfounded and the monarch added, "Next month ex-
pecting five more." One cannot help wondering what might have
been "understood" by this.

At least it made people aware of a place called Siam, which by
then of course was called Thailand, so could not be found on any
map. Nor could any scholar find anything approximating historical value in the fictitious influence and implied romance
between the two major characters.

Over the decades that followed, there were numerous reviv-
als from Los Angeles to New York to London's West End, with

---

1. It was during the run-up to the Broadway production when a young American
businessman who lived in Bangkok, Jim Thompson, first took silk to New York, showing it to the editor of *Vogue*, who featured it in her magazine. Thompson subsequently
met the play's costume designer and when *The King and I* opened, its cast was clothed
in Jim Thompson silk, perhaps the production's most authentic touch.)

Brynner eventually portraying the king over four thousand times. (Saying that he thought he was too young when he originated the role, but felt more comfortable as he aged; Mongkut was, at the time of Anna's arrival in Siam, fifty-eight.) For other productions, Mongkut was played by Herbert Lom, Ben Kingsley, Theodore Bikel, Farley Granger, Jason Scott Lee, and Lou Diamond Phillips, while the feisty schoolmarm's role went to Angela Lansbury and Julie Andrews, among many more.

The King and I was also adapted as an animated film—in which the King of Siam took a hot air balloon ride in search of his runaway son and hung from the balloon by a rope—and became a short-lived television series in the United States in which Samantha Eggar played Anna who with her son Louis now were transformed into Americans.

It has been more than a century since Anna Leonowens's books first appeared and it is reasonable to surmise that little of what she saw and experienced could possibly be left in today's modern Thailand. Yet, because most of the action in her memoirs occurred inside the walls of the Grand Palace, which has been preserved, and because the mile-square royal compound is Thailand's No. 1 tourist attraction, thousands of visitors walk in her footsteps every day.

Nearly two-thirds of the area is not open to the public, however, and few outsiders have been allowed a look. An exception was William Warren, an American writer who settled in Thailand in 1960, becoming the country's unchallenged authorial dean with more than forty books published about his adopted country. When the Royal Household wanted a book about the palace to use as a gift for visiting dignitaries—the royal family lived elsewhere by then—Warren was asked to write it. In the course of his research, he was invited to tour what Anna called "The City of Veiled Women." Anna said there were nine thousand living there, but Warren claims the accurate figure was perhaps a third of that, still an impressive figure.

This was where Mongkut's "harem" lived, a world populated by women, not only the many wives and concubines but also, quoting Warren, the "women shopkeepers, specialty cooks, and dressmakers to cater to the needs of the Inside, as well as a female judiciary and a much-feared female police force…"

Over time, many traditional practices, polygamy among them, were abandoned and according to Warren, "various Inside residences rotted away, never to be replaced. Unmarried princesses moved out to assorted palaces, where they continued to be as strictly chaperoned as ever. The pleasure gardens, scene of so many happy times, succumbed to weeds."

Although this area remains closed, even the most casual visitor to the Grand Palace today may see, exactly, much of what Anna Leonowens saw outside the "Inside." The present royal family still visits the ornate palace and adjacent Wat Phra Keaw, with its revered Emerald Buddha (actually a piece of jade), for special ceremonies, but mainly it's a tourist stop now. That said, it isn't to be missed, for there are no structures anywhere else on earth so fantastical.

In 1998, Hollywood announced still another adaptation entitled *Anna and the King*, this one starring Jodie Foster and Chow Yun-Fat, the producers requesting permission to film in some of the original sites. By now, Thailand was a location favored by film companies worldwide, serving as the location for two James Bond movies, a slew of Jean-Claude van Damme and Steven Seagal action flicks, a remake of *Around the World in Eighty Days*, *The Ugly American* (with Kukrit Pramoj portraying the prime minister of a fictional southeast Asian country opposite Marlon Brando; he was later elected Prime Minister of Thailand), *The Young Indiana Jones Chronicles*, *The Phantom*, Sylvester Stallone's fourth Rambo film, and virtually every Vietnam war movie ever made, including three by Oliver Stone, and something called *Surf Ninjas of the South China Seas*.

When the first script for *Anna* was submitted to the Thailand Film Board, the panel rejected it. It also said no to the second script and when it appeared that the smile that accompanied that verdict was more polite than promising, the film crew went south and the elephants and extras used in the movie were Malaysian. Although Chow Yun-Fat was the most "realistic" of actors so far assigned to Mongkut's role, the political aspects of the story went even further astray and at the movie's end, when the king had a final dance with Anna, the effect could only be called Disneyesque.

Thai authorities to date have not permitted any version of the film to be distributed or shown in Thailand due to scenes that were considered disrespectful to the royal family.

When Anna Leonowens, at age thirty-one, was invited to come to Siam in a letter signed by S.S.P.P.Maha Mongkut in 1862, he said, "We beg to invite you to our royal palace to do your best endeavorment upon us and our children." However much gonzo embellishment followed, by her own hand and those of others, it can be securely argued that Anna performed precisely as she was asked.

Lafcadio Hearn

Traditional Legends and Ghost Stories from Japan

His publisher called Patrick Lafcadio Hearn "almost as Japanese as haiku" and Kenneth Rexroth said he was "the most influential authority of his generation on Japanese culture," yet he was born in Greece and lived for extended periods in Ireland, the United States, and Martinique. Migrating to Japan at the age of forty, he became enchanted, some might say besotted, by what he called a "topsy-turvy world" and he remained for the rest of his life, taking a Japanese wife and name, wearing a kimono and writing his books seated on a tatami mat on the floor.

Although most of the material in his books about Japan could more reasonably be termed non-fiction, almost always they are found in a bookstore's "literature" section and when so many are legends or tales of the supernatural, as written after they were told to him by his wife and then researched as far as such research can go, it's fair to call it fiction, too. Call it "faction," a word that may fairly be applied accurately to many other works about the East that pass for fiction, short and long.

He was blind in one eye and shortsighted in the other, and although he lived in Japan for fourteen years, outside the big cities and apart from other foreigners, teaching English literature at middle schools and universities, he never learned to read or write Japanese, nor even to speak it fluently. Despite these disadvantages, Hearn was the source the West read when they wanted to know about everything Japanese, from pet crickets, plant-less gardens, and haiku to calligraphy, ghosts, and how Buddhism shaped daily life.

Hearn spent his youth in his father's homeland, Ireland, moving to the United States when he was nineteen. There, he became a journalist, first in Cincinnati and then New Orleans, producing two forgettable novels, a handful of books about Creole culture, another following two years in Martinique. Still searching for a home and direction, in 1890 he moved to Japan. Two volumes titled *Glimpses of Unfamiliar Japan* appeared four years later and half a dozen more over the next ten years. Several were reissued in the 1970s and four titles remain in print.

Hearn married a Japanese woman, took the name Yakumo Koizumi and died a Japanese citizen September 26, 1904, of heart failure.

"Elfish Everything Seems"

"Elfish everything seems; for everything as well as everybody is small, and queer, and mysterious: the little houses under their blue roofs, the little shop-fronts hung with blue, and the smiling little people in their blue costumes. The illusion is only broken by the occasional passing of a tall foreigner, and by diverse shop-signs bearing announcements in absurd attempts at English. Nevertheless such discords only serve to emphasize reality; they never materially lessen the fascination of the funny little streets."

It is as if the writer were describing a visit to Middle Earth, where hobbits lived. It is practically Disneyesque; the reader can almost hear dwarves whistling their way to work. Was this not a sort of Magic Kingdom, too? Perhaps Lafcadio Hearn was prescient. Was not Japan the place where, a hundred years later, manga and Hello Kitty were born?

Donald Richie, an American novelist, essayist, journalist and film scholar who lived in Japan for nearly sixty years, said in his introduction to a new edition of Hearn's first work, "Like many early foreign writers on Japan...Hearn was infantilizing the place but while most writers were castigating the Japanese for being (from the Western point of view) childlike, Hearn was praising them for it. Here were folk living in an innocent naturalness which he felt that Europe and America had long lost."

When Hearn arrived in Japan in 1890—fleeing the fast-grow-ing materialism of nineteenth century America and nominally on assignment for *Harper's* magazine—Japan was still emerging from two centuries of self-imposed isolation. It had been just thirty-seven years since Admiral Matthew Perry (in 1853) threat-ened to bombard the Japanese capital if the country wasn't opened to American trade. In the years that followed, the Tokugawa Shogunate was overthrown and feudalism was abolished. The samurai were sent abroad to learn about Western science and technology and then were abolished as a class, as the new Meiji government allocated more than half its budget to staffing its schools and universities with Western faculties. Japan had a lot of catching up to do and decided to let outsiders help; it was a "topsy-turvy world" in more ways than even Hearn imagined.

So Japan was still mysterious when the author arrived and his euphoric description of "My First Day in the Orient" could be excused. Nonetheless, so turned was his head that he described the rickshaw puller who spent the day taking him from place to place at a dead run romantically, failing to notice how thin and impoverished the man surely was, enthusing instead about "the little sky-blue towel, with designs of flying sparrows upon it, which the jinrikisha man uses to wipe his face."

Lest all of this seems unappreciative and disapproving, no matter how old-fashioned his flowery prose now seems and however much his fame has dimmed, Hearn's contribution to both knowing and understanding Japan at that time was enormous. His articles for *Harper's* and *Atlantic Monthly* also were widely syndicated and the books he wrote were (and continue to be) considered authoritative, even to the fussiest of Japanologists.

He came to such fame circuitously. His father was an Irish surgeon major stationed in Greece, his mother a Greek woman who named him Lafcadio, after Lefkada, the island on which he was born. He was taken to Ireland at age two, the marriage dissolved four years later, his mother returned to Greece (pregnant with a brother Lafcadio never met), his father remarrying and going to India. Hearn never heard from either of his parents again and was raised by a great-aunt in Dublin.

It was a time of recovery from the second of Ireland's "Great Famines," caused by a potato blight that over a period of fifty years reduced the population by nearly half, from eight to four and a half million, by starvation and migratory flight. After a year of school in France (missing Guy de Maupassant, who enrolled a year later) and several more in England, where he lost an eye in a playing field accident, at nineteen he joined the migration to America. There, following a year of homelessness he became a journalist in Cincinnati, Ohio, losing his newspaper position when he married a black woman, an illegal act.

In 1877, he moved to New Orleans, where again he worked for newspapers, now serving as a literary editor and translating stories by Théophile Gautier, Guy de Maupassant, Gustave Flaubert, Pierre Loti, and Anatole France, who were then little known in the US. He also began developing his luxuriant prose style along with having affection for exotic subject matter, publishing books about Creole culture and cuisine, and voodoo, and Chinese ghosts. For *Harper's* he wrote *Two Years in the French West Indies* after spending two years in Martinique. It was published in 1890, the year he went to Japan, more or less on assignment for the same publisher.

"In attempting a book upon a country so well trodden as Japan, I could not hope—nor would I consider it prudent attempting—to discover totally new things, but only to consider things in a totally new way..." he told his editor. "The studied aim would be to create, in the minds of the readers, a vivid impression of living in Japan—not simply as an observer but as one taking part in the daily existence of the common people, and thinking with their thoughts."

And that he surely did, avoiding the big cities and with the endorsement of Basil Hall Chamberlain, a professor at Tokyo Imperial University and one of Britain's foremost Japanologists, began teaching at a middle school in Matsue on Japan's provincial western coast. There he married Setsu Koizumi, changed his name to Yakumo Koizumi, and in 1895 became a Japanese citizen. For a brief period he wrote editorials for the English-language *Kobe Chronicle*, but continued teaching until 1902, first at another middle school in Kyushu, then at a small state college and finally he joined Chamberlain in Tokyo as a professor of English literature.

Not only did he embrace all things Japanese, he openly disparaged the Western culture from which he came. Although he did not fully accept the teachings of Buddhism—rejecting the connection made between karma and rebirth, for example—he made it clear how he felt about Christianity when he wrote in his preface to *Glimpses of Unfamiliar Japan*, "That the critical spirit of modernized Japan is now indirectly aiding rather than opposing the efforts of foreign bigotry to destroy the simple, happy beliefs of the people, and substitute those cruel superstitions which the West has long intellectually outgrown—the fancies of an unforgiving God and an everlasting hell—is surely to be regretted."

In the essays that followed he said the harsh disciplinary measures that characterized education in England were unnecessary in Japan, as the children disciplined themselves. The Japanese were politer and happier, as well, and while they shared the West's urge to acquire material goods, there was no urge to adopt inferior Western morals. Even in the manner of flower arranging, he said what he saw in Japan made him regard what the West called a bouquet a "vulgar murdering of flowers, an outrage upon the color-sense, a brutality, an abomination." In conclusion, he wrote, "there can remain no doubt in the mind of one who even partly understands the Japanese, that they are still the best people in the world to live among."

There were twenty-seven sketches in all, four going to newspaper syndicates in the US, publishing another six in *Atlantic Monthly*. Another eleven books followed during his lifetime, appearing at the rate of one a year; a further two posthumously. He was one of the first to write in English about haiku as an important literary form. Kenneth Rexroth, the American poet and critic, wrote an introduction to *The Buddhist Writings of Lafcadio Hearn* (published in 1977 and now out of print) in which he said, "Hearn is as good as anyone at providing an elementary grounding in Buddhist doctrine. But what he does incomparably is to give his reader a feeling for how Buddhism is lived in Japan, its persistent influence upon folklore, burial customs, children's riddles, toys for sale in the marketplace, and even upon the farmer's ruminations in the field. For Hearn, Buddhism is a way of life, and he is interested in the effects of its doctrine upon the daily actions and common beliefs of ordinary people. Like the Japanese themselves, he thinks of religion as something one does, not merely as something one believes…"

Continuing an interest developed listening to Creole and Caribbean tales of voodoo years before, Hearn was drawn to the myths and legends, the folklore and fantasy, the fairy tales and ghost stories of Japan. His wife became a primary source, sharing with him in a sort of half-English, half-Japanese lingo they formed over the years the stories she heard as a child. Others he found in old books. One ghost story he attributed to a local farmer he met.

Three books were the result: *Japanese Fairy Tales* (1898), *In Ghostly Japan* (1899), and *Kwaidan: Stories and Studies of Strange Things* (1903). Masaki Kobayashi adapted several tales from the last of these for his 1965 film *Kwaidan* and when, in 2005, a dramatization of Hearn's life, called *The Dream of a Summer Day*, toured Ireland, four of his ghost stories were a part of it.

The wonder is how he managed to accomplish so much. In describing Hearn, Rexroth said one eye was whitened and the good eye protruded from overuse, helping make the writer "a painfully sensitive and shy person for the rest of his life." While his friend and mentor Basil Hall Chamberlain wrote that, "On entering a room his habit was to grope all around, closely examining the wallpaper, the backs of books, pictures, curios. Of these he could have drawn an exact catalog, but he had never properly seen either the horizon or the stars."

In the end, he was not happy. After acquiring his Japanese citizenship, his host government rewarded him by paying him like other Japanese, slashing his salary by four-fifths. He also lamented the changes he saw, writing Chamberlain to say "how utterly dead Old Japan is and how ugly New Japan is becoming. I thought, how useless to write about things which have ceased to exist."

Poor health ended his teaching career in 1902, although he continued to write, dying on September 26, 1904, of heart failure. He asked his eldest son (of four children) to put his ashes in a simple jar and bury it on a forested hillside, but he was given a formal Buddhist funeral instead.

Lafcadio Hearn has not been forgotten in Japan, as he has by virtually everyone in the West. His former residence in Matsue is open to the public and the garden there is the one described in *Glimpses of Unknown Japan*; an adjacent museum includes cages in which he kept pet insects and birds and a specially-made desk to accommodate his blindness and short stature. The temples he described can be found on numerous websites, some of which actually take the pilgrim on a Lafcadio Hearn "temple tour."

There is also a monument in Yaizu, a small fishing village where he spent his summers while teaching in Tokyo. And he is buried in Plot 1-1-8-35 of the Zoshigawa Cemetery near Ikebukuro; the small rock and flower garden on the plot is well cared for.

Rudyard Kipling

The White Man's Burden

In 1907, Rudyard Kipling won the Nobel Prize in literature, becoming the first writer in English to receive the award and, to date, he remains the youngest (he was forty-two). In 1995, nearly sixty years after his death, in an annual poll conducted by the BBC, he was named England's favorite poet, ahead of usual winner William Shakespeare. In between those dates, the author was frequently vilified.

George Orwell called him a "good bad poet" whose work is "spurious" and "morally insensitive and esthetically disgusting." Dylan Thomas said he stood "for everything in this cankered world which I would wish were otherwise." Henry James, who was the best man at Kipling's wedding, called him an "infant monster." And W.H. Auden said he wrote poetry like a drill sergeant, never allowing the words to think for themselves.

The rise and fall in popularity of writers, actors, singers, politicians, and fashion is well documented, but few reputations have experienced highs and lows as extreme as that of Rudyard Kipling, the author known for such novels as *Captains Courageous* and *Kim*, short stories in two volumes titled *The Jungle Book* and called "The Man Who Would Be King," along with hundreds of poems that included "Mandalay," "Gunga Din," and "If—," the latter being the poem that so attracted BBC listeners. ("If you can keep your head when all about you/Are losing theirs and blaming it on you…") All are hailed as classics today, however much of a jingoist, imperialist, and racist history ultimately judged Kipling to be.

Joseph Rudyard Kipling was born on December 30, 1865, in Bombay, India, his father, Lockwood Kipling, then teaching sculpture and serving as principal of a school of art. Educated in England, he returned to India at eighteen to write for a newspaper in Lahore (now in Pakistan), his stories and poems about Anglo-Indian society destined to displace Tennyson as England's favorite author.

Although he traveled widely and frequently, lived for six years in the United States (his wife was American), spent many summers in South Africa (where he befriended Cecil Rhodes), and, for most of his life, called England home, Kipling is best remembered for his works inspired by his years in Asia. Even after his death—of a perforated ulcer in London, January 18, 1936—his characters and exotic place names lived on, in movies starring Cary Grant and Jason Scott Lee, in Disney animation, in a song popularized by Frank Sinatra, and in McDonalds' "Happy Meals."

"On the Road to Mandalay"

Few if any poetic phrases, or place names, have turned more heads toward Asia than this refrain from what surely is one of Rudyard Kipling's most memorable poems. (Superseded, perhaps, only by "If—.") It was written more than a hundred years ago, published in 1890 in a collection awkwardly but accurately titled *Departmental Ditties and Barrack-Room Ballads*, but right up to the present day it inspires dreams of the exotic sensuality the tropics are claimed to represent.

Kipling's works have long since passed into the public domain—one of the reasons, likely, that his works have continued in print—so let's quote that famous first verse:

> *By the old Moulmein Pagoda,*
> *lookin' lazy at the sea,*
> *There's a Burma girl a-settin',*
> *and I know she thinks o' me;*
> *For the wind is in the palm-trees,*
> *and the temple-bells they say:*
> *'Come you back, you British soldier;*
> *come you back to Mandalay!'*
> *Come you back to Mandalay,*
> *Where the old Flotilla lay;*
> *Can't you 'ear their paddles chunkin'*
> *from Rangoon to Mandalay?*
> *On the Road to Mandalay,*
> *Where the flyin-fishes play,*
> *An' the dawn comes up like thunder*
> *outer China 'crost the Bay!*

There's a lot very right and wrong about this poem. There's nothing wrong with fantasy, of course, but the truth is that although Kipling did visit that pagoda in Moulmein, he spent only three days in Burma in all his life, never went north of Rangoon (never mind all the way to Mandalay), there were no "flyin' fishes" in the Irrawaddy River that connects the two cities, and China is nowhere close to where he says it is located.

No matter. Because the images stuck and the promises made sang loud the Asian siren's call. "I've a neater, sweeter maiden in a cleaner, greener land!/On the road to Mandalay..." Kipling wrote in another verse. And in another: "Ship me somewheres east of Suez, where the best is like the worst/Where there aren't no Ten Commandments an' a man can raise a thirst..."—the latter a line that helped convince Anthony Burgess to accept the offer of a teacher's job in Malaysia some years later and start writing novels about Asia as well.

Thus it was no surprise the English bard was given songwriter credit in 1957 when Frank Sinatra had a hit recording called "On the Road to Mandalay." Nor that there is a five-star hotel/cruise ship called *The Road to Mandalay* that to this day carries wealthy travelers from Pagan to Mandalay. Nor that the Mandalay Bay Hotel in Las Vegas has a restaurant named Aureole (the literal meaning is "halo," but...) and a beach club with "opium beds" beside the pool with wrap-around curtains for privacy.

As an Orientalist, Kipling unquestionably was a sensualist. But it was his more serious interests that deservedly earned him his lasting reputation, his descriptions of the Anglo-Indian society of which he was a part, a massive body of work that was acidly critical but simultaneously sympathetic toward the ordinary British soldier and the Indian to whom he was so brutally superior. This was evident in several of his *Barrack-Room Ballads*, most remarkably in a long poem told from the point of view of a soldier about an Indian water-bearer who died as he saved the soldier's life. The poem closes with the famous lines, "Tho' I've belted you and flayed you/By the livin' Gawd that made you/You're a better man than I am, Gunga Din!"

No other writer of his time addressed this colonial conflict so honestly (if sometimes contradictorily) and nowhere was this more evident than in a poem called "The White Man's Burden," published in 1899 with the subtitle "The United States and the Philippine Islands," but accepted widely to be about imperialism in the broadest sense. Although Kipling warned of the risks that accompanied colonialism, many took the poem to support empire building as a noble enterprise. The title itself could be regarded ambiguously: was the colonialist holding the native up, or back? Were European wealth and modern ways helping non-Western culture or was the Western interloper merely helping himself?

The macho American president, Teddy Roosevelt, said the verses were "rather poor poetry, but made good sense from the expansionist standpoint." While some called the verses satirical, history sided with Roosevelt and the phrase "white man's burden" came to epitomize the imperialist view, and thus Kipling eventually was deemed a racist relic, in today's phrase, "politically incorrect."

Kipling's exposure to Asian culture was on-again, off-again for most of his life. His first six years were spent in Bombay, the next six with his younger sister back in England where he said his caretakers made life miserable. Back with his mom through the rest of his school years, at age seventeen he rejoined his father in India and, as "my English years fell away, nor ever, I think, came back in full strength," he began to write stories for Asian newspapers. Summers were spent in Simla, the colonial hill station where the British Raj government escaped the lowland heat. It was here that he wrote many of the stories that were published in *Plain Tales from the Hills*, published in Calcutta in 1888, a month after his twenty-second birthday.

Most of the stories appeared first for the *Civil & Military Gazette* in Lahore (now part of Pakistan), where he was an assistant editor (a job his father got for him) and at that paper's sister periodical in Allahabad, *The Pioneer*. Kipling was at his most prolific during this period and in 1889, the year he was discharged he saw another six collections of stories published—which he sold for £200 and a small royalty, giving up all rights to *Plain Tales* at the same time for another £50. Such figures sound pitifully small today, but at that time seemed a windfall to a young writer.

Among the poems published that year was the one that gets Kipling most often quoted as well as most misunderstood. This was "The Ballad of East and West," whose first line has been taken out of context countless times. The problem is that most don't hear more than the one line, missing the rest of the verse and its true meaning:

Oh, East is East and West is West,
   and never the twain shall meet,
Till Earth and Sky stand presently
   at God's great Judgment seat;
But there is neither East nor West,
   Border, nor Breed, nor Birth,
When two strong men stand face to face,
   though they come from the end of the earth!

This also was the year Kipling visited Burma so briefly and continued on around the world, writing as he traveled, returning to London in October 1889. In just seven years, he had gone from a teenager whose poor eyesight had kept him from military service to being accepted as a literary lion—publishing in 1890 two poems for which he became famous, "Mandalay" and "Gunga Din," then in the next five years, the book that included them, *Barrack-Room Ballads*, and two volumes of what appeared to be clever animal fables written for children but actually had much more to them. In what came to be called *The Jungle Books*, Kipling created stories and characters that would remain popular for more than a hundred years.

These animal tales were written mainly for magazines while he was living for five years in Vermont following his marriage to an American woman, Carrie Balestier, sister of another writer with whom he collaborated on a novel called *The Naulahka*. (About which, a little more soon.) Most of the stories were set in British India and eight of the fifteen concerned the adventures of Mowgli, an Indian boy raised by wolves. The concept was not new: the mythical tale of Romulus and Remus, the founders of Rome who were raised by wolves, inspired other authors as well and an American writer, Edgar Rice Burroughs, created Tarzan of the Apes seventeen years later, in 1912. In all his stories, Kipling also personalized the animals, to make easier the telling of moral lessons, just as Aesop did in his fables more than five hundred years B.C.

Some readers said the tales allegorized the politics and society of the time, but most took them at face value—Robert Baden-Powell, the founder of the Scouting movement among them, who asked Kipling for his permission to use Akela, the head wolf in *The Jungle Book*, to lead his Cub Scout "packs." Both books—the first illustrated by Kipling's father—were immediate and lasting bestsellers and usually regarded as "children's books."

Although many other Kipling characters and stories have been adapted in other media over time, none underwent the cosmetic surgeon's scalpel more frequently than *The Jungle Books*. Predictably, there were numerous comic books and Disney experienced a great success with an animated film in 1967 (much praised when Walt died soon after its completion), then in 1994 returned to the Kipling fount and starred Jason Scott Lee as Mowgli in a live-action version that made a mockery of Kipling, "casting the British as stupid, cold-hearted and greedy imperious villains." (Quoting William Cash in *The Daily Telegraph*.) Another animated version appeared in Russia and there was a Japanese anime television series called *Jungle Book Shonen Mowgli*. Additional artistic adjustments were made for the dance and stage. It is likely Elvis will never be challenged when it comes to merchandising, but numerous manufacturers did well with Mowgli and his animal friends, marketing towels, bedding, clocks and watches, notepaper, keychains, clothing, a variety of games and toys, and in 1989, a McDonald's Happy Meal with all the attendant effluvia.

In this fashion, Kipling's reputation was "restored," though he likely would not yet find himself bagged with Hans Christian Andersen, Beatrix Potter, and Dr. Seuss.

At the same time, many of his earlier and most important works have been sidelined or forgotten. (Save for that inspirational poem "If—.") One of these was *The Naulahka: A Story of West and East*, the novel written with Wolcott Balestier, whose sister married Kipling shortly after Balestier's death of typhoid fever. (Naulakha—the accurate spelling of the Hindi word for nine-hundred thousand rupees and of a pavilion in Lahore—also was the name Kipling gave his home in the United States.) Although it was not a commercial success, as an adventure tale in the genre epitomized by H. Rider Haggard's more popular *King Solomon's Mines*, it didn't disappoint. As was true for most of what Kipling wrote, there were lessons to be learned. In this case, it included a dire warning:

> Now it is not good for the Christian's health
> to hustle the Aryan brown,
> For the Christian riles and the Aryan smiles
>   and he weareth the Christian down;
> At the end of the fight is a tombstone white
>   with the name of the late deceased,
> And the epitaph drear: 'A fool lies here who
>   tried to hustle the East.'

It was in such lines where Kipling revealed most clearly what he meant when he said his English heritage "never came back in full."

So too was this evident in a short story called "The Man Who Would Be King," published in 1888 and brought back to life nearly a hundred years later (1975) when John Huston cast Sean Connery and Michael Caine in the film of the same name. (With Christopher Plummer portraying Kipling himself, as narrator.) This tale epitomized another Asian fantasy, inspired by the true adventures of James Brooke, the Brit who became the "white Rajah" of Sarawak in Borneo, and a nineteenth century American adventurer named Josiah Harlan who established himself in Afghanistan and western India (now Pakistan), where in exchange for military advice and aid, not to mention a heavy dollop of regal posturing, he won the title "Prince of Ghor" in perpetuity for himself and his descendants. Thus Kipling set down for all who followed the premise (promise?) that in Asia, the white man could be a king, in lifestyle if not in fact.

However, once again Kipling's consistent warning was made clear. The author's two adventurers may have made themselves gods in the fictitious nation called Kafiristan. When one of them (the one played by Sean Connery) starts to bleed after he is bitten by his bride and with his humanity revealed he is then killed. The populace turns on his partner as well, but he survives, although he loses his mind. In the final scene, in order to prove his story is true, he gives the narrator his partner's head, still wearing its crown.

In the years leading up to winning the Nobel Prize in 1907, Kipling was as successful as he was prolific—publishing another collection for children, *The Just So Stories*, and a novel placed mainly in India and Tibet, taking its title from the central character, *Kim*. This is the book that many critics regard as the author's masterpiece.

Kim (Kimball O'Hara) is the illiterate orphan son of an Irish soldier who grows up on the streets of Lahore, is taken care of by a half-caste keeper of an opium den, befriended by a horse trader and British spy, educated by a Tibetan lama, and zipped through a string of adventures that might give Indiana Jones the shivers. Dressed as a Hindu beggar child, Kim accompanies the lama on a quest for a holy river that sprang from the arrow of Buddha, at the same time, after having learned espionage from an Indian gem dealer and other colonial agents, he serves the empire by combating the infiltration of Russians through the Khyber Pass.

(Oddly, it wasn't until 1950 that a movie was made, starring Dean Stockwell in the title role and Errol Flynn as the horse trader. Another version was broadcast by the BBC in 1984 with Peter O'Toole portraying the lama. In between, a one-hour adaptation was shown in 1960 in the US as an episode of *Shirley Temple's Storybook.*)

Kipling seemed to have peaked with *Kim's* publication and being awarded the Nobel Prize. He served briefly as a reporter during the First World War, but the battlefield death of his son at age eighteen and the death of one of his two daughters took a heavy toll. He continued to write and publish, yet as the imperial tides turned worldwide, in some ways he came to be better known for the use of a phrase from one of his most popular poems, "Recessional," originally written to honor Queen Victoria's Diamond Jubilee. The final line, "Lest we forget," now appeared on countless tombstones white.

The cottage where he was born in Bombay on the campus of what is now the Sir J.J. Institute of Applied Art (where his father was the first principal) is long gone and when plans were announced in 2007 to turn a newer structure into a museum in Kipling's memory, there was such a public uproar over recognizing the author of "The White Man's Burden" that a museum of art was opened instead. However, there is a plaque acknowledging the site.

In England, following the death of his widow in 1939, the Kipling home in Burwash, a village in East Sussex, was given to the National Trust and it's now a museum, open to the public. The large shingled home called Naulakha where he wrote *The Jungle Books* also still stands, on Kipling Road in Dummerston, Vermont (three miles outside Brattleboro); it was designated a National Historic Landmark in 1993 and is privately owned, so don't go knocking on the door.

Most important, there is still all of Kipling's India (including what is now Pakistan, Bangladesh and Burma), much of it little changed. I suggest travelers take a well-read and flagged copy of *Kim*—because it ranges over much of the subcontinent and from place to place can be an essential complement to whatever guidebook you may be following. It will be especially helpful in Lahore, where Kipling spent five of his early years writing for newspapers (his father was curator of the local museum) and later the city was the site of many of the novel's dramatic scenes.

Other Kipling works serve elsewhere. On a trip to Simla (now Shimla), take *Plain Tales from the Hills*. You might also put *Departmental Ditties and Barrack-Room Ballads* in your backpack when visiting the old Victoria Terminus in Mumbai (renamed the Charapati Shivaji Terminus). This is the magnificent Gothic railway station that looks like it wants to be a palace or cathedral, where some of Kipling's father's sculptures are still visible, if you've got binoculars and know where to look. Upon arrival, select a poem and read aloud, arm held aloft, triumphantly. I recalled reading somewhere that when Anthony Burgess was sailing from England to Malaya to work as a teacher for the British Colonial Service, he stood at the ship's bow and recited Kipling's "Mandalay," because he liked the sound of it. So I did the same outside the railway station, choosing the final words to Kim:

> 'E carried me away
> > To where a dooli lay,
> > An' a bullet come an' drilled the beggar clean.
> > 'E put me safe inside,
> > An' just before 'e died,
> > 'I 'ope you liked your drink,' sez Gunga Din.
> > So I'll meet 'im later on
> > At the place where 'e is gone—
> > Where it's always double drill and no canteen;
> > E'll be squattin' on the coals
> > Givin' drink to poor damned souls,
> > An' I'll get a swig in hell from Gunga Din!

Yes, I actually did that, and I don't think anyone even noticed. I was just another crazy Westerner standing in a crowd of whirling Indians.

André Malraux

XXX

Christopher Hitchens called André Malraux a "supreme con artist" and "one of the most prolific self-inventors of the twentieth
century." Philip Roth described Maleraux's memoirs as "autobiography grandiosely enlarged." Philosopher Raymond Aron said
Malraux was "one-third genial, one-third false, one-third incomprehensible," and Malraux himself wrote in one of his novels that
"every adventurer is born a mythomaniac."

The exceptional truth should have been enough. He was arrested by French authorities (with his first of four wives) at twenty-
one for stealing statues from ancient Cambodian temple sites,
edited an anti-French newspaper in Saigon, helped organize an air
force for the Republicans in the Spanish Civil War, fought with a
French tank unit during World War Two, endorsed and then re-
futed Communism, and when Charles de Gaulle became France's
president was appointed the nation's first cultural minister, a
position he held for ten years, during which time he became
friends with Jacqueline Kennedy and promised her he would
bring the "Mona Lisa" to the United States, and did so. He talked
politics with Trotsky, met T.E. Lawrence, Nehru, and Mao, and

was invited to brief Nixon and Kissinger before their history-making 1972 trip to China.

But everything was wrapped in exaggeration and tied up with lies. Even his memoirs were fictionalized. All to support a towering ego. "There are only two men in France, de Gaulle and me," he told Francois Mauriac, believing, or at least supposing, that he would be the president's successor. Trotsky himself said Malraux was "organically incapable of moral independence."

His true legacy was in his writing, novels largely forgotten outside France today but ranked among the finest for their time. Four published between 1926 and 1933 were placed in Asia: *The Conquerors*, which told the story of China's fight against foreign domination in Canton; *The Temptation of the West*, a fictional exchange of letters between a European and an Asian intellectual; *The Royal Way*, an adventure story placed in Cambodia; and his masterpiece, *Man's Fate*, a tale of conspiracy set against the failed 1927 Communist uprising in Shanghai.

André Malraux was born in Paris November 3, 1901. A lifelong chain smoker, he died of a pulmonary embolism following lung cancer surgery in Créteil, outside the capital, November 23, 1976, and on the twentieth anniversary of his passing, for his contributions to French culture, his ashes were moved from the original gravesite to the Panthéon.

The Great Pretender

André Malraux was like a rock star. His preferred music certainly wasn't rock and roll, yet in the 1950s and 1960s when Elvis Presley and his friends—and in France Johnny Halliday and his friends—ruled the airwaves and the hearts and nether regions of the young, as his nation's first cultural minister, the acclaimed author-adventurer behaved rather like one, creating a legend, or myth, that nearly overwhelmed the talent that lay behind it.

Born in a small town outside Paris in 1901 and raised by an aunt and grandmother after his parents divorced, he dropped out of university, married a wealthy German writer and promptly lost her fortune in the stock market. That sent the couple to Cambodia, then part of the French colony called Indochine, where he removed some bas-relief statuary from an ancient temple and was arrested and sentenced to three years in prison. A petition circulated by his wife and support from such luminaries as André Gide, Francois Mauriac, and André Breton, got the conviction reversed.

Malraux returned to Southeast Asia to help organize and edit an anti-colonialist newspaper in Saigon, during which time he also become enamored of the Communist movement in China, where the young Mao Tse-tung was fighting what seemed to be a losing battle against Chiang Kai-shek. This inspired his career as a successful novelist in the late 1920s and early 1930s (about which, more soon), which was interrupted in 1936 when he went to fight the fascist Franco forces in the Spanish Civil War (along with but apart from Arthur Koestler, George Orwell, and Ernest Hemingway). It was then that Malraux's embellishments began moving toward the grandiose.

Enamored of Gabriele D'Annunzio and St. Antoine de Saint Exupéry (both of them acclaimed novelists and aviators) and determined to provide the Republicans with air cover, he raised funds and helped organize a shambles of an air force of what one observer called "flying coffins," one of which crashed with "Colonel" Malraux in it, giving him the opportunity to claim a war wound. In a novel written years later, he also made it appear that he was an eyewitness to events occurring simultaneously in Barcelona and Madrid.

There's more. Not only did he say he had long, meaningful conversations with Stalin and Mao when, in fact, he never met the Russian leader and was introduced to China's top gun only formally, he also claimed falsely to have met Goebbels on a 1934 trip to Berlin. By which time he had championed both the Soviet Union and Nazi Germany, calling the Communists the world's leading hope for Democracy and the Third Reich "the type of civilization from which Shakespeares emerge."

There were early biographical lies, too, when he told *Who's Who of France* he had attended the Lycée Condoret and graduated from École des Langues Orientales when neither was true, and that he had learned Sanskrit and Persian and could converse in Russian, when in fact he could speak only French and didn't understand basic English. One can't help wondering how he got away with all this.

Of course, he sometimes didn't. He spent most of World War Two with a mistress in a country house in the south of France—then under the control of the Nazi-cooperating Vichy French "government"—emerging from his cocoon just ahead of the D-Day invasion at Normandy, whereupon he again appointed himself a colonel and joined a tank unit and got shot in the leg and captured. He was released within forty-eight hours, however, and a few days later at the Ritz Bar in newly liberated Paris he finally met his macho match, Ernest Hemingway. Telling the American author that he had commanded two thousand soldiers, one of Hemingway's pals said, "Papa, shall we shoot this asshole?"

Undaunted, Malraux then put his fiction-writing talents to work on his military record, thereby earning a chest-full of spurious medals, while claiming, among other things, that he had faced a German firing squad and liberated Alsace-Lorraine. His biggest wartime feat, however, was in capturing General Charles de Gaulle, becoming his minister of information during the year that de Gaulle led France from 1945-1946, remaining his confidant and Number One groupie for the next twenty-five years, ten of them as France's first minister of culture when de Gaulle returned to the presidential palace in 1958.

Some called him the "in-house intellectual," others preferred "court clown"—an image sadly abetted by a facial tic and a nasal sniff that was attributed to Tourette's Syndrome—but all agreed that he was, to the dismay of his leftist friends, one of the most consistent voices in defense of the Gaullist right. Proving once again that among his numerous talents was knowing how to ride a horse in the direction it was going in and if it seemed like a good idea, how to change horses mid-stream.

It was during this period he supervised the restoration of the Louvre colonnade and construction of numerous provincial art museums and libraries, arranged an important retrospective Picasso exhibit (refusing to meet the artist, fearing the artist would humiliate him), and wormed his way into Kennedy's Camelot and, fulfilling a promise to Jackie, had the "Mona Lisa" transported by luxury liner to Washington where it was viewed by two million Americans. He also reissued six volumes of art theory that were published between the two de Gaulle administrations, densely written screeds criticized for their lack of scholarship but hailed for a concept he called *le musée imaginaire*, usually translated as "the museum without walls," a notion that really didn't gain much meaning until the invention of the Internet.

In the 1970s, with de Gaulle in what seemed to be permanent eclipse, Malraux made a final political score. Believing that he had played a role in Mao's revolution or at least to be some sort of expert, he was invited to brief Nixon and Kissinger ahead of their diplomatic journey to open China to the West in 1972, whereupon he blew some inspired smoke you know where and got away with it.

It was his early novels that saved him, *La Condition Humaine* (*Man's Fate*) alone putting him in his country's and perhaps the century's writing top rank. With a fictional exchange of letters that was more an essay than a novel, *Le Temptation de l'Occident* (*The Temptation of the West*) and his earlier novel, *Les Conquérants* (*The Conquerors*), forming a trilogy chronicling China's communist revolution during the 1920s, Malraux was, along with Pearl Buck in a distant but complementary fashion, one of the few

Western writers to take that part of the world at that time as a serious subject for their fiction. Maugham was another, but his collection of sketches, *On a Chinese Screen*, was without a storyline and numerous others such as Sax Rohmer and Earl Derr Biggers, creators of Dr. Fu Manchu and Charlie Chan, were pulp writers, enjoyed by a large audience but rarely taken seriously, even if they did influence how the West regarded the Chinese.

Malraux was more China's champion and friend, taking the opposite tack. Where the pulp writers influenced how the West came to think and feel about the Chinese, *The Temptation of the West*, published in 1926, lamented the damage done to China's cultural identity by exposure to European music, movies, and technology. The message in this fictional exchange of letters between Chinese and Western intellectuals concluded that China had been "seduced" and the result was China's "disintegrating soul."

Two years later Malraux published his first true novel, *Les Conquérants (The Conquerors)*. This was an exciting war story that described the struggle between Chiang Kai-shek's Kuomintang and Mao as the Nationalists broke away from the Communists in Canton (now Guangzhou) in the 1920s. The four major characters were intellectuals, what The University of Chicago Press, the book's US publisher, accurately described as "a ruthless Bolshevik revolutionary, a disillusioned master of propaganda, a powerful Chinese pacifist, and a young anarchist." Each of these "conquerors" came to a sorry end.

"China has always conquered her conquerors," Malraux wrote. "Slowly, it is true. But always."

Malraux's next novel, *The Royal Way*, published in 1930, was less successful, maybe because it was inspired by his own shameful and shameless behavior in Cambodia as an antiquities thief, although in the book the thieves fail to secure the bas-reliefs. Abandoned by their guide in the jungle to deal with swamps, giant insects and an injury that eventually kills one of them (in the same manner that conquerors are defeated, slowly), the book turns into a discourse on how adventure can be an attempt to affirm the significance of the human presence in the face of a meaningless universe. When it came to wrapping action in metaphysical imponderables, Malraux knew no equal.

In 1933 came his most celebrated work, *Man's Fate*, the third in the China trilogy, sometimes called "the greatest novel of revolution in this century." This novel was set mostly in Shanghai in 1927, when Chiang Kai-shek's forces teamed up with the Communists to liberate the city from the Imperial government, only to have Chiang turn on his pals three weeks later and slaughter the rebel troops.

Because Malraux himself was such a consistent fabricator about his own life, it is natural to wonder how accurate he was about his story telling. Because the foreign governments doing business in China supported Chiang's betrayal and the subsequent massacre (epitomized in the novel by a sleazy French banker), Malraux concocted a story about Chiang's brutality that was criticized in the West. Chiang had not gone so far as to make his prisoners stand in line to be thrown, one by one, into the firebox of a steam locomotive and with each execution blow the train whistle. There was little question about where Malraux's sympathies lay in the 1920s and 1930s; like many other writers of the period, Malraux embraced Communism.

Man's Fate was a title that would demand much of any author and like Tolstoy with the similarly labeled *War and Peace*, Malraux delivered lots of action, important themes, and memorable characters. Combat scenes were mixed with psychological examinations of the novel's several protagonists; in the opening scene, a Chinese terrorist agonizes over assassinating a man sleeping beneath a mosquito net, wondering whether he should lift the net or stab through it. Once past that whimsical opening, it got really dark and by the end, everyone was either dead or wounded, at least psychologically.

This is not an easy book. Philosophical notions about the human condition—the inevitability of death and what we might do on our way to meet the reaper—appeared like shell-shot buildings in Shanghai's international district during the revolution he wrote about. Political intrigue and murder and war in the streets in a city whose name alone spelled adventure and mystery came together as a challenge as big as the intellect that created it.

Yet, this was the book that made Malraux a star. The novel won the prestigious Prix Goncourt, putting him in a league with Marcel Proust. Even after his death, the company he kept embellished Malraux's name. On the twentieth anniversary of his death his remains were moved to the Panthéon to spend the rest of eternity with Voltaire, Rousseau, Victor Hugo, Jean-Paul Marat, Emile Zola, and Alexandre Dumas.

Malraux wanted to be recognized as both an adventurer and an intellectual. In this, he was a success. He was also considered to be one of the world's finest conversationalists, a popular early television talk show guest, his arm gesticulating dramatically, the cigarette in his hand diving and darting like a biplane in a dogfight over 1930s Madrid. And then suddenly came that nasal sniff, a long silence, and then more brilliant sparkle dust. A man whose fate it was to become more interesting, in retrospect, than the books he wrote; as happens with so many rock stars, the image overwhelmed the work.

Is there a visitable path in Malraux's life? One could visit the schools and battlegrounds he lied about in his life and visit the Louvre, whose columns he once had cleaned and whose primary attraction, the *Mona Lisa*, is still to be viewed if you don't mind badly dressed crowds. A visit to Angkor Wat to look at all those headless Buddha figures might give you another peek into Malraux's fabled past. And of course, more seriously, one can visit the Panthéon.

George Orwell

Burmese Days

Perhaps no other writer of the last century was so sanctified and damned by conservatives and liberals alike, while making such an impact on all—hailed for his "uncompromising intellectual honesty" (Arthur Koestler), an "unusually high moral sense and respect for justice and truth" (Evelyn Waugh), and for taking "some of the supposedly Christian virtues and [showing] how they could be 'lived' without piety or religious belief" (Christopher Hitchens).

He was skeletal, clumsy, and socially inept, described by *The Times* as an "old Etonian chain-smoker and socialist with a terrible haircut," a man who threw himself at women (who usually retreated in horror); he distrusted intellectuals, was more than mildly anti-Semitic, disparaged homosexuality; and woe to the editor who changed a word of his spare, frequently self-contradicting prose. He was, said Malcolm Muggeridge, easier to love than to like.

Best known for his satirical novels *Animal Farm* and *Nineteen Eighty-Four*, George Orwell produced more than two million words of fiction, journalism, opinion, and poetry, and by the centenary of his birth more than forty million copies of his books were sold in sixty languages.

Taking the impoverished underdog's side in early reportage, Orwell became one of the fathers of participatory journalism and thereafter, he said, "every line of serious work that I have written...has been written, directly or indirectly, against totalitarianism and for democratic socialism, as I understand it." Who can forget the words and phrases he concocted—Newspeak, double-think, reality control, the Thought Police, cold war, Big Brother is watching? Even his name became an adjective, "Orwellian," when used to measure language separated from moral reality. Yet, he once called himself "a sort of a pamphleteer."

He was one of the few Western writers identified with Asia actually born there, in what was then Bengal, India, on June 25, 1903, and named Eric Arthur Blair, the son of a French woman raised in Burma (then a province of India) and a British agent in the imperial opium trade.

While an infant, his mother took him to England, where he lived the rest of his life, save for five years as a colonial policeman stationed in Burma, an experience that led to his writing his first novel, *Burmese Days*, published in 1935.

Early success eluded him and when *Nineteen Eighty-Four* was published to worldwide acclaim, he was in a London hospital with tuberculosis. He died six months later, January 21, 1950, aged forty-six.

Orwell's Burmese Days

How many novels about Asia did George Orwell write? One, of course. Or was it actually three? There is no question about *Burmese Days*, the story that came out of his own experience as a colonial policeman in the 1920s, but some critics of the totalitarian generals who rule that country today insist that *Animal*

Farm and *Nineteen Eighty-Four* fit the repressive government so well, they should be included at the very least as "prophesy."

Emma Larkin—a pseudonym for an American writer based in Bangkok—is one of the most recent Orwell seekers to sneak into Burma by saying she was something she was not (a tourist), using the author of *Burmese Days* as a vehicle by which to take another swipe at the Southeast Asian country that held the Nobel Peace laureate, Aung San Suu Kyi, under house arrest for fifteen years. In her idiosyncratic book, *Secret Histories: Finding George Orwell in a Burmese Teashop*, published in 2004, a Burmese man exclaims on the first page that Orwell is "the prophet" for accurately predicting in his best-known novels what the Burmese would come to experience.

George Orwell's place in history and literature will never be disconnected from *Animal Farm* and *Nineteen Eighty-Four*, but at the end of the twentieth century and into the twenty-first, his seminal novel about life in Burma under the repressive British Raj in a way moved to the head of the queue. This could be explained in large part by the increased media coverage of Burma, which led to greater worldwide curiosity, but also because *Burmese Days* could be regarded as a sort of prism through which present-day Burma might be viewed.

The ironies abound. When he was in a good mood, Orwell called his time as an imperial cop "five years in an unsuitable profession." In a short story titled "Shooting an Elephant," he went much further, saying, "I had already made up my mind that imperialism was an evil thing and the sooner I chucked up my job and got out of it the better. Theoretically—and secretly of course—I was all for the Burmese and all against their oppressors, the British. As for the job I was doing, I hated it more bitterly than I can perhaps make clear. In a job like that you see the dirty work of Empire at close quarters. The wretched prisoners huddling in the stinking cages of the lock-ups, the gray, cowed faces of the long-term convicts, the scarred buttocks of the men who had been bogged with bamboos—all these oppressed me with an intolerable sense of guilt."

Does this not sound like what's happening today, the only difference being that the uniformed successors to the British Raj are now Burmese? By itself, that is ironical. Add to this the fact that the generals permit copies of Orwell's novel to be sold openly—because (apparently) they consider it anti-British. Yet, in first calling itself the State Law and Order Restoration Council and then the State Peace and Development Council, isn't the military junta toeing the Orwellian line? Doesn't changing so many of the place names—Rangoon is now Yangon and no longer the country's capital and Moulmein, city of Orwell's mom's upbringing and one of his postings as a cop, is now Mawlamyine, for example—fit Orwell's declaration in *Nineteen Eighty-Four*, "Who controls the past controls the future: who controls the present controls the past"?

However much irony may echo today, Burma was a far different place when Orwell arrived in 1922. Burma was considered the "backwater of India," with the Empire's highest incidence of crime, the murder rate in some districts six times of that in Chicago during the days of Al Capone. It was politically unstable and there was a growing hatred of British rule. In addition, in a land of thirteen million people with a large native-born police force of thirteen thousand men, just ninety British officers controlled almost all the police operations.

Any posting outside Rangoon was considered "remote" as nowhere were there more than a handful of other Westerners, and few of them of the female sex. Add threatening fauna ranging from crocodiles and tigers to elephants and poisonous snakes and a wide range of tropical diseases. So low was the appeal of a Burmese assignment, those sent were given a sort of consolation prize, a "Burma allowance" that put several extra pounds in their monthly pay packets. Yet, this was Orwell's first choice, because he still had family there.

The first year was as comfortable as colonial service got and it passed mainly in Mandalay in a police training school. His studies were as demanding as they were tedious, but he and two other candidates there at the time were provided individual apartments, a library, and a billiards room, along with two butlers, two cooks, several gardeners, a punka-wallah (fan-puller), a billiard marker, a lamp-trimmer, and for each a personal valet. For a nineteen-year-old, it must have been a heady experience. And yet, what Orwell remembered of Mandalay was that it was famous for having "five main products all beginning with P, namely, pagodas, pariahs [an Anglo-Indian term for stray dogs], pigs, priests and prostitutes."

And then it was into the jungle and swamp, serving in six different districts in under four years, ranging from some near the capital city of Rangoon, another at Insein where a jail housed 2500 prisoners (and more recently has been home to many of Aung San Suu Kyi's supporters), another in Moulmein in the south, where he finally met his maternal grandmother (he was appalled that in forty years she hadn't learned a word of the native tongue, whereas he had learned Burmese, Hindustani, and a smattering of Karen), spending his last year in Katha, two hundred miles north of Mandalay, the most remote of all his assignments. This last became the setting for *Burmese Days*.

By now, he had successively climbed the ladder of cop success, to where he commanded a force of three hundred men. He had witnessed executions—as recorded in his short story written years later, "The Hanging"—and if you believe what he wrote in "Killing an Elephant," he had done that as well. "As a police officer I was an obvious target and was baited whenever it seemed safe to do so," he wrote in that story. "The young Buddhist priests were the worst of all. There were several thousands of them in the town

[Moulmein] and none of them seemed to have anything to do except stand on street corners and jeer at Europeans."

Orwell was angry and depressed, ready to piss on the Empire he represented, the Asians over whom he had what he regarded as unjustified power, as well as on himself. By admitting that he beat the Burmese with a cane and said in "Shooting an Elephant" that the "greatest joy in the world would be to drive a bayonet into a Buddhist priest's guts." Thus, he discovered that the oppressor was more damaged than the oppressed.

"It is a stifling, stultifying world in which to live," he wrote. "It is a world in which every word and every thought is censored… Free speech is unthinkable. All other kinds of freedom are permitted. You are free to be a drunkard, an idler, a coward, a backbiter, a fornicator; but you are not free to think for yourself. Your opinion on every subject of any conceivable importance is dictated for you by the *pukka sahib's* [colonialist's] code."

So it was no surprise that his novel based on his years in Burma, like so much of his work, was angry and depressing. *Burmese Days* was a brilliant, early evocation of the work that was to follow, but like so much of Orwell's output, it didn't leave the reader in a cheery mood. Reality at its most honest seldom does. Stripped of all pretense, *Burmese Days* was, as noted by others, a book that "took no prisoners." While innocent Burmese are reviled, flogged, and killed by their imperial overlords, a corrupt Burmese civil servant devises a way to cheat his karma. "He would devote his closing years to good works, which would pile up enough merit to outweigh the rest of his life," Orwell wrote. "Four pagodas, five, six, seven—the priests would tell him how many."

The deeply flawed "hero" of the novel is John Flory, an English timber merchant who sponsors an Indian doctor for membership in the colonial outpost's European Club. He is opposed by a corrupt Burmese magistrate who, in his own desire to be the club's first non-English member, sets out to destroy both men's reputations. An English woman enters the plot and Flory wins her, loses her, and wins then loses her again, as he tries to live in both worlds and fails at that as well. The book ends with Flory's suicide.

Orwell's tour of duty itself was ended by dengue fever—the Indian physician attending him is thought to have been the model for the doctor in his novel—and once back in England, he resigned from the colonial police. He began writing the novel a year later, in 1928, an effort that would take, off and on, four years. Two British publishers rejected the manuscript, fearing lawsuits, but Harpers in the United States agreed to take it with some editing and when it appeared in 1935, (a year later in England with more changes), Orwell's friend Cyril Connelly praised it in the *New Statesman* for its "efficient indignation, graphic description, excellent narrative, excitement and irony tempered with vitriol."

So what was the novel's appeal? It was, of course, a good read, an engaging story driven by fully developed characters, set against an exotic background as realistically as the short stories being written about colonial life in British Malaya at approximately the same time by Somerset Maugham. Orwell and Maugham had little in common aside from their occupation and nationality, but their literary characters would have shared sundowners at the local British club most compatibly, their complaints about the locals and fellow expats perfectly matched while, quoting Orwell, "playing bridge and getting three parts drunk." From the 1920s through the final collapse of the Raj following World War Two, there was a ready audience for tales of such expatriate behavior and their predictably juicy consequence.

In addition, Orwell's detailed descriptions of the jungle with its screaming parrots and mist that "poured through the valleys like the steam of enormous kettles," of the colorful morning markets, of the dancers in Mandalay whose buttocks moved independently, offered an enticement to the wannabe travelers who found their adventure in pre-tourism days mainly by reading books. However piqued Orwell may have been by individuals—writer

Paul Spencer Sochaczewski called him an "equal opportunity misanthrope"—his enthusiastic respect for and enjoyment of the Burmese culture and its exotic environment never flagged.

"I wanted to write enormous naturalistic novels with unhappy endings, full of detailed descriptions and arresting similes, and also full of purple passages in which my words were used partly for the sake of their sound," he said in "Why I Write" (1946). "And in fact my first complete novel, *Burmese Days*…is rather that kind of book."

Orwell's trail is frequently traveled nowadays, for at least two reasons: the seeker finds more of Orwell's old haunts still more or less intact, thanks to the isolation and lack of development that accompanied Burma's dictatorial government; you put a country in mothballs and when the doors are finally opened a bit, it may smell a little, but not so much has changed as eighty years would seem to justify. Additional reward comes from the frisson of excitement the traveler experiences when gathering information somewhat surreptitiously, just as contemporary journalists must.

I remember my first visit to Burma, in 1996 when I was part of one of the first tour groups booked to travel the Irrawaddy River from Bagan (formerly Pagan) to Mandalay on a new, five-star hotel/cruise ship called *Road to Mandalay*. Asked my occupation on arrival in Rangoon, I said, "writer," and was pulled aside for questioning. Not until it was clear that I was on assignment from four magazines to write about the cruise, which would be good for the Burmese economy, was I permitted to rejoin my group. In subsequent visits, I said I was "retired."

Thus it was when Emma Larkin lied her way through Burmese immigration and visited the various Orwell sites over a period of several years, meticulously tracking the author's life, while talking surreptitiously in Burmese with new friends usually met in tea shops. For anyone wishing to follow in Orwell's

Burmese footsteps, her book is key, though it might be advisable to put a false cover on it if you take it along.

In Mandalay, she found the Police Training School and Officers' Mess where Orwell lived not only still standing, but also still serving and housing cops. So, too, the police stations in Twante and Insein, while in Rangoon the old Strand Hotel where Orwell (and his character John Flory) fled whenever possible for a touch of home, has been completely restored by the Raffles hotel group.

In the southern city of Moulmein, once a prosperous trading center famous for its seafood, where Orwell's mom grew up, there is no trace of the family save for a short residential street bearing the family name, Limouzin. But here, as elsewhere, to evoke Orwell, one has only to visit surviving (sometimes relocated) Christian cemeteries and when passing old colonial homes and government buildings, merely add a coat of paint.

Because Orwell's eight postings were so widespread, and given the restrictions, both logistical and political, connected to modern travel in Burma, most of the author's followers content themselves with a visit to Katha, the novel's primary setting. Much has changed, as would be expected in a place whose population has gone from four thousand to eighty thousand; even the river has altered its course. But there is still sufficient remaining to make the journey by plane, bus, and riverboat rewarding. And so long as visitors keep their questions and conversations with the locals apolitical, talking about Orwell is not only acceptable but also expected. (Whereas by the time Larkin got to Katha, she was sure she had people following her.) So far, there are no maps or brochures available, nor are there any signs identifying the sites, but the *Lonely Planet* guide in 2005 devoted two pages to the town, whereas five years earlier, before Larkin wrote her book, it didn't even mention the place.

The hospital and Indian physician's home have been remodeled and the tennis court has been modernized, but the police station is little changed and the "European Club" is still a simple wooden building with a corrugated metal roof, occupied today by a government-run agricultural cooperative, the exterior gardens replaced by warehouses where the commodities are stored. There is still a colorful morning market and much of Orwell's beloved jungle is there, too—you just have to travel farther out of town to get to it.

W. Somerset Maugham
On Asia's Edge

Where the exotic settings, characters and events of the Orient established, propelled or defined numerous other writing careers, W. Somerset Maugham was a literary and theatrical colossus well before he made his first visit to the Orient and it is for his non-Asian writing that he is most solidly hailed. At the same time, his tales of post-World War One Southeast Asia established him as one of the best short fiction and travel writers of his time. They also got him called a predatory gossip.

Born on January 25, 1874, in Paris, the youngest of six sons of an English legal advisor to the British embassy, his mother died when he was eight of tuberculosis, his father two years later of cancer. Raised next by an uncle, a vicar in Kent, he studied for and abandoned a career as a physician, wrote a bestselling novel when he was twenty-three, and was famous at thirty, with ten plays and ten novels produced, at one time having four dramas playing in London simultaneously. He then topped himself with *Of Human Bondage* in 1915, *The Moon and Sixpence* (based on the life of Paul Gauguin), becoming one of the most important and highest earning authors of the twentieth century. (Adding *The Razor's Edge* to his bibliography much later, in 1944.)

His short stories about British colonial life in today's Indonesia, Singapore, and Malaysia won him further notoriety, some of them picked up in the bars at sundowner time and so thinly disguised that Graham Greene said colonial Asia was comprised "of British clubs, of pink gins, and of little scandals waiting for a Maugham to record them."

The writer's interest in Asia was not shallow, encompassing a collection of vignettes describing journeys in China; a novel set in Hong Kong; a travel memoir that took him to Burma, Siam, and Indochine; and before making a swami an important character in *The Razor's Edge*, to an Indian ashram. He trekked remote jungles in Burma on a mule, was sunk by a huge wave on a river in Borneo, tried opium in Cambodia (and threw up), and nearly died of malaria in Bangkok.

Although he married and fathered a daughter, he was openly, if reservedly, gay, living most of his adulthood with male companions. All his life he had a persistent stammer and some believe his mother's death left him traumatized; her photograph was at his bedside until his death at his home in Cap Ferrat on the French Riviera, December 16, 1965. He was ninety-one.

The Gentleman in the Parlor

He was a welcome visitor, even when unannounced. Virtually anyone would be, especially if you're a British plantation manager or a district officer or a constable in remote Southeast Asia, or married to one. When your social group is limited to other homesick Brits and their sad wives, sucking up sundowners at the bloody, boring club, and W. Somerset Maugham walks through the door, you know you're going to have a drink with him.

It was 1921 and Willie Maugham's linen suit may have been wrinkled, but his hair was cut and his mustache was neatly trimmed. He was rich and famous and had interesting stories to tell. He brought news from the outside world, which now was recovering from a world war and entering a period of great prosperity. He was, as described by Anthony Burgess, "at home in Paris and Vienna but also in Seoul and Djakarta, convivial and clubbable, as ready for a game of poker as for a discussion on the Racine Alexandrine, the antithesis of the slippered bookman." He even paid for most of the drinks. All he wanted in return was your life story, including all the gooey bits. He seemed a nice man, so you spilled every bean in your pot. And then he went home and exchanged the beans for buckets of cash.

Young writers are told to write about what they know and Maugham did that in his early novels and plays. Yet, his prolific skills quickly outdistanced his life experience, so he turned to the histories of others. In his novel *Cakes and Ale*, his good friend Hugh Walpole and half a dozen other of his contemporaries only had their names changed. His supernatural thriller *The Magician* was so closely modeled on Aleister Crowley, the real-life occultist and mystic wrote an article for *Vanity Fair*, accusing Maugham of plagiarism. Another novel, *The Moon and Sixpence*, was openly modeled on the life of Paul Gauguin.

So it also was in Singapore, Hong Kong, and the present-day Malaysia, where the difference was that instead of writing about himself or other well-known personalities—legitimate fodder for the mill by their own device, after all—Maugham now zeroed in on people he met casually over bridge and gin.

The Painted Veil, a novel published in 1925, was revised at least twice to eliminate references to and change the names of people living in Hong Kong who had sued his publisher and won. Even more invasive was a story he gleaned from a Singapore lawyer and his wife. Retold in a short story without overmuch fictionalizing as "The Letter," it subsequently appeared successfully on the London stage in 1927 and was adapted repeatedly for the movies and TV, most famously in 1940 in a film starring Bette Davis, but again in 1982 with Lee Remick in the lead. It was even staged as an opera, in 2009. Good gossip is good business.

Surely his best-known story after "Rain," "The Letter" told of
a married Englishwoman in Malaya who shot her lover on the
verandah of her home and then claimed self-defense, saying he
was trying to rape her. As Maugham told it, the man had a Chinese mistress as well and a letter the accused Englishwoman wrote
asking him to visit her was now in the Chinese woman's posses-
sion. The defendant's attorney purchased the letter, eliminating
the piece of incriminating evidence. The killing was found to be
justifiable by the Kuala Lumpur court and the woman was freed.
In reality, there was no letter and the woman was found guilty
and sentenced to hang. The public responded sympathetically, a
petition was circulated, and the Sultan of Selangor pardoned her,
whereupon she returned to England alone and died in a sanato-
rium. So Maugham made significant changes, but in Asia the
original subjects were instantly recognized.

This was typical. In Singapore he stayed at the Hotel Van Wyck,
which became the Hotel Van Dyke in a story called "Neil Mac-
Adam." Years later, when some of his tales were televised, he explained each one's origins. Of "Footprints in the Jungle" he said,
"It is one of those stories that I can hardly claim the authorship
of, for it was told me word for word one evening in a club in one
of the towns of the Federated Malay States." Introducing "The
Vessel of Wrath" he admitted, "all the people I have described in
this story I met at one time or another. I only had to bring them
together to invent the story." When *The Letter* appeared on the
London stage, he sent a copy of the play to the lawyer and his
wife, thanking them.

Some thought of Maugham as closely connected to Malaya
as Kipling was to India. Yet his time there was not long, six months
in 1921 (half of that in sanatoriums in Java, ill), four months in
1925. "He stayed in no one place very long," Anthony Burgess
wrote in an introduction to a repackaged collection of the tales,
"but he usually managed to absorb something of the atmosphere
of each town, village, or rubber estate he visited, and he always

made quick contact with the local residents. These residents were invariably Europeans—planters, colonial officials, businessmen, or just men living in exile to escape from trouble or sadness at home—and there is little evidence that Maugham gained, or wished to gain, any direct knowledge of the lives and customs of the native peoples of the East."

Years later, Burgess tempered this faint praise, saying (in a review of Paul Theroux's collection of stories set in Malaysia, *The Consul's File*, as well as surely recalling his own Malayan trilogy), "Willie Maugham, who knew the country least, has unfairly effected a literary near-monopoly of it…Maugham is always around somewhere, even in the post-Vietnam age, sardonically sipping gin *pahits* on the club veranda, observing exilic adulteries, defiled by mold on the termite-eaten shelves of the Carnegie Library."

Yet he captured the expat community so perfectly it was as if it were set in amber. Pico Iyer wrote, "It's hard not to go to an expat dinner party in Hong Kong, Paris, Buenos Aries, and not realize that you're in a collection of half-exotic types that you've met before in a Maugham short story."

When he mounted his 1938 pilgrimage to India, it was only after he obtained letters of introduction to a variety of maharajahs from the Aga Khan, one of his Riviera neighbors. Maugham had resisted going to India for many years, believing it was Kipling's patch, but he wanted to have the protagonist of his next novel, *The Razor's Edge*, adopt the Hindu idea of renunciation. So at sixty-four, Maugham packed his mountain of bags and found his way to a Vedanta ashram in southern India, where he promptly fainted upon meeting the resident swami, who sat with his unconscious visitor until shortly before he woke up, feeling fine. This was thirty years before ashrams became mandatory R&R stops on the hippie trail to Kathmandu and sixty-five years before Elizabeth Gilbert, an American writer, wandered into an ashram in her mega-selling *Eat Pray Love*.

(Years later, Paramahansa Yogananda, the Indian guru who wrote the worldwide bestseller *Autobiography of a Yogi* inscribed a copy for Maugham, thanking him for "spreading the seed of India's teachings.")

Of course Maugham did what he could to make his travel comfortable. He obtained letters of introduction to local British authorities, knowing that it guaranteed him a roof and meals. When you read his account of a backcountry tour of Southeast Asia in 1923 that took him from Rangoon to Bangkok to Siem Reap to Haiphong, readers may get the impression he traveled rough. In fact he was accompanied by his secretary and lifelong intimate friend Gerald Haxton, a cook, a Gurkha orderly, and a group of Yunnan tribesmen leading a train of mules that carried, among other things of course, dozens of books for the author to read. And when they halted, bamboo shelters sometimes were especially erected for him.

That said, it was 1923, after all, and potable water had to be found and food had to be gathered and shot and there were leeches and mosquitoes and snakes; in fact, he did contract malaria, his fever raging by the time he reached Bangkok (where the management of the Oriental Hotel fretted about his possibly dying there). The result was his only real travel book, appropriately titled *The Gentleman in the Parlour* and published in 1930, between his two collections of Malaysian tales, *The Casuarina Tree* in 1926 and *Ah King* in 1933.

In the introduction to *The Skeptical Romancer: Selected Travel Writing of W. Somerset Maugham* (2010), Pico Iyer wrote that "travel lay behind nearly all his work, and the traveling impulse—the wish to steal into the untried alleyway, to slip into a foreign heart, the wish to be away from the stuffy drawing-rooms he knew too well, and out among dramas and mysteries that would challenge and expand his mind—was really the engine that drove all his writing."

In a novel published when he was thirty, *The Merry-Go-Round*, Maugham himself had a character say, "My whole soul aches for the East, for Egypt and India and Japan. I want to know the corrupt, eager life of the Malays and the violent adventures of the South Sea islands...I want to see life and death, and the passions, the virtues and vices, of men face to face, uncovered." Such romantic notions were good for business, too.

Maugham was a cosmopolite: born in Paris, educated in Canterbury and Heidelburg, trained in medicine in London, a refugee in the United States during World War Two (when he worked on the film script for *The Razor's Edge*), and finally a resident of France (migrating there when his companion Gerald Haxton, an American, was deported from England on morals charges). He was also a man of his time, when Victoria was Queen and the time carried her name: always, always a proper gentleman, parlor or no parlor.

The Villa Mauresque at Cap Ferrat became his fortress, as noted by his biographer, Ted Morgan (in 1980): "Maugham in residence was the anti-bohemian, the writer as man of means who had by his pen alone been able to afford a style of life available only to tycoons and princes of the blood. The Maugham legend began with the Mauresque. Here was the ageing writer in his setting, the neighbor of millionaires and duchesses, surrounded by paintings, servants and cypresses, retiring at designated hours to his study, host to the Windsors, Churchill, and Beaverbrook."

In this setting he became a grumpy old man (of letters). In 1957, when he was eighty-three, he urged all his friends to burn any letters they kept. In his last will, signed in 1964, he directed his literary executor and trustees of his estate "to refuse permission for any such publication and any assistance to any person who wishes or attempts any such publication." He and his secretary, Alan Searle (who had moved into the villa after Haxton's death) held "bonfire nights," setting alight correspondence and unpublished manuscripts.

Is there anything left of what the intrepid gentleman in the parlour experienced in Asia for his readers to see today?

The *New York Times* sent a writer to the ashram of Sri Ramana Maharshi in Tiruvannamalai in the southernmost state of Tamil Nadu in 2010 and reported, "These days, the jungle surrounding the ashram has given way to semi-urban sprawl. On a recent visit, the place was humming with quiet activity, as Indians and Westerners alike ambled in and out to chant, meditate, pray before the tomb of Sri Ramana, who died in 1950, or just to chat or nap in the courtyard." Simple curries were eaten off a banana leaf, he concluded, with your hands.

Malaysia is one of the three largest producers of rubber (with Thailand and Indonesia) and some plantations and factories offer tours or can be talked into opening their gates if you seem to have no hidden agenda. Much has changed in the industry since Maugham was there, but the Dickensian work conditions largely remain in place in factories and almost nothing has changed in the pre-dawn tapping of the trees. In some of the scattered old camps and town, the old British club buildings still exist and depending on their present use (often by the local governments), a visit might be arranged.

E. M. Forster

A Passage to India

Edward Morgan Forster was born in London on January 1, 1879, the son of an architect who died before the boy was two, leaving him with a domineering mother, with whom he lived for much of his adult life, until her death in 1946. Although there were two earlier novels, the next two, *A Room With a View* and *Howards End*, published in 1908 and 1910, established Forster as a critical and commercial success. This was followed in 1924 by *A Passage to India*, his only work placed in Asia and his last novel, although he lived for another forty-six years.

Set in Raj India when the independence movement was young, and though praised for its multiple points of view, the novel nonetheless angered his fellow countrymen by damning—often in dialogue alone—the upper middle class "public school attitude" he felt characterized the colonial administrators and their wives. They were, he sniffed, elitist, prudish, censorious, lacking subtlety, complacent, self-satisfied, racist, and dull.

Discreetly, but openly gay to his friends, publicly he remained in the closet, lamenting (in his diary) the dishonesty he felt was forced upon him by society. A novel inspired by an affair he had with a young Egyptian train conductor, *Maurice*, was to be with-held from publication until both he and the empire were dead.

Considered one of the finest novelists in the English language of the twentieth century, Forster also wrote short stories, essays, plays and scripts, biography and literary criticism, the libretto for an opera based on Herman Melville's *Billy Budd*, and *Aspects of the Novel*, which is still being read by aspiring writers. Among his numerous honors was a knighthood, which he declined (in 1949).

Forster died of a stroke June 7, 1970, in Coventry at the home of his longtime lover, a policeman named Bob Buckingham, the cop's wife holding the author's hand. He was ninety-one.

"A Little Bridge of Sympathy"

"When I began the book," Edward Morgan Forster said of his classic *A Passage to India*, "I thought of it as a little bridge of sympathy between East and West, but this conception has had to go, my sense of truth forbids anything so comfortable. I think that most Indians, like most English people, are shits, and I am not interested whether they sympathize with one another or not."

These are strong and surprising words for a man always por-trayed by his biographers and friends as a humanist, a writer who seemed dedicated to the reconciliation of the differences between cultures and classes, whose epitaph on his gravestone reads, "Only Connect." Did it mean that he finally said the hell with it? And that it was for that reason he quit writing novels, nearly half a century before his death?

The truth is, *A Passage to India* almost didn't get written. For-ster was thirty-three years old when he first voyaged to the sub-continent, in 1912. A graduate of King's College, Cambridge, where he was befriended by future members of London's liter-ary Bloomsbury group, he was the author of four highly praised novels and a considered overly sensitive—given to easy tears and temper tantrums as a child—still living with his highly demanding mother. He had traveled in Europe with her—using the time spent in Italy as a setting for *A Room With a View*—and when World War One broke out, he volunteered for the Red Cross and was sent to Alexandria in Egypt, where he discovered another way that travel broadens you: he began an affair with a young Egyptian who inspired his homosexual novel, *Maurice*.

By now he also had begun *A Passage to India*, calling upon his experiences in 1912, when he visited a Moslem friend he had known in England, Syed Ross Masood, to whom the book would be dedicated and the object of the author's secret love as well as the model for the novel's Dr. Aziz. During that trip, he realized that Masood did not share his feelings, leading him to make the theme of his novel the difficulty of maintaining friendship across racial and cultural divides.

Yet another eight years passed, the novel, like Forster, seeming without impetus or direction, Virginia Woolf called him "a vaguely rambling butterfly." Forster said later that if her husband, *Bloomsbury* editor and publisher Leonard Woolf, hadn't kept after him, likely it would not have been finished. In 1921 he returned to India for nine months, serving as a personal secretary to a Rajah in Dewas in the dusty reaches of central India's Madhya Pradesh. Here he wrote a non-fiction account called *The Hills of Devi* and upon his return to England, he returned also to *A Passage to India*.

The story was a simple one. A Moslem physician, Aziz, befriends some British visitors, an elderly woman and a young schoolteacher who has come to India to marry her companion's son, who is serving the empire as a city magistrate. Aziz plans a picnic with the two women at the Marabar Caves, a religious site known for an unusually loud echo. Once inside, the older woman is spooked by the noise and claustrophobia caused by a thronging crowd. They leave and become separated. The schoolmistress then goes missing. A guide says she went into another cave and Aziz begins an unsuccessful search. Back outside, he sees the bloodied and disheveled woman drive away with a mutual friend, the British headmaster of a small local college. Returning to town, Aziz is told that the young woman has accused him of attempted rape.

In an early draft of the novel, Aziz was found guilty of the assault in court. But in the published version, the woman withdrew her charge while testifying, saying she doesn't know what happened inside the cave, and Aziz was carried away on the shoulders of his Indian friends. The British community turns against the false victim, her fiancé ends their engagement, and when the headmaster shelters the schoolteacher as she awaits a ship that will take her back to England, Aziz refuses to talk to him, although he was the only Englishman to support him in the trial.

The two men desire continued friendship as the novel ends. "But the horses…the earth…the temples, the tank, the jail, the palace, the birds, the carrion, the guest house…they didn't want it; they said in their hundred voices, 'No, not yet,' and the sky said, 'No, not there.'" Many call the book one of the greatest "Orientalist" novels, for its view that man's inability to overcome the individual and traditional differences made it impossible for the two cultures to meet. (Orientalism was an amorphous term that referred to a field of study describing a Western tradition, both academic and artistic, of hostile and disapproving views of the East. Some modern scholars use the term to describe writers of the Imperialist era with something positive to say about the Orient rather than slant everything to favor the West. Which of course describes Forster precisely.)

The novel was hailed as Forster's masterpiece—later appearing at number twenty-five on the Modern Library's list of hundred best novels of the twentieth century—contributing an alternative voice to the jingoistic chest-thumping of Kipling, taking its place on a shelf next to Orwell's *Burmese Days*.

Forster disliked and distrusted the cinema and even after his death, many respected filmmakers were turned away. Much impressed by a stage adaptation for the West End and Broadway in 1960 by Santha Rama Rau, David Lean was finally approved as director for a much-hailed filmed version of *Passage* released in 1984, fourteen years after Forster's death. Lean ignored both the opening and the ending of the novel and removed nearly all of Forster's criticism of British imperialism. The film was hailed, nonetheless, nominated for eleven Academy Awards, winning two.

Following the novel's publication, during the 1930s and 1940s, Forster appeared regularly as a talking head on BBC Radio and associated himself with various ethical and humanist societies. For the last twenty years of her life, he lived with his mother (who died in 1945, aged ninety) not far from the home of a London policeman named Bob Buckingam, the second serious affair of his life. Although Forster moved his base of operations to Cambridge after being elected an honorary fellow, this was an open relationship that continued until his death, despite the policeman's marrying. His wife, May, accepted it.

However satisfying that may have been for Forster, he blamed his inability to create fiction out of his gay desires—and do so publicly—for making *A Passage to India* his last novel, published forty-six years before his death. He wrote a number of short stories with gay themes, but they, like *Maurice*, also were published posthumously.

Reviewing a biography of Forster published in 2010, *A Great Unrecorded History* by Wendy Moffat, Colm Toibin disagreed with the author in *The New York Times*, saying the explanation for the long dry spell was "too easy, and perhaps even untrue. It may be more true to say that Forster wrote the five books on which is reputation rests because he desperately needed to create characters and situations that would expose his own plight in ways that were subtle and dramatic without being obvious or explicit. His true nature was not only homosexual, it was also wounded, mysterious and filled with sympathy for others, including foreigners and women. Despite his best intentions, he allowed all of himself into the five novels published in his lifetime, and only part of himself in *Maurice*."

I'll give Forster the final word on this. When told by friends that he should follow André Gide's example and publish his gay writing during his lifetime, he replied, "But Gide hasn't got a mother!"

Forster was meticulous about his physical descriptions of Indian sites and changed their names only slightly. Thus, the Marabar Caves so key to *A Passage to India's* plot were inspired by the Barabar Caves (and the nearby Nagarjuna Caves), which are in unfriendly bandit country thirty-five kilometers (twenty-two miles) north of Gaya, one hundred kilometers (sixty-two miles) south of Patna, in the northern district of Bihar. They are now, as they were to Aziz and his English guests, popular religious sanctuaries, but seldom visited by foreigners. (And, yes, the echo is real.) The *Rough Guide* to India suggests making arrangements through a travel agency and if you go alone, hire a local cop to accompany you. A journey for only the most dedicated Forster readers.

So, too, the location where Forster served his Rajah. Although the palace is closed to visitors and there are no hotels in Dewas, there are frequent bus connections with Ujjain, Indore, or Bhopal, where readers might meditate on the chemical plant meltdown and that disaster's role in the bumpy history of relations bridging East and West.

James Hilton

Lost Horizon, Shangri-La

James Hilton was born September 9, 1900 in Leigh, Lancashire, England, the son of a teacher and a headmaster. He grew up in London and was still an undergraduate at Christ's College, Cambridge, when at the age of twenty he published his first novel. Working as a journalist in Dublin, he wrote another ten before delivering a one-two literary punch that made him famous and rich—*Lost Horizon* in 1933, creating the legendary and mythical Shangri-La, and a year later, a story about an elderly, much-loved schoolmaster called *Goodbye, Mr. Chips*. Both became immediate bestsellers and successful films.

That led directly to California, where he became a naturalized citizen, divorced his English wife (after just two years), married his second (a starlet) seven days later, and started writing for film. He continued to publish novels—seven over a period of thirteen years; all sold well, but none won the praise and sales of the two for which he is remembered.

Now he became known for his movie work, providing dialog for Alfred Hitchcock's *Foreign Correspondent* in 1940 and, two years later, sharing the screenplay credit for *Mrs. Miniver*, a film that won six Oscars, including Best Picture, and was credited with rallying American support for its British allies during World War Two.

Hilton's name may not be known widely today, but four versions of *Goodbye, Mr. Chips* have been filmed (the last in 2002) and Shangri-La, depicted in two movies, remains part of the vocabulary, keeping his work alive.

He died December 20, 1954 in Long Beach, California, of liver cancer. After divorcing his second wife, he had reconciled with his first, who nursed him until the end.

In Search of Shangri-La

Elysium, Eden, Paradise, Arcadia, Valhalla, Utopia, New Atlantis, El Dorado, Fantasia, Walden, Erehwon, Nirvana, Heaven, Shangri-La. And these are only the *English* words for it. (Erehwon being "nowhere" spelled backwards.)

Everyone has a word for it and a notion about whether it does or does not exist, and no one knows where it is located…or if, indeed, it exists only in desire.

In 1933, when a British writer named James Hilton published a novel called *Lost Horizon*, he contributed to the world both a conundrum and a fantasy. When a small propeller-driven plane crashes somewhere in what is believed to be Tibet, the four passengers, three Brits and an American, find themselves in a hermetically sealed kingdom characterized by what the author called "sumptuous tranquility…a delightfully favored place…an enclosed paradise of amazing versatility…a landlocked harbor touched with the mystery that lies at the core of all loveliness."

Although there is little sexual play in the plot, there is even something said about a young Chinese musician who becomes of interest to two of the men saying, "…the ivory doll has manners, good taste in dress, attractive looks, a pretty touch on the harpsichord, and she doesn't move about a room as if she were playing hockey. Western Europe, so far as I recollect it, contains an exceptionally large number of females who lack those attributes."

The year was 1932 and here, cut off from the outside world—a world still recovering from World War One and dealing with the anxiety that accompanied the run-up to Number Two, not to mention the Great Depression—was a most unusual paradise, where Buddhist monks ruled benevolently and the lamas lived for hundreds of years and breathed clean air, but also had central heating, modern plumbing (described as being from Akron, Ohio) and a library of leather-bound classics to while away the cold, blustery hours between morning ambrosia and afternoon tea. Hilton called this lamasery Shangri-La.

That the novelist hadn't been any closer to the world's highest mountain range than the British Museum to do his research didn't matter. That his primary inspiration were articles in *National Geographic* by a botanist and explorer named Joseph Rock was irrelevant. (Rock introduced the rhododendron to the United States along with medicinal plants used to treat Hansen's disease and his manuscripts and photographs are part of the Tibetan collection at the US Library of Congress, the rare plants collected going to Harvard University's Arnold Arboretum.) One takes paradise where one can find it without too many questions asked and the book became a runaway bestseller.

The book's plot was fairly simple. After the crash landing, the pilot dies, but first tells his passengers that they can find shelter at a nearby lamasery called Shangri-La. Learning upon arrival that they've stumbled into a sort of utopia, where longevity comes with the tranquility, three of the four decide to stay—a female missionary who wishes to introduce the local population to the concept of sin, another (the sole American) because he is wanted by police and sees an opportunity to exploit gold mines in the area, and the third, a British diplomat, merely because the notion of sitting down and enjoying life appeals to him. The fourth, another British foreign officer, wants to leave.

Time passes, as it does even in utopia, and when it is time for the High Lama to finally die at age 200 or so, he tells the diplomat he wants him to lead the lamasery. Meanwhile, his rival has won the young harpsichordist's heart and is planning to take her home with him to the Real World, refusing to believe a warning that she is not as young as she appears but old and that she will age when she leaves. At the last minute, the diplomat decides to accompany them, but once outside, he again changes his mind and the last we hear of him, he's trying to find his way back, leaving the younger Brit with a story he cannot prove.

The message is simple, too. The High Lama believes Man seems determined to destroy the world and his goal was to preserve what the world was losing and provide sanctuary for those who agreed with him. "Here we shall stay with our books and our music and our meditations," he said, "conserving the frail elegancies of a dying age, and seeking such wisdom as men will need when their passions are all spent."

(Ironically, war and politics came into play when in 1942 following comment by President Roosevelt, the film was re-released as *The Lost Horizon of Shangri-La*, with twelve minutes cut to soften the pacifistic tone for wartime audiences. More scenes were removed in 1952 when Cold War censors thought all that utopianism sounded too much like communism and also wanted to make China seem less attractive to the American public. Eventually, all the missing footage was restored.)

When Frank Capra made a film of the book in 1937 starring Ronald Coleman and US President Franklin D. Roosevelt named his weekend retreat outside Washington "Shangri-La" (President Eisenhower renamed it Camp David after his grandson), the word entered the language as a synonym for utopia. In time, a US aircraft carrier would carry the same name during World War Two, as would the No. 1 singing group of the 1960s with No. 1 hits called "Remember, Walkin' in the Sand" and "Leader of the Pack." There were many other books that included Shan-gri-La in the title, ranging from *Prisoners of Shangri-La: Tibetan Buddhism and the West* to *Shangri-La: A Travel Guide to the Hi-malayan Dream.*

A second Hollywood version of *Lost Horizon* opened on Broadway as a musical comedy for a mercifully short run in 1956 (music by Burt Bacharach), it was done again as a movie in 1973 starring Peter Finch and Liv Ullmann, and in 1996 a sequel was published, *Shangri-La: The Return to the World of Lost Horizon.* Written by Eleanor Cooney and Daniel Altieri, this told the story of a Chinese general who planned to plunder the riches of Shan-gri-La; it, was a failure. Shangri-La more successfully became a brand by a host of entrepreneurs who wished to cash in on the feel-good mystique. In China there was a company that manu-factured traditional Chinese medicines and cosmetics, in the Philippines a upscale Shangri-La Plaza, in Nepal a Shangri-La Development Bank. The name also was used by a construction company in Los Angeles—a city that fancied itself somewhat utopian—and by Hamilton Beach as a design on its stoneware cookers. Most remarkably it became the name of a Hong Kong-based chain of sixty-five five-star hotels with expensive rooms for rent in nineteen countries. (Did these hotel people not take note of the novelist's name?)

Although more than ten million copies of the book eventually sold, it did not catch on right away. Published in England in 1933, it found a readership only after the author's *Goodbye, Mr. Chips* became a bestseller a year later and *Lost Horizon* was awarded the prestigious Hawthornden Prize, comparable, more or less, to America's Pulitzer. In the US, the *New York Times* called the pro-logue and epilogue "inept" and "maladroit" and said the charac-ters were "too vaguely realized and their problems were too evasive to matter then or now" and Shangri-La remained unknown until Alexander Woollcott praised it on his popular radio show. That was when American readers took it as an antidote to war talk and the failed economy and in 1939 the book was republished as the industry's first pocketbook by Ian Ballantine. Seventy-six years later, it's still in print.

Okay, so where is Shangri-La? Putting aside all rational thought about the futility of chasing literary white rabbits down fictional holes, it's a question that has not gone away.

For many years, the reasonable location-of-choice was Tibet, because that's where Hilton said it was located. In 1959, when the Chinese government decided to reclaim Tibet and replace its culture with its own, many Shangri-La searchers and theorizers shifted their attention to Bhutan, which was, then, and now, the most remote and pristine country in Asia. The rulers of this tiny Buddhist nation bordering Nepal and Tibet, like the lamas in Hilton's Shangri-La, have made it clear that not only do they wish to preserve the peacefulness that accompanies their isolation, that notion is also now government policy.

Until the early 1960s, the only way to get there was walk. Now there are roads and airports, but tariffs must be paid before entering—$165 per night per person during the low season (July and August), $200 per night per person the rest of the year; this is for groups of three or more—add $40 per night if traveling alone, $30 for each if you travel with a friend—plus a $20 visa fee. Some discounts are offered for students and children, but there are heavy "fines" for cancelling your visit.

This keeps the riff-raff out, so there are none of those ganja gangstas in parachute pants, backpacks and tattoos, and small money in their belly-packs; Bhutan figures this represents a step in the right direction. Then came the big breakthrough in 1972 when King Jigme Singye Wangchuck in an interview suggested an alternative to the Gross National Product, the economic yardstick by which countries measure their success or lack of it. Instead of using the GNP, he urged his small kingdom to adopt as its guiding philosophy the GNH, the "H" standing for "Happiness."

(The king's tutor, a distinguished British citizen, suggested to the monarch that the "H" should be for Harmony rather than Happiness, but it was too late.)

Was he serious? Yes, he was, and by 2008 it had been fine-tuned sufficiently for a new Constitution to mandate that all government programs—from agriculture to transportation to foreign trade—must be judged not by the economic benefits they may offer, but by the happiness they may produce. (Thus trumping America, a country that only guarantees the "pursuit" of happiness in its constitution.) At the same time, the king resigned—against the wishes of his subjects—and turned over the throne to his son, Jigme Kesar Namgyel Wangchuck, who now reigns as a constitutional monarch without executive power.

Kinley Dorji, Bhutan's secretary of information and communications, told the global edition of the *New York Times* in 2009 that GNH was an idea whose time had come. "You see what a complete dedication of economic development ends up in," he said, referring to worldwide economic crisis. "Industrialized societies have decided that GNP is a broken promise."

As charming and idealistic as all this sounded—one could almost hear those tie-dyed backpackers cheering from the other side of the Bhutanese border—it was no surprise when the World Bank and the International Monetary Fund said, in effect, "What the hell are you talking about? How do you measure happiness?"

An answer came in a report n the *New York Times* that said Bhutan "produced an intricate model of well-being that features the four pillars, the nine domains, and the seventy-two indicators of happiness. More specifically, the government has determined that the four pillars of a happy society involve the economy, culture, the environment and good governance.

"It subdivides these into nine domains: psychological well-being, ecology, health, education, culture, living standards, time use, community vitality, and [again] good governance, each with its own weighted and unweighted GNH index.

"All this is to be analyzed using the seventy-two indicators. Under the domain of psychological wellbeing, for example, indicators include the frequencies of prayer and meditation and of feelings of selfishness, jealousy, calm, compassion, generosity, and frustration, as well as suicidal thoughts.

"'Every two years, these indicators are to be reassessed through a nationwide questionnaire' said Karma Tshiteem, secretary of the Gross National Happiness Commission, as he sat in his office at the end of a hard day of work that he said made him happy."

Bhutan was not the only Shangri-La candidate. The Chinese government had one, too, after it had effectively wrecked Tibet. (In 1958, the year before the Chinese army moved in and began destroying all the temples and monasteries, there were 115,600 monks in Tibet; in 1976, there were just nine hundred and seventy.) With Shangri-La still in the dictionary and all those high-priced hotels bearing the name springing up, Zhongdian County in southwestern Yunnan province in 2001 renamed itself Shangri-La after gaining approval from the State Council, the national cabinet in Beijing.

In fact, Zhongdian, the capital city of a huge province, wasn't a bad or arbitrary choice, its terrain widely recognized as fitting Hilton's description of a verdant valley crowned by a Tibetan Buddhist lamasery and encompassed by snow-capped peaks. And Joseph Rock had been based just one-hundred kilometers south of Zhongdian in Lijiang, a town that for many years also made a claim to the mythical name, drawing a goodly crowd of, you guessed it, those banana pancake eating people in tattoos and parachute pants.

In an article in the *China Daily* in 2005, it was also pointed out that the sacred mountain that Hilton called Karakal was described almost word-for-word as Rock wrote in his journal of his first sight of Konkaling, a mountain now part of the Yading National Nature reserve northeast of Zhongdian.

Today's tourism folks in Beijing weren't slow to recognize all this. Today there is domestic airline service and five-star accommodation in both Lijiang and the former Zhongdian. Oddly, there is no Shangri-La Hotel in either city, nor anything that would prevent any existing or new hotel from using the city's new name in its own so that there could, say, be a Sheraton or Marriott Shangri-La.

There was, of course, still another candidate, this one aptly put forward by *National Geographic*, the magazine where this all began. Hilton may have been inspired by the generic word for "pass" in Tibetan, which is *la*, the magazine theorized, and the pass called Changri La in particular, which was located near Mount Everest, a place frequented by the legendary British climber George Mallory in the 1920s. The snowcapped peaks are there but the lamasery is missing.

One thing is certain, if Shangri-La is in Tibet or in the new province that has taken the book's title for its name, China claims it as its own and copies of the book now available come from the Yunnan Publishing Group Corporation, Yunnan People's Publishing House. With royalties presumably going to Beijing.

Pearl S. Buck
The Good Earth

Pearl Sydenstricker Buck, who spent the first half of her eighty years living in China, the other half in the United States, was one of the first champions of women's rights, children's rights, the rights of racial and inter-racial minorities, the rights of what were then called the mentally retarded (her only natural child being profoundly so)—all of this before such issues were even talked about in public.

She also wrote between seventy and a hundred and twenty books (depending on whether anthologies and new editions were counted), won a Pulitzer Prize for a novel about peasant Chinese farmers called *The Good Earth*, published in 1931, and seven years later became the first American woman to be awarded the Nobel Prize for literature. Through her novels, short stories, biographies, children's books, political journalism, essays, drama, poetry and numerous translations from the Chinese, she also became the twentieth century's most important interpreter of China to the West, contributing more to cross-cultural understanding between East and West than even Kipling might grudgingly have thought was possible.

Buck's humanitarian beliefs led to her establishing the first interracial and international adoption agency in the world (adopting seven of her own) and the Pearl S. Buck Foundation, dedicated to helping Ameriasian children, kids abandoned in the Orient by their love-'em and leave-'em American dads. Both organizations are still active.

She was the fourth of seven children (and one of only three who lived to adulthood), born to American Presbyterian missionaries on June 26, 1892, in Hillsboro, West Virginia, and taken to China when she was five months old, where Mandarin became her first language. She was educated by her mother and a Confucian tutor as a child and earned two university degrees in the United States.

She died of lung cancer March 6, 1973, in Danby, Vermont. Her tombstone, of her own design, does not record her name in English, but is inscribed with Chinese characters.

The Original Pearl of the Orient

When I first read the book as a student, it was puzzling, at least to me, why Pearl Buck's novel *The Good Earth* had been so popular. Yes, it was well written, but it also told a story that for its time—it was published in 1931, during the worldwide Great Depression—was so depressing itself, I would have thought people would have not just ignored it, but run away from it.

It told the story of Wang Lung, a poor farmer who marries a plain but hard-working young kitchen slave named O-lan and fathers five children, among them a daughter who is mentally handicapped and the last of whom, also a girl, apparently was strangled at birth by O-lan. A period of good crops is followed by drought that forces the family to migrate to the city, where O-lan and the children beg on the streets and Wang Lung labors as a rickshaw puller, a work category below which there is only unemployment.

There is talk of revolution in the country and when Wang and O-lan loot a rich man's home, they use the gold and jewels they stole to return home, fix up the old house, and buy additional land. After a period of prosperity, the crops now are destroyed by flood, the marriage by a woman Wang meets in a teahouse, who is soon found in bed with his oldest son. He then acquires a former prostitute for his "second wife" and takes her slave as a concubine while O-lan continues to cook and clean for him.

He feeds opium to a threatening uncle and aunt to keep them quiet. His youngest son becomes a revolutionary leader and is killed. Then O-lan dies, there is more flood, then famine, then locusts, or maybe it was the other way around, but through it all, Wang Lung holds on to his beloved land, "the good earth" of the book's title. The book ends when he is on his deathbed, as he overhears his two surviving sons planning to sell the land, Wang Lung begs them not to and they say they will honor his wishes. The reader knows they're lying. And these are just some of the "high" spots in the plot; there's much, much more trouble and tragedy and rarely even the smallest laugh.

Is this the kind of story you'd want to read during the Great Depression, when the world's economy hung in tatters? Was it a matter of misery loving company? Did readers in the West think: well, at least my life is not *that* grim? I figured there had to be something more. There had to be a reason the novel was so popular, selling one million, eight hundred thousand copies over a period of two years, and then won a Pulitzer for best novel of the year and got made into a movie by MGM that cost $2.8 million—a huge sum for the time—and took three years to film, a motion picture that not only was nominated for best picture of the year but was a hit at the box office as well.

For decades I didn't understand and then, as the twentieth century came to an end, seventy years after book's publication, I married a poor rice farmer's daughter in Thailand and built a house in a tiny, rural village where it became clear: in extreme circumstances you do whatever you have to do to survive—some of those acts to be regarded by others as unfavorable, unacceptable, or despicable—but you do not abandon what was so incisively phrased by the Permanent Secretary of the Swedish Academy in 1938 when presenting Buck with her Nobel Prize.

"As her hero," said Per Hallstrom, "she took a man who led the same existence as his forefathers had during countless centuries, and who possessed the same primitive soul. His virtues spring from one single root: affinity with the earth, which yields its crops in return for a man's labors."

That was it. That connection to the soil existed at that time in America, before Big Agribusiness distanced the "farmer" from his crops, introducing harvesting machinery as large as a house and government guarantees of profit with import protection and subsidies not to plant. America had a similar tale in John Steinbeck's epic, *The Grapes of Wrath* (he later won a Nobel, too). That novel was published a few years later, in 1939, but readers during the Depression understood what he and before him, Buck, were talking about. China may have been unknown to the West, but Wang Lung rang a familiar bell. I remembered something I'd been told at mealtimes by my parents when I was growing up in the years immediately following the Depression and I didn't want to clean my plate: "There are people starving in China…" Thus, Buck had reached into everyone's home.

This is not to say Buck was always praised. William Faulkner called her "Mrs. Chinahand Buck" and John Hersey, also raised in China by missionary parents, in a reference to the outpouring of books that followed, said she produced "probably seventy too many." While many in the religious community expressed shock at the novel's candid talk about sex and other bodily functions.

Pearl Buck's parents were Presbyterian missionaries and when they took her as an infant to China, settling in Chinkiang (called today Zhenjiang), she was tutored by her mother but also by a Confucian scholar whose teachings softened the sharp edges of the Calvinist doctrine that otherwise might have dominated her instruction. Her parents also encouraged her to write from the time she was scarcely literate and she published stories in the weekly children's edition of the *Shanghai Mercury*, an English language newspaper.

Her life in China was not always pleasant. When she was eight years old, in 1900, hatred against foreigners led to what was called the "Boxer Uprising (or Rebellion)," forcing her family to flee first to Shanghai, then to the United States, where they remained for a year before returning to China. Through it all, her parents provided a moral compass. Her father, Absalom Sydenstricker, spent months away from home in search of Christian converts and at home, was what she described as a stern and humorless man who devoted much of his time to translating the *Bible* from Greek to Chinese, while her mother ministered to Chinese women in a small dispensary. So it was no surprise when at fifteen, their only child volunteered at the Door of Hope, a shelter for Chinese slave girls and prostitutes.

Still, when she went to the United States to attend the Randolph-Macon Women's College in Virginia, she studied not theology, for which the school was famed, but psychology, graduating in 1914 and after teaching at the school for one semester, returning to China to nurse her mother through a long illness.

In 1917 at age twenty-five she married a young Cornell University graduate, an agricultural economist named John Lossing and they migrated to impoverished rural Anhwei (Anhui) province. It was here that while he did some pioneering work on Chinese agriculture, she gathered the background for what eventually became *The Good Earth*, two sequels, *Sons* and *A House Divided*, as well as other stories of China.

"It is people that have always afforded me my greatest pleasure and interest," she once said, "and as I live among the Chinese, it has been the Chinese people. When I am asked what sort of people they are, I cannot answer. They are not this or that, they are just people. I can no more define them than I can define my own relatives and kinsmen. I am too near to them and I have lived too intimately with them for that."

That being said, it was as much for the separate biographies of her parents that she was given the Nobel. And whatever it was she wrote about the Chinese, she did so in a fashion that struck a loud and emotional chord—making it clear that Fu Manchu and Charlie Chan, two contemporaneous literary figures, were not even remotely what real Chinese were like. Those two figures were good and evil stereotypes, made for Hollywood and comic books, where the Chinese Buck described were, as she said, just like you and me.

Buck's marriage lasted eighteen years but was not a happy one, complicated by their only child's severe mental disabilities and surgery that made Buck's further pregnancy impossible. Both held teaching positions at Nanking University as she began to publish stories and essays in American magazines. Her first novel, *East Wind, West Wind*, was published by the John Day Company in 1930. John Day's publisher, Richard Walsh, also took *The Good Earth* and after they both received divorces, in 1935 they married and Buck joined him in the United States, where she put her daughter in an institution. (In my hometown in New Jersey.)

Thus ended the Chinese half of her life, at least so far as her residency. Her life was similarly divided, as Buck became not only a prolific writer about Asia (with interests that spread to India and Korea) but also one of the planet's most outspoken and innovative humanitarians. Sometimes, these two sides seemed in conflict, often when Hollywood intruded into her life.

When MGM bought the rights to *The Good Earth* and she asked that Chinese be cast in all the film's roles, the leads went instead to two Caucasians, Paul Muni and Luis Rainier, both of whom had won Oscars the previous year, Rainier for her role in *The Great Ziegfeld* and Muni for the lead in *The Story of Louis Pasteur*. This was not a problem that went away. Wishing to duplicate its success with *The Good Earth*, MGM in 1942 adapted another novel, *Dragon Seed*, and this time made Katharine Hepburn the star.

Buck had no voice or choice in such matters. Big name writers nowadays frequently maintain some control when films are based on their work (often by taking percentage points of any profit in lieu of cash and sometimes serving as "producers") but in the 1930s and 1940s it was as Ernest Hemingway said: when you sell one of your books to the movies, best thing to do is meet them at the California state line where you toss the manuscript over the line and they throw a bag full of money back and you return to your typewriter to write the next one.

Buck always had another story to tell and from the telling found her reward. "I feel no need for any other faith than my faith in human beings," she said in 1939. "Like Confucius of old, I am so absorbed in the wonder of earth and the life upon it that I cannot think of heaven and the angels…If there is no other life, then this one has been enough to make it worth being born, myself a human being."

It was with this reverence for life that she ran her public life. She published essays in *Crisis*, the journal of the NAACP, and *Opportunity*, the magazine of the Urban League. For twenty years she was a trustee for Howard University, America's first university for what then were called Negroes. In 1942, she and her publisher-husband started the East and West Association, dedicated to serve as a bridge between those two cultures.

When in 1949 she learned that existing adoption services considered Asian and other mixed-race children unadoptable, she started Welcome House, the world's first international, interracial adoption organization. (With more than five thousand placements made since and still counting.) She followed this by publishing, in 1959, a book exploring the ethics of dropping the atomic bomb on Japan, and in 1964 founding the Pearl S. Buck Foundation, an organization that more than fifty years later continues to provide sponsorship funding for thousands of Amerasian children in half a dozen Asian countries. What this means is that she became the individual who went in and helped clean up after the American military had left an Asian country with its women pregnant, and its villages burned to the ground.

Sadly, in her final years, her life was a bit of a mess. After her second husband's death, she formed still another foundation, this time with a much younger Arthur Murray dance instructor. She became estranged from her adopted children and wore a white mink coat while driving a limousine with her monogram on the door. In the end, following a scandal in which her partner was accused of improper behavior with young Asian boys, they retreated to Vermont, where he sold antiques and she sold her books from his shop.

China today is much changed since Buck lived among the poor peasant class, but in many rural areas, disturbingly little has changed at all and if the nation at large has bulled and bullied its way into becoming the world's second largest economy, as well as a force to be kowtowed to internationally, it has done so at great cost to the same desperately poor, who now work in unsafe coal mines and thousands of factories to drive this growth, and are no better off than the farmers in their own genealogy.

Add brutalized Tibetans and numerous other minorities, the shame of Tiananmen Square, displacement of millions to build the world's largest dam on the Yangtze (a river the young Pearl Buck once lived beside), the excess and braggadocio of Beijing's Olympics and Shanghai's World Expo, the planet's highest execution-of-troublemakers rate, and a paranoiac suppression of all dissident thought, even when the "crime" was no more threatening than meditation. Despite all that, China acquired a worrisome tidal wave-strength force.

China may now have more dollar millionaires than the United States and own over twenty-five percent of America's bonds (thus control a potentially threatening portion of its debt) and

Shanghai, where the young Pearl Buck once sought refuge from Boxer bad guys, may some day overtake London, Hong Kong and even New York as a financial capital, yet if Buck were alive today and sitting at a computer instead of a manual typewriter or paper and pen, she would not have to look far to find kindred souls to write about. The new wealthy get the headlines, but the poor still get the leavings at the same time they form the heart and muscle of China's boom.

So the visitor to modern China sniffing for the scent of Pearl Buck doesn't have to look far to see identical poverty. That pilgrim can also find, both in China and the United States, places where Buck once lived and worked, visiting the past mementoes as well as volunteer to serve her legacy.

Initially, the Communists didn't like Buck, thought she made China look repressive, but today there are two onetime homes of the author in China open for tours—the house in Zhenjiang where she spent her early childhood, established as a Cultural Heritage in 1992 on the hundredth anniversary of her birth (go to www.pearsbcn.org/e/), and what today are called the Pearl S. Buck Villas in Lushan Mountain in Jiangxi Province, originally a retreat used by the Presbyterian Church for its foreign ministry to escape the summer heat. This home has a splendid view and has been restored, complete with wax figures (see www.china-lushan.com/english/). A former residence of Mao Tse-tung is also nearby.

In Perkasie, Pennsylvania, about an hour's drive north of Philadelphia, visitors may tour Buck's Bucks County stone farmhouse and grounds, dedicated on her seventy-fifth birthday to further help disadvantaged children. Here, her Pulitzer and Nobel are displayed, along with many other artifacts, and fans may rent the site for weddings and other social or business events. Graceland it is not, but with its vast archives and the "Artifact of the Month," it's definitely worth the trip.

John Masters

Bhowani Junction

John Masters had a goal. Born into a family that had served in
the British military in India for six generations, he planned to tell
the whole story of the English in their most remarkable colony
in thirty-five historical novels covering three hundred years. He
didn't live long enough to accomplish that, but the body of work
he did produce was as impressive as it was popular.

Best known for a novel set during the bloody partition and
transition to Indian independence in 1947, *Bhowani Junction*,
which became a film starring Stewart Granger and Ava Gardner.
Masters finished twenty-two novels and three volumes of autobiography as well, not bad for a man who turned to writing after
retiring as a lieutenant colonel and emigrating to America. (Another film adaptation, *The Deceivers*, starred Pierce Brosnan and
was produced by Ismail Merchant.)

Inevitably he was compared to Kipling. One Indian novelist,
Khushwant Singh, said that while Kipling understood India,
Masters understood Indians. "He couldn't avoid being British,"
said another, Darshan Singh Maini, "but he had developed a
keenly neutral, observant eye and, therefore, he treated both the

masters and the subjects with equal justice and authority," while Kipling was "derailed in his formulations, and the concepts of 'the East-West divide' as well as 'the White Man's Burden' became the staple of his song."

Masters was born in Calcutta January 1, 1914, taken to England when he was two, and, upon graduation from Sandhurst, served in Iraq during Britain's short war. He was a staff officer in Delhi, and behind the Japanese lines in Burma during World War Two, where, before his brigade was ordered to withdraw, he had nineteen of his own men shot, believing them to be past recovery or escape. His biographer described him as an impatient man, but extremely disciplined.

Unhappy with life in Britain following the war, he immigrated to New York, where he started a travel agency that offered treks of the Himalayas, an idea ahead of its time. When it failed and rumors of a hidden Indian ancestry that had dogged his career were confirmed in his genealogy, he began to write, dedicating seven of his novels to telling the story of the Savage family in its multi-generational service in India.

He and his wife—who was married to a fellow officer when they met, a scandal at the time—spent their last years in Santa Fe, New Mexico, where he died on his sixty-ninth birthday, January 1,1983, following heart surgery. His ashes were strewn from the air on hiking trails in the nearby mountains.

"Murderous at Times"

"I have a very low tolerance for yogis and transubstantiation and meditation and anything like that, especially when people associate a higher spirituality with it, if only because it's not American or not English," the middle-aged John Masters said. "They chant, the Indians are holy as hell, but we're not. And there are all kinds of secrets that they know that our people don't know, in a spiritual sense. And I have never been able to accept that. You see, my family have been in India for six generations and if anybody should know something about it, we would and all we know is that Indians are very nice people, very warm and generous, and murderous at times, and just like everybody else."

He was a career military officer, a lieutenant colonel who was the son of a lieutenant colonel in the British Army assigned to maintain order in India during the waning days of empire. Yet, he also steadfastly maintained that Indians were just like him, friendly chaps, only sometimes "murderous." That he was of mixed blood himself was a rumor eventually confirmed that, some said, explained his attempted neutral stance. He may also have realized that his own genealogy and experience as a military man could have contributed some of the violence.

This was made clear in the first novel, *Nightrunners of Bengal*, published in 1951. Because the book is set at the time of the Indian Uprising (or Mutiny) of 1857, he captured the murderous nature of both the "natives" and the British, both of whom were wearing the same uniform. This is how it happened.

In understanding India's history, it is essential to recognize that at its root much of the violence has been religiously motivated, and so it was with the Mutiny, the causes of which even today remain somewhat muddled. Virtually all of the men in the Army were Indian—only the officers were Brits—and the grievances were various and numerous. However, when a rumor, quite possibly true, spread that a new type of bullet issued to the troops was wrapped in paper containing pig fat, and a similar rumor claimed that it was greased with cow fat, both Muslims and Hindus rebelled. Pigs are unclean to Muslims and cows are holy to Hindus.

When the British were slow to address the rumors, or make and announce changes if they were true, forty-seven of the seventy-four battalions in the Bengal army mutinied. The outbreak quickly led to the fall of Delhi and swept across north India, lasting a full year. There were massacres on both sides, killing thousands. So, too, in the novel, which ended, with most of the soldiers in the Bhowani garrison in Bengal and their families dead, including the wife of the book's hero, the provocatively named Rodney Savage.

The novel was selected by the Literary Guild in the United States as its book of the month, making it a bestseller and launching both his career and the start of a long series of tales featuring Savage, a captain in the Indian army. The officer reappears in other novels—advancing to general and old age—as do his father, son and other family members, one of whom is a Thug, short for Thugee, a murderous cult that preyed on innocent travelers by garroting them for their possessions, then burying them so that they appeared to have disappeared. That was in his second novel, *The Deceivers*, published in 1952 and made into a film by Merchant-Ivory that starred Pierce Brosnan, but after the author was dead, in 1988.

It was his third novel that put Masters over the top. This was *Bhowani Junction*, a multi-racial romance set against the eruptive violence that accompanied the empire's withdrawal from India in 1946, an event still fresh in public memory when it was published just six years later. It, too, was adapted for film, but this time by Hollywood and starring Stewart Granger as Savage (now a colonel) and Ava Gardner as an Anglo-Indian nurse in the British army.

The novel had a little of everything in it: three men competing for the nurse's love in a time when races and religions didn't mix (besides Savage, a Sikh and another Anglo-Indian); an attempted rape of the nurse, during which she kills her attacker; a showdown between Savage and protestors halting railway traffic by lying on the tracks, broken when the colonel orders his Gurkha troops to piss on them and as the locomotive releases it's steam with a hiss, the humiliated men take flight; and a Communist plot to kill Gandhi with a bomb. In the end, Gandhi's life is saved but Savage loses the girl, although in the Hollywood version, he *got* the girl.

The books appeared at the rate of one a year (occasionally two) right up to the time of his death, when he was working on a trilogy set during World War Two. Four of Masters' novels were adapted for an eighteen-part series for posthumous broadcast on BBC Radio. The majority sold well during the 1950s and 1960s, although today Masters is largely forgotten and most of his work is out-of-print.

In much that has been written about Masters he is called an "Anglo-Indian" writer, as if that tinted the way he wrote. But his mixed blood was no more than a rumor during most of his adult life. Surely those rumors gave him something to think about as he wrote his early novels, but there is little doubt that mainly he was thinking as a military Brit, a descendant of other British soldiers. So if he made his Indian characters "murderous at times," he also tried to make them sympathetic, in an effort to be fair. When asked how he felt about his fellow Imperialists, he was ambiguous even about them.

"There was an overall British emotion towards India," he said, "—a kind of possessiveness, a sort of scorn and great affection at the same time."

He was hard on other British writers as well. He faulted *The Razor's Edge* because Maugham had made a yogi such a force in it. Forster's was not a great book because "it was too clear-cut" and India was not. He did not like Kipling much, either. "I think *Kim* is a superb book because of atmosphere," he said in an interview a few years before his death. "You stay to the end. Which, if you've read *Kim* and have read it carefully and felt it, you can go to India and say, 'My God, I know India. I know, I've seen this before, I've felt it. I've smelt it, without understanding much. You know, you shouldn't understand. It's much too big, much to complicated for one book to clarify any situation, that's my opinion. But *Kim* is also one of the few books where Kipling does not show a sort of mean streak, a want to hurt somebody or stick a ramrod up somebody's behind to smarten them up."

He was kinder toward what he called the Indo-Anglians, "those who are Indian who write in English, like Kushwant Singh and Ved Mehta and Naipaul. Kamala Markandaya, I believe she'd count as an Indo-Anglian. And together, if you read them one after the other, then alternately, you get an extremely good picture of India."

The British are now long gone, of course, and India has become an Asian powerhouse, yet those who wish to walk in Masters's footsteps today can easily do so if they stick to the still-impoverished rural countryside, where the struggle to survive hasn't changed a bit. It's also still murderous…at times.

There's a restaurant in Delhi called Bhowani Junction, but the junction itself does not exist. It was modeled on the central Indian town of Bhusawal, which has the biggest railways junction and one of the largest rail yards in Asia.

Graham Greene

The Quiet American

Graham Greene was born into privilege in 1904 in England, a committed communist as a youth, a prodigious drinker and opium smoker, a troubled Catholic convert, by his own description "a bad husband and a fickle lover" and arguably one of the most prolific and acclaimed writers of his time, producing twenty-five novels, four books of autobiography, three travel volumes, a book of verse, nearly twenty plays and film scripts, a relentless stream of essays, newspaper reportage, short stories, film and book reviews, and at his peak an average of some two thousand post cards and letters a year.

It was for his novels that he won his greatest praise, much of his best work, *The Heart of the Matter, The Power and the Glory, A Burnt-Out Case, Brighton Rock* and *The End of the Affair*, marked by a struggle between the secular and the spiritual. Other themes included betrayal and treachery, as epitomized by two of his best-known novels, *The Third Man* and *The Quiet American*.

He traveled broadly, and adventurously, for much of his life, drawn mainly to trouble spots—to Liberia in 1935 by a map of the region marked "cannibals," to Mexico apparently for its seediness and poverty, and to wars and revolutions in the Congo,

Kenya, Indochina, Malaya, Israel, Haiti, Cuba, Argentina, Panama and Nicaragua, "not to seek material for novels but to regain the sense of insecurity which I had enjoyed in the three blitzes on London [during World War Two]." So obsessed was he by living "on the dangerous edge of things" and at the same time so easily bored, he once tried Russian roulette.

A lifelong manic-depressant, his Catholicism denying him divorce, chronically unfaithful to his subsequent partners, a habitué of whores, probably alcoholic, and an opium smoker, not to mention his secret life as a spy, he didn't need to look far for material.

When *The Quiet American* was published in the US in 1956, it was widely condemned as anti-American. More recently, the writer's condemnation of what he saw as America's ignorant, high-handed and idealistic involvement in Vietnam has been recast and compared to that country's undeclared war with Islam.

Greene was born October 1, 1904. He lived his last twenty-five years in the south of France, dying in April 3, 1991, at the age of eighty-six.

Vietnam, Quite by Chance

Ask anyone to name the best novels about Asia written by Westerners and Graham Greene's *The Quiet American*, will always be on the list. Always. And frequently at the top of it.

When this slender novel placed in Vietnam during its war with France was published in London in 1955, the conflict had been over for a year, concluding with France's ignominious defeat. Later, of course, France's war was eclipsed by America's. Nonetheless, more than fifty years after publication, critics, readers and old Asia hands agree that *The Quiet American* still offers one of the most insightful portraits of any Asian country in print, as well as a gripping read. A film based on the book appeared in 1958, starring Michael Redgrave and Audie Murphy, and another, starring Michael Caine, went into theaters worldwide in 2002.

The plot was not complex. A young, idealistic American named Pyle took a young Vietnamese woman away from an older, married British journalist named Fowler, then Pyle was murdered. The police suspected the journalist, who in face had been innocently duped into helping set up the young American, while wishing only to win back the woman's love. The story unfolded gently—even the grisliest violence was delicately described—against locations mainly in and near what then was called Ville de Saigon and now is Ho Chi Minh City, but also in the north under an hour's drive from Hanoi.

When Greene first went to Vietnam, in 1951, he was well established as a novelist and foreign correspondent, his passport already bulging with stamps from three continents and two of his strongest novels (of a total of fifteen), *The Power and the Glory* and *The Heart of the Matter*, set in Mexico and Sierra Leone. Greene returned to Vietnam, representing *The Times* of London and *Paris-Match*, eventually remaining to watch the French defeat in 1954 at Dien Bien Phu. Greene said in his autobiography "perhaps there is more direct reportage in *The Quiet American* than in any other novel I have written."

There was stunning description, too. When Pyle went to Fowler for guidance, Greene wrote, "He would have to learn for himself the real background that held you as a smell does: the gold of the rice fields under a flat late sun: the fishers' fragile cranes hovering over the fields like mosquitoes: the cups of tea on an old abbot's platform, with his bed and his commercial calendars, his buckets and broken cups and the junk of a lifetime washed up around his chair: the mollusk hats of the girls repairing the road where a mine had burst: the gold and young green and the bright dresses of the south, and in the north the deep browns and the black clothes and the circle of enemy mountains and the drone of planes."

As he sought danger, he found beauty, too—they were inseparable.

The Quiet American was greeted harshly in the United States, in 1956. The review in the *New Yorker* said Greene was "anti-American" and Fowler was called "a middle-class English snob," a label that was pasted onto Greene as well. The author told Gloria Emerson in *Rolling Stone* in 1978, "Nobody liked it in America at that time. They only began to like it when they became involved. Then I began to get lots of nice letters from people and correspondents who were there. But before that I don't think I had any good reviews when I came out in America."

England liked the book, on the other hand, and as Greene said, once the US found itself mired in the same Southeast Asian rice paddy mud, the novel became a steady seller, many of its readers considering the author prescient.

As the story unreeled, Fowler met several times in a go-down in Saigon's Chinatown with one of Ho Chi Minh's undercover men, who told him that Pyle had imported a container of "plastic." Pyle claimed it was for the manufacture of toys, but Fowler, and we the readers know that it was the infamous French *plastique* that was and is still used in terrorist bombs.

Soon, the bombs began going off. First there were scattered blasts outside cafes frequented by foreigners, part of Pyle's plot to discredit the communists. There followed a massive car bomb that killed many civilians in the square in front of the Hotel Continental. Fowler confronted Pyle, who admitted responsibility, but said he was told there would be a parade; the explosion was intended as a political statement and he didn't know the parade was cancelled. In a telling aside to the reader—which many took as Greene's view of America—Fowler said, "I never knew a man who had better motives for all the trouble he caused." Another time, Fowler said, "God save us always…from the innocent and the good."

Fowler was, in fact, enraged by the bombing, so when Ho Chi Minh's man in Cholon asked him to invite Pyle to dinner at a remote restaurant near a bridge that crossed a tributary of the

Saigon River, the journalist agreed and the next day Pyle's body was discovered beneath the bridge. Phuong returned to Fowler, whose wife finally agreed to a divorce, and—one hopes—someone lived happily ever after.

A film was made in 1958, written and directed by Joseph Mankiewicz and starring Audie Murphy (the most decorated soldier of World War Two) as Pyle and Michael Redgrave playing Fowler. In the film, Pyle was made a representative of a charitable organization rather than a US government (CIA) employee and the story's focus was shifted to the love triangle, removing almost entirely Greene's anti-war message. And the actress playing Phuong was Italian. Unsurprisingly, the author disavowed the film.

Following the end of America's war, in 1975, which it lost even more shamefully than the French, the United States disavowed Vietnam, enforcing an economic embargo and denying its citizens permission to visit. Not until 1994 did President Bill Clinton end the economic blockade, after Vietnam agreed to assist in finding the remains of some two thousand, two hundred Americans missing in action.

I started visiting Vietnam in 1991, after the Vietnamese announced a policy of *doi moi*, welcoming visitors and foreign investment; on the street in Saigon, renamed Ho Chi Minh City, the souvenirs for sale besides maps and post cards included models of wartime jet fighters and helicopters fashioned from beer and soda cans, fake Zippo lighters with slogans like "Let Me Win Your Heart and Mind or I'll Burn Your God Damn Hut Down," and, to my great surprise, counterfeit copies of *The Quiet American*.

In 2001, Hollywood adapted the novel again, this time so faithfully the script convinced the Vietnamese government to permit filming in Vietnam, a postwar Hollywood first. Phillip Noyce, the Australian who wrote and directed the film, kept the novel's anti-American message and ending, and concluded with a montage of images of newspaper accounts of the American war. (Greene was openly scathing about the war, telling V.S. Naipaul in a 1967 interview, "The Vietnam war is not only horrible but foolish… There is something menacing about great power combined with great foolishness.") It also became the first American film about the war to win approval for distribution in Vietnam.

Ironically, in the US, the film's release was delayed for nearly a year by the 9/11 attack on the World Trade Center in New York. Because the film's (and book's) plot turned on a terrorist bombing, the production company, Miramax, thought American audiences would be offended. Only after the star, Michael Caine, made a personal plea to the company's chief was the movie given a limited film festival distribution to qualify for the 2002 Oscars. Caine was nominated but did not win. When international release followed, it was a commercial hit as well and book sales predictably increased.

What is Greene's Vietnam like today? With the isolation imposed on the country for so long following the war, led by the US embargo, the nation remained in something approximating a time capsule. However, few nations have played catch-up faster, so many of the old Greene landmarks still evident today have been remodeled beyond recognition.

A tour must begin, of course, at Saigon's Hotel Continental, where from 1952 to 1954 Fowler and his friends did much of their drinking and gossiping. Greene's view has been spoiled by the erection of numerous highrises in the neighborhood, the hotel's outdoor terrace has been glass-enclosed and turned into an Italian restaurant, and the building has been given a glossy makeover that changed virtually everything but the address.

During Vietnam's period of colonial subservience, the street running past the hotel was called rue Catinat, named for the French gunship that led the assault on Danang harbor in 1856. At one end was the red brick Notre Dame Cathedral that Greene, a Catholic convert, rarely entered and the Post Office, where Fowler first met Pyle; at the other, the Saigon River and the Majestic Hotel, the author's preferred address. Occasionally, Greene stayed at the more modest Mondial Hotel just up the street. Nearby is where the opium parlors frequented by both Fowler and his creator used to be. Opposite the Continental is the Lam Son Restaurant, in Greene's time the Cafe Givral, fictionalized in his book as a "milk bar" visited by Phuong for her daily ice cream fix.

Following France's defeat, when the Americans took their place in the fight against Ho Chi Minh, it was renamed Tu Do Street (meaning "victory") and soon was lined with noisy bars catering to American GIs. Today it's called Dong Khoi (for "uprising"), a corridor of restaurants offering Vietnamese, French or Chinese cuisine, art galleries, cafes and shops with expensive crafts for the tourist trade. The street remains narrow and tree-lined, for Greene it was an avenue for bicycles, today it's Honda City. While in upmarket bars beneath the Municipal Theatre, within earshot of the Continental, the music played on state-of-the art sound systems is jazz and new age rock.

Cholon is the next destination. It was described by Greene as a "Chinese suburb," but today is part of the city, another teeming, commercial neighborhood, Chinatown. Mass-produced household items are displayed in abundance on the sidewalks, as television sets and microwave ovens from China and Korea are snapped up by Saigon's newly rich, but Cholon still looks and feels much as it did to the novelist:

"In Cholon you were in a different city where work seemed to be just beginning rather than petering out with the daylight. It was like driving into a pantomime set: the long vertical Chinese signs and the bright lights and the crowd of extras led you into the wings where everything was suddenly so much darker and quieter."

The action for Fowler shifted sometimes to Phat Diem, a Catholic town in Vietnam's north, the scene of fierce battles and one of the last pockets of resistance against Uncle Ho. It wasn't surprising that Greene used an area with a large Catholic population and a city with a huge cathedral as the site where the novel's plot would turn. There, Fowler saw one of the town's canals so full of bodies he was "reminded of an Irish stew containing too much meat." A small boy's corpse intensified his hatred of war and his mood was further strained when Pyle unexpectedly arrived after dark and told him he planned to take Phuong away from him.

There are scarce signs of war in Phat Diem today. One-hundred and twenty kilometers south of Hanoi on Hwy. 1, turning toward the sea at Ninh Binh, the town has grown but you can still see what Greene described as "one long narrow street of wooden stalls, cut up every hundred yards by a canal, a church, and a bridge."

Pyle returned to Saigon before Fowler and by the time the journalist arrived, Phuong had left his flat. Fowler had asked his wife back in England for a divorce so he could marry Phuong and now he wanted his mistress back.

The final stop on the tour is Tay Ninh, northwest of Saigon. This was then, and is today, the center of the eccentric and colorful Caodai faith that combines fragments of several Eastern and Western religions, whose saints include such unlikely altar mates as Sun Yat Sen, Napoleon Bonaparte, Louis Pasteur, Victor Hugo, Winston Churchill, and Joan of Arc. Greene was drawn to the odd religion at first, perhaps by a priesthood based partly on the structure of the Roman Catholic Church, but turned disdainful, describing the temple in his novel as "a Walt Disney fantasia of the East, dragons and snakes in Technicolor...the private army of twenty-five thousand men, armed with mortars made out of the exhaust-pipes of old cars." In a dispatch to *The Times*, he wrote, "What on my first two visits had seemed gay and bizarre (was) now like a game that had gone on too long."

Today, the Caodai army is long gone, but the garishly decorated and painted temple remains the same and the hour-long service at noon on Sunday has become a popular tourist attraction, well worth the two-hour drive from Ho Chi Minh City. As Greene hinted in his description four decades ago, amid all the chanting and incense, you cannot help looking for Goofy or Donald Duck.

When the war finally ended and he was asked if he wanted to return, Greene said no, he preferred to remember it as it was.

Still, he took a worldly, and timeless, view. It was, he said, as he had Fowler tell Pyle: "If I believed in your God and another life, I'd bet my future harp against your golden crown that in five hundred years there may be no New York or London, but they'll be growing paddy in these fields, they'll be carrying their produce to market on long poles wearing their pointed hats. The small boys will be sitting on the buffaloes."

"It was quite by chance that I fell in love with Indo-China," Greene wrote in his autobiography, *Ways of Escape* (1980). "Nothing was farther from my thoughts on my first visit than that I would one day set a novel there… The spell was first cast, I think, by the tall elegant girls in white silk trousers, by the pewter evening light on flat paddy fields, where the water-buffaloes trudged fetlock deep with a slow primeval gait, by the French perfumeries in the rue Catinat, the Chinese gambling houses in Cholon, above all by that feeling of exhilaration which a measure of danger brings to the visitor with a return ticket."

Sax Rohmer

The Yellow Peril

His name may not ring loud bells today, but during the first half of the twentieth century, a man with the pseudonym Sax Rohmer created a literary villain who set a standard for Asian bad guys right up to the present day.

The British author's Dr. Fu Manchu, a sinister Chinese master criminal inspired by an Ouija board and introduced in 1912 in a monthly magazine, gave readers a character that personified the imagined threat from Asia known as "the Yellow Peril," thus catering to anti-Asian prejudice then widespread in the West.

Rohmer was born Arthur Henry Ward in Birmingham, England, February 15, 1883, of Irish immigrants, the son of a stonemason and a boozy mom. When he was three, the family moved to South London and at twenty-one, he married Rose Knox, the daughter of a music hall singer who was working with her brother as a juggler, a connection that would lead to his writing sketches for comedians. He published his first stories at age twenty under his birth name and from the first Fu Manchu novel onward used a pseudonym, taking "Sax" from ancient Saxon for its meaning "blade," adding "Rohmer" as a spelling variation of "roamer."

A lifelong devotee of the occult, he rejected his family's Catholicism for membership in the Hermetic Order of the Golden

Dawn, a secret society, and also was admitted (along with Rud-yard Kipling) to the Rosicrucian Society, a sect believing wisdom could be handed down only to the initiated.

The thirteen Fu Manchu stories, forty-one novels in all, eleven collections of short stories, and the production of a slew of movies, television programs and comic strips, made Rohmer one of the most successful and well-paid authors of the 1920s and 1930s. The insidious doctor also served as a model for many contemporary clones as well as such later villains as the James Bond adversary Dr. No, The Celestial Toymaker in the Doctor Who story named for him, Dr. Yen-Lo from *The Manchurian Candidate*, and Wo Fat from the CBS television series *Hawaii Five-O*.

Despite the large sums earned from the films, Rohmer's final years were spent in relative poverty, many of them in an un-heated flat in New York City. Soon after his return to England, Rohmer died in London, ironically, of "Asian flu," June 1, 1959, aged seventy-six. He is buried with his wife and parents in that city's Kensal Green Catholic cemetery.

"The Yellow Peril"

In the long, torturous history of fictional evil and skullduggery, can there have been any character more fearsome than Dr. Fu Manchu?

Here is a description from the first book, *The Mystery of Dr. Fu Manchu*, as it was titled in England (in the US, *The Insidious Dr. Fu Manchu*): "Imagine a person, tall, lean and feline, high-shouldered, with a brow like Shakespeare and a face like Satan, a close-shaven skull, and long, magnetic eyes of the true cat-green. Invest him with the cruel cunning of an entire Eastern race, ac-cumulated in one giant intellect, with all the resources of science past and present, with all the resources, if you will, of a wealthy government—which, however, already has denied all knowledge of his existence. Imagine that awful being, and you have a mental picture of Dr. Fu Manchu, the yellow evil incarnate in one man."

An opium smoker who dressed in long, yellow robes, Fu Manchu's arsenal in his quest to control of the world included drugs, potions, and poisons that caused amnesia, made men mad or turned them into zombies. There were lethal fungi and orchids from which an elixir was made to prolong life (his own). He developed a fly that could transmit a plague worldwide, invented a "Chinese wire jacket" that could be tightened until the victim's flesh pushed through the mesh, and created a fifteen-inch-tall killer dwarf. He was a hypnotist and a master counterfeiter and an alchemist who turned base metals into gold, a man described as being "more formidable than the Catholic Church." (As Dave Barry says, I'm not making this up.) Even the books' titles seemed as if someone were attempting satire—including *The Hand of Fu Manchu*, *The Mask of Fu Manchu*, and so on, changing but a single word in successive books (*Bride, Drums, Shadow, Wrath*, et cetera.).

What seems preposterous today is easily explained. The phrase "Yellow Peril" appeared in a *Los Angeles Times* headline as early as 1886 and in the years following, real events helped convince Westerners that they had much to fear from China and Japan—the Sino-Japanese War (1894-1895), the Russo-Japanese War (1904-1905), and the Boxer Uprising that involved the United States (1898-1901). At the same time, most remarkably in the US and the American territory of Hawaii, indentured Chinese and other Asians imported to build railroads and work in sugar cane fields had earned their freedom, they represented a threat to American jobs.

"Conditions for launching a Chinese villain on the market were ideal," Rohmer said. "I wondered why it had never before occurred to me."

If we think Rohmer's villain still overstepped credulity, we should also now recall how villains in silent movies of the same period twirled their mustaches, slapstick comedy won all the laughs, and cliff-hanger serials ruled the movie houses on

Saturday afternoons. It was a time of broad and outrageous strokes; it was not a time of villainous subtlety.

(Fu Manchu's long drooping mustache, which caused all such growths to be so named ever since, was Hollywood's invention; Rohmer's character was clean-shaven.)

In fact, Rohmer's books—the first appearing in 1913—were not the first in the genre and the concept of the "Yellow Peril" in fiction dated back to 1892 when a story called "Electric Sea Spider or The Wizard of the Submarine World" was published as part of a dime novel, one of the predecessors to what later was termed pulp fiction. This featured a Mongolian or Chinese (it wasn't clear) named Kiang Ho, a pirate dedicated to sinking all Western shipping in China's offshore waters with his super-submarine.

Four years later came a series of stories by Robert Chambers about Yue-Laou, ruler of an empire in central China and the Yellow Peril's first black sorcerer. There followed two novels by M.P. Shiel called *The Yellow Danger* and *The Yellow Wave*, set against the murder of German missionaries in China in 1897 and the Russo-Japanese War, and a third, *The Dragon*, which was later rereleased and retitled *The Yellow Peril*, fictionalized China's revolution of 1911-1912. These featured a half Japanese, half Chinese military leader, Dr. Yen How, who united the nations of his parentage and sent armies from both countries to destroy the West.

Still, it was the success of Fu Manchu that spawned a parade of pulp magazine evil-doers as outrageous as their names, including Li Ku Yu, Ali Singh (from a 1916 series called *The Yellow Menace*), the Blue-Eyed Manchu, Wang-ba, Dr. Yen Sin (created by Donald E. Keyhoe, who found greater fame later when he wrote *Flying Saucers Are Real*), Li Shoon, Wu Fang, Fing-Su, Wun Wey (get it?), Wo Fan, Dr. Chu Lung, the Red Dragon, Fui Onyui (these are not my jokes), Ssu His Tze, Shiwan Khan, Pao Tcheou, Ming the Merciless (from *Flash Gordon*), Taronago, and that dynamic duo, Kong Gai and the Nameless One. Even with the jokes removed, it's difficult for many Westerners to keep a straight face.

Making all of this possible was a new market for the stories and the birth of what came to be called "pulp fiction," blossoming in the 1920s and so named for the cheap wood pulp paper on which the tales were printed.

The Pulps were produced for a largely male audience—although there was a category featuring lesbians—and for every possible genre, including sports, detective/mystery, western, romance, gangster, "spicy/saucy" (not by today's standards), railroad, war, horror/occult, science fiction, sword and sorcery. Their sensational storylines, outrageous heroes and villains, and lurid cover art defined pulp fiction. And authors in all genre visited the Orient—or in a pinch the nearest Chinatown—for the color and exotic change of pace or an over-the-top evil threat.

In the 1930s and 1940s, the periodicals multiplied to the point where they blanketed newsstands. One company, Popular Publications in the US—the pulps were mainly an American phenomenon—claimed to have marketed over three hundred titles and at its peak was cranking out forty-two a month.

The success of the pulps, both in magazine and pocketbook format, was credited to a rapidly rising literacy rate in the US and the need during the long Depression years and World War Two for escapist entertainment with comic book plots, pretty girls in various stages of distress and undress, and exotic locales that would take the reader away from reality. And good always, always triumphed over evil. In times of such uncertainty, that was key.

Rohmer's career began somewhat mundanely, when as a young journalist living in London he ventured on assignment into the city's Chinatown, called the Limehouse for the limekilns in the potteries that served the London port. Here he visited opium dens that had been visited earlier by Charles Dickens in his fiction, witnessing a tough waterfront way of life that provided the backdrop for his early Fu Manchu novels.

Other writers of the period went to the Limehouse, too, among them Thomas Burke. His anthology of what one critic called "melodramatic stories of lust and murder among London's lower classes," *Limehouse Nights*, was published in 1916. One of the tales, "The Chink and the Child," became a film three years later, called *Broken Blossoms*, directed by D.W. Griffiths and starring Lillian Gish. The same book also inspired Charlie Chaplin's *A Dog's Life* and much later, was sourced frequently by the television show *Alfred Hitchcock Presents*. The response from city authorities was negative, however, when the scandalous marriage of white women to Chinese men in the tales caused the generally ignored Chinese immigrant community to come under public examination.

Chinatowns around the world became a common background in pulp fiction, allowing the writers to bring the exotic threat to their backyards. Rohmer wrote a six-part serial about an international ring of posh opium dens headquartered in the Limehouse, publishing them in book form in 1916, calling it *The Yellow Claw*. Three years later came *Dope: A Story of Chinatown and the Drug Traffic*, inspired by the real life overdose of a London showgirl. Even Dashiell Hammett, in one of his weaker short stories, "Dead Yellow Women," took his action into the Chinatown in Washington, D.C.

Rohmer's first three Fu Manchu novels—serialized in *Story-Teller* in the UK, *Colliers* in the US—were enormously successful, but not wanting to be categorized as a one-trick pony, Rohmer shelved the evil doctor from 1917 to 1931 to write as many as three novels a year, remaining faithful to his main area of interest, the occult, as evidenced in such titles as *Brood of the Witch Queen*, *Tales of Secret Egypt*, *Moon of Madness* and *The Day the World Ended*. Then came the Great Depression. By now, he was living in New York and with the book market collapsing along with all others, he returned to Fu Manchu. There followed another ten books, between 1931 and 1959.

The character was perfect for film serials, a popular "short subject" usually shown with a feature film, each of the weekly episodes (called cliffhangers) that ended with the innocent in unimaginable peril. The first of these came in 1923 with the Irish actor Harry Agar Lyons in the title role of *The Mystery of Dr. Fu Manchu*. A second serial appeared in 1924. It would be 1940 before a serial was produced in the US, but *Drums of Fu Manchu*, told in fifteen episodes and starring an American character actor named Henry Brandon, was regarded by some as Republic Pictures's best.

Feature film adaptations were numerous, too, beginning in the US in 1929 when the Swedish actor Warner Oland was cast in the lead role of *The Mysterious Dr. Fu Manchu*. He starred in two more films in 1930 and 1931 (*The Return of Dr. Fu Manchu* and *Daughter of the Dragon*), when he also appeared in a musical, *Paramount on Parade*, where he murdered both Philo Vance and Sherlock Holmes. A year later the English actor Boris Karloff took the title role in *The Mask of Fu Manchu*, a film that later was banned for a while for its blatant racist dialog and shocking torture scenes, but today is regarded as a camp classic. The racial stereotyping was criticized, without effect.

In the 1940s and 1950s, world politics shifted allegiances and so did Fu Manchu. From the beginning, he had a constant nemesis, a British agent named Denis Nayland Smith, who was joined by a variety of different helpmates as the series left the London dockside and moved around the world, from Egypt to Persia, France, Haiti and, because his books were so popular there, the United States. By the 1950s, Smith and Fu Manchu found themselves in an unholy alliance in shared combat against Communism, weakening the books' original dynamic and causing them to resemble spy thrillers.

His final authorized appearance was in *The Fiendish Plot of Dr. Fu Manchu*, a 1980 parody with Peter Sellers playing both Fu Manchu and Smith. It was the actor's final film and a commercial and critical failure.

The novels also were adapted for television by Republic Pictures, for radio on CBS, in newspaper comic strips and a Marvel comic book series, *Master of Kung-Fu*, and then reprised posthumously in two more stories by Rohmer's friend and biographer, Cay Van Ash, one of them titled *Ten Years Beyond Baker Street: Sherlock Holmes Matches Wits with the Diabolical Dr. Fu Manchu* (1984). Still another writer, William Patrick Maynard, again revived the character in *The Terror of Fu Manchu* in 2009—ninety-seven years after the first story appeared.

Because Rohmer never actually traveled to research his foreign settings, there is not much visitable past available to readers. In London, the Limehouse Basin was one of the first docks to close in the 1960s, old Chinatown is long gone as well, all falling to gentrification.

Yet a remnant from the past exists. Untouched in what is otherwise a comfortable residential neighborhood, a part of the London Borough of Tower Hamlets on the northern bank of the Thames, is a pub built in 1720 called the Grapes. Dickens called it Six Jolly Fellowships in a story titled "Our Mutual Friend" and tales are still told to visitors of men taking drunks from the pub, drowning them in the river and selling their corpses to a medical faculty. Today the pub is as spiffy as the neighborhood and the food is perceived to be so good you have to book ahead.

More stimulating for Rohmer fans would be a visit to the next PulpFest, the convention held annually for pulp fiction fans in Columbus, Ohio. It's unashamedly commercial—the most recent one had a hundred tables selling stuff—but there are author readings along with all those salacious magazine and paperback books to drool over. Take a poster home. The pretty damsel in distress depicted on it will be wearing less than Lady Gaga and there'll be an evil Chinese arch-criminal twirling his mustaches leering over her shoulder.

Websites worth visiting: www.pulpfest.com, www.thepulp.net (best source for links to the entire pulp world), www.pulpmags.org/default.htm, www.thepulp.net.com, and for a look at more than two thousand illustrations and covers, www.pulpcovers.com.

Earl Derr Biggers
Charlie Chan

If Dr. Fu Manchu was the image of evil incarnate and the epitome of racial stereotyping in the first half of the twentieth century, the fictional creation of Earl Derr Biggers—a Chinese detective named Charlie Chan—was the lovable opposite, representing a positive step for the Asian image. True or false? Many now call him a "Yellow Uncle Tom."

Biggers was born August 26, 1884, in small-town Warren, Ohio, and following graduation from Harvard University, he worked for daily newspapers in Cleveland and Boston, wrote a play that failed, and then at twenty-nine published *Seven Keys to Baldplate*, a novel that combined mystery, satire, and romance. It was adapted for Broadway by George M. Cohan—who also starred in it—and over a long period of time was made into seven films by the same name and two more with different titles. This was followed by more plays—which were successful, one of them a collaboration with Christopher Morley—and two more novels. Then at age forty-five came the book and character that hijacked the rest of his life, a novel called *The House Without a Key*, featuring in a minor role a Chinese detective on the Honolulu police force who sounded like a test marketer for a fortune cookie factory.

Serialization in the *Saturday Evening Post*, followed by publication as a hardcover book and a multi-episode film serial of *The House Without a Key*, made Biggers wealthy, and with some of the first money, he moved his wife and son to Pasadena, California. He wrote only five more novels in the series before dying at forty-eight, but more than forty more films were commissioned posthumously, as were comic strips, a magazine that featured original Chan novellas, and numerous radio and television shows (including a 1970s Hanna-Barbera cartoon series), arguably making Chan the most famous detective since Sherlock Holmes.

Chan also remained a controversial figure—one side insisting he created respect for Asians in a time when no one else did, the other side arguing that the subservient, cartoonish way the detective was portrayed both in print and on film—and by Caucasian actors in most the films—made him as much a racial stereotype as Fu Manchu. So heated did this issue become, work by young Asian writers were collected in anthologies called *Charlie Chan Is Dead* and in 2003 ethnic rights crusaders wrapped in political rectitude got the Fox network, which owned the Chan movies, to ban their broadcast from their own network.

Biggers survived two heart attacks and died (reportedly with an unfinished novel in his typewriter) on April 5, 1933, in a Pasadena hospital after suffering a massive stroke.

Charlie Chan

Earl Derr Biggers said he created Charlie Chan to counter the likes of Dr. Fu Manchu.

"Sinister and wicked Chinese are old stuff," Biggers told an interviewer a few years later, "but an amiable Chinese on the side of law and order had never been used."

That was Biggers looking back, making it appear as if Chan were conceived as a fully realized if somewhat gimmicky character, a roll of the authorial dice. The fact is that in the series' first novel, *The House Without a Key*, published in 1925, Chan was not essential to the plot, he didn't speak his first words until page eighty-two, and although he figured out the mystery at the end, it was a Caucasian who got to arrest the murderer. It might also be argued that those first words made Chan no less a stereotype. "No knife are present in neighborhood of crime," the detective said.

Thus, Biggers hedged his bet. Racist feeling had not changed that much in the US and the same year the writer submitted his manuscript to his Ohio-based publisher, 1924, the US Congress passed a law withholding citizenship from all foreign-born "Asiatics," a reaction to the thousands of Chinese immigrants who arrived to work in California's gold fields and then to build the railroad linking ithe East and West coasts. Chan may have entered *The House Without a Key* late, as Biggers later said, "supposedly a minor character, providing some local color, but by introducing a likeable Chinese man in a role normally granted respect in society required some courage."

Set in 1920s Hawai'i, when a young bond trader from Boston is found dead, his mainland US family is surprised that the detective assigned to the case is Chinese. Yet, when he confronts the Boston spinster who discovered the body, he bows and says, "Humbly asking pardon to mention it, I detect in your eyes slight flame of hostility. Quench it, if you will be so kind." In this fashion, Chan hijacks the novel and Biggers's career, as a good character often will.

Unsurprisingly, Chan stepped front and center in the follow-up book, *The Chinese Parrot*, published in 1926. Accompanying a valuable string of pearls to California as a favor to a onetime employer—Chan was her houseboy before joining the police force—Biggers introduced the non-Hawaiian settings that dominated most of the books (and films) to come.

It was also in this story that the police inspector began spouting the fortune cookie aphorisms that became so cherished by fans there now are websites listing them: "Detective business consist of one unsignificant (sic) detail placed beside other of same. Then with sudden dazzle, light begins to dawn." In another story, Chan quipped, "Mind like parachute—only function when open." In keeping with his self-effacing personality, he said, "Even great detective steps off on wrong foot. My wrong foot often weary from too much use."

In such a manner, Chan endeared himself to readers and, soon afterward, in dozens of serial and feature films. He may have been described by Biggers in the first novel as walking with "the light dainty step of a woman" and "very fat indeed," but he was a devoted family man who was so patient, wise, modest, commonsensical, unflappable, and et cetera, he seemed the personification of the Boy Scout oath. And he had a sense of humor, too—something Sherlock Holmes sorely lacked—even if many of the smiles he won came from his broken English and amusing faux Confucionisms.

Many have called Chan's manner of speaking "pidgin English." It is not. Hawaiian pidgin is a recognized creole language with distinct rules of grammar, construction, and vocabulary, the latter incorporating words from half a dozen immigrant languages, and what Chan spoke was no more than English over easy, sometimes scrambled. For example, in *Behind That Curtain*, the third mystery, Chan cautions against "hoarsely barking up incorrect tree" and in *The Black Camel*, the fourth in the series, he tells a suspect, "I could place you beneath arrest."

Unfortunately, this is what is remembered of the writing, as Chan's quirky persona overwhelms the text. "Biggers was a good writer, possessed of a simple, straightforward prose style and a gift for patient, plausible plotting," said Richard Schickel in 2010 in the *New York Times*. "I've sampled some of his novels recently and can testify that they can be read today without condescension."

There is some confusion regarding the detective's origins. One story says the inspiration for Chan likely came when Biggers was vacationing in Hawai'i in 1919, lodging at Gray's Hotel on the beach at Waikiki. There, he spent some of his evenings at the nearby Halekulani Hotel, beneath a big kiawe tree, drinking and talking with High Sheriff of the Territory Arthur Brown, who owned Gray's, and a Chinese detective with the Honolulu Police Department named Chang Apana, who had been handpicked many years before by the sheriff as Honolulu's first Chinese cop. At least this is the version found in the Hawai'i State Archives in notes by Richard Kimball, a son of Clifford and Juliet Kimball, owners of the Halekulani from 1917 through 1962.

Biggers himself claimed that he read about Apana's exploits in a Honolulu newspaper in the New York Public Library reading room a full five years later and that he didn't actually meet the fabled detective until four years after that on a visit to Hawai'i, in 1928, three years after *The House Without a Key* was published. The meeting, at the Royal Hawaiian Hotel, was real enough, but it has been established since then that the library did not subscribe to any Hawaii newspapers during in the 1920s and the number of similarities in Apana's and Chan's lives, expressed in books published before the meeting, was just too much coincidence to accept.

Whatever the truth, Biggers did admit that the illiterate, five-foot-tall Chinese policeman was the model for Chan. Known for bringing in forty gamblers single-handedly using only the threat of his homemade bullwhip, capturing an escaped leper who scarred his face permanently with a scythe, while leaping from rooftop to rooftop in Honolulu's Chinatown in pursuit of opium addicts, how could Biggers resist? In the years following, many said it might have been nice if the author had shared some of his financial wealth with Apana, but Apana himself said he was happy with being able to visit the movie set when one of the films was shot in Hawai'i and sign books when people asked. Around the police department, his friends actually called him by the fictional detective's name. (For a detailed biographical sketch of Apana, read *Charlie Chan: The Untold Story of the Honorable*

Detective and His Rendezvous with American History by Yunte Huang, a scholarly Chan fanatic who further suspiciously pointed out that Chan greatly resembled Hercule Poirot, the overweight, somewhat delicate, proverb-speaking Belgian detective created by Agatha Christie in 1920, five years before Chan. Was Biggers a secret Christie fan?)

Following Biggers's death at forty-eight, further sequels were commissioned and, in all, a total of forty-seven serials and movies were released. So formulaic were these efforts, their titles—*Charlie Chan in Paris, in Egypt, in Rio, in Shanghai, at the Circus, at the Wax Museum, at the Race Track, at the Opera, in the Desert*, etc.— made them sound like the Bob Hope-Bing Crosby "road" movies. Hollywood's rule was then, as it is now, when you stumble onto a good thing, you keep doing it over and over again. They call it a "franchise," like McDonald's or 7-Eleven or Spider-man.

It's little remembered that Japanese and Korean actors were cast in the first three Chan films, all of which won poor reviews. It wasn't until Caucasian actors played Chan that the character succeeded—sixteen of them with the Swedish actor Warner Oland as Chan (often with Keye Luke, who *was* Chinese, as Chan's "Number One Son"), another twenty-two with Scottish-American actor Sidney Toler (who bought the rights to the character when Oland died), a final six with another American actor, Roland Winters. Then, in 1981, the year following release of Peter Sellers's Fu Manchu parody, a movie starring Peter Ustinov called *Charlie Chan and the Curse of the Dragon Queen* went into the theaters. It was one of Ustinov's worst performances. *Chan Is Missing*, a spoof directed by Wayne Wang, and released a year after, was slightly more credible.

Like Fu Manchu, Charlie Chan was a worldwide multi-media star and from the early 1930s to the late 1940s, the detective appeared on the radio and in the 1950s on TV. There were comic strips and comic books as well, and board and card games, and, for a time, *Charlie Chan's Mystery Magazine*. So popular was

Chan in China, that country produced its own series of Chan movies, casting a Chinese actor to play Chan, who then played him exactly as the Swedish Warner Oland did.

From the beginning, there were critics decrying both Fu Manchu and Charlie Chan as racial stereotypes, calling their names "interchangeable epithets," although more found the Honolulu detective to be a positive role model. David Kehr wrote in the *New York Times* that Chan "might have been a stereotype, but he was a stereotype on the side of the angels" and Ellery Queen (Erle Stanley Gardner) called Chan "a service to humanity and to inter-racial relations." In the second novel, *The Chinese Parrot*, after solving a murder and still encountering racist remarks, Chan smiled and said, "Perhaps listening to a 'Chinaman' is no disgrace."

Other critics pointed to the phony broken English dialog given Chan and went so far as to say the detective's glib aphorisms mocked the wisdom of Confucius. For all of his bowing and scraping, he was called the Asian equivalent of an "Uncle Tom." He also came off, both in the books and films, as a bit of a wimp and asexual, despite the fact that he had thirteen children. Some wimp.

Nor was it just Chan's character that came under fire. In 1935 in *Charlie Chan in Egypt*, an actor called Stepin Fetchit—mind you, this is a name derived from a command to serve—played a character called "Snowshoes," while in other movies a chauffeur named "Birmingham Brown" was played by Mantan Moreland, whose reaction to danger was chattering teeth and the line, "Feets, get me out of here!" No one denied the racism there.

At the time, Asian actors rarely found work in Hollywood, as the movie industry seemed determined to use Caucasian actors in Asian roles, a policy that eventually led to Marlon Brando's silly performance as a Japanese houseboy in *The Teahouse of the August Moon*, John Wayne as Genghis Khan in *The Conqueror*, and Mickey Rooney as a buck-toothed Asian in *Breakfast at Tiffany's*, among too many more. This obviously was a cinematic problem, not a literary one. Still, the effect on Chan's legacy was clear and finally, in 2003, the Fox Movie Channel, which by then owned the Chan films, surrendered to ethnic pressure groups and halted a Charlie Chan Film Festival before it started, later releasing restored versions on DVD instead.

All copies of the three earliest adaptations, silent films starring Asian actors, apparently have been lost, but all others (starring white actors in yellowface) are still available online in a variety of boxed sets. The radio shows are available, too, as are reproductions of the original movie posters and lobby cards, film scripts, and black-and-white newspaper comic strips; hardcore fans may even purchase copies of the felt hat that was as much a Chan trademark as his bow tie, goatee and mustache. Project Gutenberg Australia offers the six novels online and there are a couple of dozen websites. (For links, visit http://charliechanfamily.tripod.com.)

In the visitable past, there isn't a great deal to track. You can drive by the Biggers home in Pasadena and Chang Apana's in Honolulu, at 3737 Waialae Avenue in the still-racially mixed area called Kaimuki. That city's Chinatown played an occasional role in the Charlie Chan stories, and many of the buildings of the real Chang's and fictional Chan's time have been restored or are still in place. In fact, much of the city's Chinese section was under reconstruction at the time of Biggers's 1919 visit to Honolulu. The long-ago gambling parlors and opium dens are now occupied by pricey restaurants and art galleries, but the lava rock Minatoya Sukioki building where Apana had his office is still at the corner of Maunakea and Pauahi Streets, 102 Pauahi and 1152 Maunakea. Apana's grave can also be visited, in the Chinese Cemetery in Manoa Valley, and Apana's bullwhip is displayed in a small museum at Honolulu police headquarters.

More compelling is the beachfront cocktail lounge called the House Without a Key at the modernized Halekulani Hotel, where the hundred-plus-year-old kiawe tree has a team of tree doctors keeping it alive and the view of Diamond Head remains unchanged from the one on the book's original cover. Sunset is the best time, when Kanoe Kaumehe'iwa Miller dances the hula to music as old as Chan and twice as charming. Please tell her I sent you.

Mr. Moto

The Charlie Chan stories were serialized in the *Saturday Evening Post*, a popular weekly magazine, and when their author died, the editors wanted another Asian hero to take his place. Thus was created by American novelist John P. Marquand, the small, fastidious Japanese secret agent with gold teeth who spoke with a breathy sibilance yet performed acts of great brutality, Mr. Moto.

As was true with Chan, the Moto character was inspired by a real police detective, who followed Marquand during a visit to Japan partly sponsored by the magazine. And like Chan, Moto didn't always play a central role in the stories, appearing instead when the plot needed him. But there the likenesses stopped. Both characters were endlessly polite and seemed outwardly self-effacing, but Moto had a license to kill, so the Moto series was far more violent.

Because the first four novels were published between 1935 and 1938, Mr. Moto was an agent serving an expansionist Imperial country. Marquand got around this problem by putting Moto in a position of extracting Westerners from danger encountered while traveling in the Orient. The brutal invasion of China by Japan (in 1937) caused anti-Japanese feeling to spread in the West and the Moto series was stopped for the duration of the world war that soon followed.

By that time, eight movies were produced starring Peter Lorre, an Austro-Hungarian Jew who admitted to darkening his skin to play the role and using a stunt man for all the action scenes. Moto also was changed from a spy to a policeman and a deadly martial arts expert. None of the films were taken seriously but the magazine serializations, books and movies all found large audiences.

In the middle of his Mr. Moto success, Marquand surprised many of his critics by winning a Pulitzer in 1938 for *The Late George Apley*, a satirical novel about Boston's upper crust. Marquand was himself from an old Massachusetts family and his marriage into another one bound him firmly to the social background that he nonetheless continued to use as fodder for subsequent books.

Martha Spaulding wrote in *The Atlantic Monthly* in 2004 that "in his day, Marquand was compared to Sinclair Lewis and John O'Hara, and his social portrait of twentieth century America was likened to Balzac's *Comédie Humaine*, [but] critics rarely took him very seriously. Throughout his career he believed, resentfully, that their lack of regard stemmed from his early success in the 'slicks' [magazines]."

Marquand was born November 10, 1893 and died in the same town where he was born, Newburyport, Massachusetts, July 16, 1960.

James Michener

Sayonara

Before we had so many wars to teach us geography, we had James Michener, a prolific author whose forty-some books girdled the globe several times and sold an estimated seventy-five million copies during his lifetime. Fourteen of his stories were made into movies and television mini-series and a bibliography of his works published in 1996, the year before he died, listed more than two thousand, five hundred entries in all, including sixty some articles profiling foreign cultures for *Reader's Digest*.

Michener is best known for such novels as *Tales of the South Pacific*—his first, published when he was forty, winning the Pulitzer Prize in 1948—and blockbusters that sometimes ran to a thousand pages and whose titles told their locations (*Hawaii, Alaska, Texas, Poland, Caribbean, Mexico, Chesapeake, Iberia,* and *Space*), but it was one of his earlier, shorter tales, set in Japan, that struck closest to home. This was *Sayonara*, a story of a romance between an American Air Force pilot and a Japanese woman he met on leave during the Korean war. In this novel, and others that both preceded and followed it, Michener was an early champion of racial tolerance and soon after *Sayonara* was published in 1954 he himself married a Japanese-American who was among those interned in a wartime camp.

James Albert Michener was an orphan born in New York City February 3,1907, and raised in Doylestown, Pennsylvania, by Mabel Michener, a poor Quaker widow. After teaching for several years and working as an editor, he enlisted in the Navy, serving much of World War Two in the Pacific as a military historian. From his notebooks he wrote the title that was shortened to *South Pacific* when adapted for Broadway and Hollywood.

He taught and funded writing courses throughout the US and under his wife's direction gave $100 million to the University of Texas and the Iowa Writers Workshop, among others. He received honorary doctorates in five fields from thirty leading universities and was given the Presidential Medal of Freedom, his country's highest civilian award. In 2008, the US Postal Service put his face on a stamp.

On October 16, 1997, Michener halted the dialysis treatment that kept him alive, dying of kidney failure at age ninety. He is buried in Austin, Texas. Preceded in death by his wife, he left his entire estate to Swarthmore College.

East Marries West

The concept of a war bride was not new when America's military men returned home with foreign wives after World War Two. But for the first time, thousands of them were Asian, citizens of Japan, the country that the US had just defeated in a devastating four-year-long war.

At the time, interracial marriage was illegal in many American states, including Oregon, Washington and California, where approximately one hundred thousand (mostly West Coast) Japanese-Americans were locked up in internment camps without due process, all of their property confiscated, their rights as citizens denied. In other parts of the country, notably in the South, the mixing of the racial bloodlines was called "mongrelization" and worse, and although most of the epithets were reserved for the descendants of African slaves, Asian races were not made to feel welcome

Then along came James Michener with a book about the war in the Pacific, where the United States military forces conquered the Japanese and then romanced and married them. *Tales of the South Pacific,* the title of his first novel—in fact, a collection of short stories with a unified setting and the recurrence of several characters—was also full of attractive native Pacific islanders, long established an object of Western desire, dating back to the days of Captain Cook and lauded by many other, earlier novelists.

One of his stories, called "Those Who Fraternize," told the story of a half-Javanese girl who married her American boyfriend in a wedding dress made from his old parachutes. Another, "Fo' Dolla," took its title from the price of a grass skirt and was about Bloody Mary, a Tonkinese (Vietnamese) and her desire to find an American husband for her daughter. Although Michener used terms like "Jap" and "Tonk" freely—everyone did in the 1940s—when *South Pacific* was touring the Southern United States, the musical came under attack for its casual approach to interracial marriage. One of the characters said racism was "not born in you! It happens after you're born..." It was suggested that the song that followed, "You've Got to Be Carefully Taught," be cut from the show. Michener was pleased when the Broadway team that adapted his book, Richard Rodgers and Oscar Hammerstein, insisted that even if it led to the play's rejection by audiences, it was going to stay in.

Two more books about the region followed—*Return to Paradise,* another collection of stories about the South Pacific, published in 1950, and *The Bridges at Toko-ri,* a straightforward war novel about US Navy support of ground troops in the Korea, in 1953. Thus by 1954, with the appearance of *Sayonara,* another interracial love story, Michener sealed his fate, becoming known as something of an expert on the Pacific and Asia, and among those who insisted upon separation of the races, a grade-A troublemaker.

In fact, Michener did not initially endorse intermarriage, not even in the novel that was blamed for encouraging it. *Sayonara* actually told the story of two East-West romances, both ending tragically, one of them fatally.

Captain Lloyd Gruver, a Korean war flying ace, engaged to a general's daughter and himself critical of interracial relationships, nonetheless falls in love with the star of a Japanese theatrical troupe named Hana-Ogi. Despite the US military's stern opposition, Gruver is best man for an Air Force friend's marriage to another Japanese in the face of strict penalties. Soon afterward, both relationships begin to unravel, with Gruver's pal being ordered back to the US, forcing him to leave his bride behind, leading both to commit suicide. When the general's wife urges her husband to enforce existing non-fraternization rules more rigidly, the Air Force arranges to have Hana-Ogi sent into hiding by her own fellow actors and in the novel's final scene the general drives Gruver to the airport where his daughter is waiting for them.

"And you, Japan, you crowded islands, you tragic land," Gruver intones on his departure, "*sayonara*, you enemy, you friend."

All in all, it was a solid condemnation of the US military's non-fraternization policy and lingering American racist attitudes. Although Michener researched his novel while working for the State Department in Japan to help discourage such relationships, it was clear where his sympathies lay. What was not known at the time, even to the author, was how close the fiction in his novel would turn into fact and change his life. But first, the world shifted.

With Congressional passage of the McCarren-Walter Act in 1952, eliminating race as a barrier to immigration, the incidence of Japanese war brides stopped being an oddity and moved toward becoming a commonplace. Where fewer than nine hundred

Japanese war brides entered the US before 1952, the number jumped to four thousand, two hundred and twenty in 1953. (Another popular novel about a Western man's romance with an Asian woman, *The World of Suzie Wong*, also was published the same year. See "In Search of Suzie Wong," page 149.) A year after that, *Life* magazine, the nation's most popular and widely distributed weekly, commissioned Michener to write an article about the phenomenon. It was then, at a lunch in Chicago hosted by the magazine, he met Mari Yoriko Sabusawa, the daughter of Japanese immigrants with whom she spent part of the war in a US government internment camp.

She approached the author and introduced herself as someone who worked with Japanese war brides, helping them adapt to life in America, and told him that not all such marriages failed. As she assisted him in researching the story, he also learned hers. She was born in Colorado, the only child of a cantaloupe farmer who moved the family to California when she was fifteen. Six years later, after the start of the war, she was among more than one hundred thousand Japanese-Americans who were rounded up as suspected spies or, at best, sympathizers with the enemy.

For the first four months, she was held in a horse stable at Santa Anita racetrack south of Los Angeles, then transferred to a camp in Colorado, where after about a year she was permitted to attend Antioch University in Ohio. After working for the American Council on Race Relations, she now was an editor for the American Library Association and in her spare time, helping Japanese war brides.

With his earlier books paving the way and *Sayonara* serialized in *McCall's* magazine and then appearing in hardcover, and now, an interracial romance of his own, it was fitting when Michener was described by the editors as "one of the more sympathetic interpreters of the East."

In February, 1955, in an article titled "Pursuit of Happiness by a GI and a Japanese," Michener reported Frank and Sachiko

Pfeiffer's experience as a triumph over "barriers of language and intolerance." He told of their courtship in Japan and the rejection by his mother and racist threats from neighbors that greeted them in Chicago. The story ended happily, however, when they moved to a suburb, where their new neighbors—two World War Two veterans who had fought the Japanese—and their wives welcomed the Pfeiffers as close friends.

Eight months later, after divorcing his second wife, Michener married the Japanese farmer's daughter.

Sayonara sold modestly at first, but became a bestseller when the movie adaptation was released in 1957, directed by Josh Logan (who also directed *South Pacific*, both on stage and film) and starring Marlon Brando. Although the movie remained generally faithful to the book, there was one crucial change: at the conclusion, at Brando's insistence, the flying ace got the girl.

In the film's final scene, Brando finds Hana-Ogi backstage in full *geisha* costume and makeup and proposes marriage. She talks about the difficulties they will encounter and asks, "What will our children be?" He says, "Well, they'll be half of you and half of me, they'll be half-yellow and half-white! That's what they'll be!"

The couple then confronts the press outside the theater, where Gruver is asked what he'll tell critics of their union. He says, "Tell 'em we said, '*Sayonara!*'" Up music, roll credits.

Michener's novels emerged from his typewriter following long periods of residence in the books' locales—big, ponderous things that sometimes had "dead spots" (quoting the writer himself), many of them epics that covered centuries of time, entertaining but always educational, too. *Centennial* began with the formation of the North American landmass in prehistoric times and *Hawaii*, which took seven years to research, with the first volcanic isle rising from the sea. By the time he finished *Texas*, he said he had read more than four hundred books on the subject.

"Some of this research manifested itself in chunky ethnological, philosophical or historical essays awkwardly stuck into his narratives," the *New York Times* said in its obituary. "The former educationalist didn't deny his didactic intent and indeed was the first to express surprise that his works were so popular since parts of them were often indigestible."

He traveled constantly, whenever possible with his wife, a small woman scarcely five-feet tall, but feisty. Because of the way she was treated in California in wartime, she forbade him to write a book about the state, and the second time he used "Jap" in her presence, back when they met, she said the next time he mouthed the word she'd knock his teeth out with a ketchup bottle.

Throughout his long and prolific career, Michener upheld the Quaker ideal of tolerance and it showed in all his works. Before the bloom of feminism in the 1970s, he said the subjugation of women deprived the human race of half its talent and while working for NASA as he researched a book about outer space, he advocated the training of more female astronauts. And while it could hardly be termed "block-busting," Michener lived for many years in Bucks County, Pennsylvania, a neighborhood that might fairly be described as conservative and white, and then ended his life in Austin, Texas. His outspoken, Japanese-American post-war bride may have been his third wife, but they were together until her death of pancreatic cancer in 1994, a total of thirty-nine years.

Racial harmony still seems distant in much of the post-John-and-Yoko world, but Michener's feelings on the subject played a significant role, coming at a critical time, when East and West were at war and coping with its tumultuous after-effects. Conflicts between Western nations and the Orient continue today, both on battlefields and in corporate boardrooms, and possibly they always will. Some will conclude Kipling was correct, but the war bride statistics alone indicate otherwise.

Asian war brides came to represent the single largest migration of Asian women ever to come to the United States. Between 1947 and 1964, there were nearly seventy-three thousand—some forty-six thousand of them Japanese, fourteen thousand Filipinas, and six thousand each from China and Korea. In a later demographic report, covering the period from 1964 to 1975, Asian war brides totaled approximately one-hundred and sixty-six thousand—some sixty-seven thousand coming from Japan, another fifty-two thousand from the Philippines, twenty-eight thousand from Korea, more than eleven thousand from Thailand, and eight thousand from Vietnam. Another six thousand married Chinese-American soldiers and were not included in the count, called "proxy brides" of arranged marriages instead.

Certainly, Michener cannot be credited with causing much of that, but it is safe to say that no other novelist using East-West romance in his or her fiction made the positive impact that his did. Where the likes of Somerset Maugham, Herman Melville, Jack London, James Norman Hall and Eugene Burdick, among others, praised the women of Hawaii, Tahiti and other South Pacific islands, and dozens more did the same for Asian females through the last quarter of the twentieth century and into the twenty-first, the motivation often seemed more hedonistic than humanistic, and Michener was, above all else, a humanist.

He was also reasonably called "prescient," seeming to have his finger on the world's pounding pulse. He wrote *Poland* before the turmoil and change. *The Source*, set in the Middle East and his own favorite (along with *Iberia*), came ahead of more upset there. And *Caravans* profiled troubled Afghanistan.

He also wrote books about Hungary and Kent State—two of more than thirty nonfiction books in all—coming down in both on the side of the revolutionaries. More books chronicled Japanese art and he donated a $25 million collection of some five thousand, four hundred prints to the Honolulu Academy of Arts. There is a James A. Michener Art Museum in Doylestown, Pennsylvania, and a Mari Michener Art Gallery on the University of Northern Colorado University campus.

Michener's works continue to attract new audiences. On its fiftieth anniversary, in 2008, the Broadway musical *South Pacific* was revived at New York's Lincoln Center. In 2011, it went to London. And many of his books all remain in print.

Michener fans wishing to walk in the author's footsteps, and those of his enduring characters, are fortunate. Much has changed, of course and most of the rough, undeveloped territory that Michener chose as a setting for his South Pacific and Asian stories today is unrecognizable. But the exotic—and, undeniably, erotic—charm of the region remains, bruised and commercialized, perhaps, but still in place and welcoming.

Richard Mason

The World of Suzie Wong

Richard Mason was born near Manchester, England, May 16, 1919, the son of an electrical engineer, inspired to write, he said, when the poet W.H. Auden was his English master at a public (in the US, private) school. A first book, written at fourteen, was given to Auden, who reportedly judged it to be "no bloody good."

At nineteen, Mason was inducted into the Royal Air Force, serving first in Europe and then, after learning Japanese, in Burma, where he was a translator and interrogated prisoners-of-war. It was there, in his tent at night, that he wrote *The Wind Cannot Read*, a love story about a student and his Japanese instructor. It was published in 1947 and made into a film called *The Passionate Summer* starring Dirk Bogarde, the script co-written by Mason with director David Lean.

After the war, he traveled to Africa and Jamaica, the latter to serve as a setting for his second novel, *The Shadow and the Peak* (1949), and he wrote a number of screenplays, one of them based on Neville Shute's *A Town Like Alice* (1956), placed in a Japanese prison camp for British female POWs. It was then that he went to Hong Kong to write the novel that not only changed his life, but also created an Asian stereotype that continues to the present day.

The World of Suzie Wong, published in 1957, was an international bestseller that was adapted successfully for the Broadway and West End stages and then for Hollywood and eventually for a ballet company in Hong Kong.

Mason published a fourth novel, a spy thriller placed in India and Nepal, *The Fever Tree*, in 1962. He then moved to Rome and never wrote another word. "That was my last book," he said later. "Don't ask me why, because I can't answer. Perhaps I got lazy, or perhaps it was because I didn't have any more inspiration. You need tremendous drive for the thousand words or whatever every day. And I don't think I've got the ideas or the energy any more. Fortunately, the books I'd already written let me live a modestly comfortable life."

A lifelong cigarette smoker, he died of throat cancer in 1997. He was 78 and had lived in Italy for nearly forty years.

Looking for Suzie Wong

A novel about a hooker with a heart of gold and a sad story was hardly a new idea when, in 1956, a thirty-five-year old British writer stepped off the Star Ferry in Hong Kong, looking for material for a new book. The way he told the tale, he checked into the harborside Luk Kwok Hotel and next morning when he went downstairs for a plate of *chow fan* (fried rice) and saw the hotel bar packed with young women who called themselves "yum-yum girls," he realized that he'd picked not an ordinary hotel but a brothel that catered to British and American sailors.

"I was absolutely thrilled," he said years later. "I thought, 'This is fabulous, I've found it!' From that moment, I knew I had my book. I thought that was unbelievable, like a gift from God."

The novel that Mason wrote after spending five months in the "brothel" told the story of a young Englishman named Robert Lomax who, while working on a plantation in Malaya (now Malaysia), began painting in order to take his mind away from the native women—this, to satisfy his employer's rule against any mixing of the races. Still distracted by the beauty he saw in Asian women, he finally quit and moved to Hong Kong for inspiration and the freedom he hoped to find there to paint whatever, and whomever, he wished.

His first day he met a woman who said she was Wong Mee-line, and that she was rich. But when he encountered her again after checking into his hotel, she said she was called Suzie Wong and she worked in the downstairs bar. They became friends and although the artist initially insisted upon not sleeping with any of the women, although he was using them for models, Suzie and Robert fell in love and thus began, in the words of Steve Rosse in an introduction to the French translation of the book, "a fantasy, a lovely fairy tale written for adults."

Rosse, an American who lived for many years in Thailand, rightly criticized Mason for his shallow reporting and narrow view. "Of three million Chinese in Hong Kong," he wrote, "Mr. Mason gives names to the prostitutes and the waiter who serves them tea. The European characters all have names and elaborate histories, but the non-European characters who don't sell sex are only 'the Indian shopkeeper' or 'the rickshaw coolie with the torn shirt.'

"And certainly we would make a big mistake if we came to this book looking for pornography. While sex is the center of the lives of these women, constantly in their thoughts, their only source of power in a world dominated by men and the only reason the Nam Kok Hotel exists, what sex that actually occurs is described demurely, never graphically."

And this is precisely why the novel was such a great success: it offended no one, save perhaps a seeker of truth. Of all the Asian fantasies spun from fake silk by Western authors, *The World of Suzie Wong* surely was one of the least believable, yet also the most believed.

Suzie wasn't the first literary prostitute. Writers have been making "the world's oldest profession" a resource for characters and plots at least since John Cleland wrote *Fanny Hill* in 1748, and, in fact, dating back to the *Bible's* Old Testament. Since then, hundreds of other fiction writers have done the same—Fyodor Dostoevsky (*Notes from the Underground*), Emile Zola (*Nana*), Charles Dickens (*David Copperfield* and *Oliver Twist*), Daniel Defoe (*Moll Flanders*), Stephen Crane (*Maggie: A Girl of the Streets*), John O'Hara (*BUtterfield 8*), William Faulkner (*Sanctuary*), Upton Sinclair (*The Jungle*), John Steinbeck (*East of Eden*), J.D. Salinger (*The Catcher in the Rye*), Henry Miller (you pick the title), Mickey Spillane (*My Gun Is Quick*), and Gabriel Garcia Marquez (*Memories of My Melancholy Whores*), among them.

But when *The World of Suzie Wong* became an international bestseller and was adapted for the Broadway and West End stages in 1958 and then in 1960 for Hollywood, she became both a symbol and an icon, fantasy posing as fact, the personification of safe sex. That the future Captain Kirk of Star Trek, William Shatner, played Lomax on the New York stage (opposite France Nuyen) and for the Hollywood adaptation he was turned into an American architect played by William Holden (Suzie by Nancy Kwan), gave the property added wholesomeness.

The *New York Times* critic, Bosley Crowther, made it clear why Suzie was such a popular figure when he reviewed the film, saying, "East is East and West is West and never the—hold everything! Who dares be so unromantic as to state that Western boy and Eastern girl cannot meet, separate, and then get together, just like they do in Hollywood films? If such there be (outside Rudyard Kipling), let him witness *The World of Suzie Wong*, wash himself free of skepticism and go forth convinced and purified.

"For here in this wildly romantic, vividly imagined color film, which the new producer, Ray Stark, delivered to the Music Hall yesterday, there is packaged the glowingest commercial for love conquering everything including the taint of prostitution, these old eyes have ever seen. Nothing, including social stigma, can keep Western boy and Eastern girl from walking off into the sunset in it, an absolute twining of the twain."

Crowther went on to say that Mason's story was "so purely idealized in the telling that it wafts into the realm of sheer romance. But the point is that idealization is accomplished so unrestrainedly and with such open reliance upon the impact of elemental clichés that it almost builds up the persuasiveness of real sincerity. Unless you shut your eyes and start thinking, you might almost believe it to be true." Which of course is what happened to the rest of us.

When *The World of Suzie Wong* was published in 1957, it was not so well received as the film. In fact, it was attacked by some critics for reinforcing stereotypes of Asian women as being promiscuous and submissive, especially to foreign men.

All this said, over the years Suzie and her creator had numerous champions, including the American writer Steve Rosse. Not only did Mason devise a character of modern English literature whose name was likely more familiar (and certainly friendlier) than that of Lady Macbeth, he said "Suzie Wong, the fair tale princess who sells her body in a bar, raised the profile of Hong Kong internationally, had her story adapted for the Broadway stage and a Hollywood motion picture, loaned her name to a cartoon character, a reggae song and dozens of taverns all over the world. She also made the author and anybody attached to the book, play or movie rich and famous. But her biggest effect will always be on the millions of readers who have fallen in love with her. To enter the world of Suzie Wong is to be enchanted. The spell lasts forever."

And if that weren't enough to be thankful for, *Asia Inc.* magazine in 2008—by which time the novel had stood the test of a half a century's time—called the book an "uplifting inter-racial love story [with] underlying messages about overcoming racial (and class) prejudice, without being preachy about it."

Today there are bars bearing her name all over Asia, the club in Beijing being regarded as one of the city's finest and described by Frommer's as "the see-and-be-seen venue for *nouveau-riche* Chinese and newly arrived expatriates." Thus along the way this yum-yum girl has been gentrified, as has the Hong Kong neighborhood in which she bloomed

As a red light area, Wan Chai peaked during the 1960s, when the city became a favorite R&R destination for Americans fighting in Vietnam. There were more than a hundred clubs there then. After that, to turn the cliché on its head, it's all been uphill.

The model for Mason's Nam Kok Hotel—real name: Luk Kwok—survived until the 1980s when it was torn down and replaced with a mirrored highrise whose only connection today is the name; rooms now start at US$230 and go to $700 a night. The Star Ferry still docks at Wan Chai, but today the journey from Kowloon has been, amazingly, halved, as land reclamation took the Hong Kong shore out to meet the boat.

Wan Chai has always been bang up against the city's business district, and now it is its equal. One of Hong Kong's eighteen districts, Wan Chai now has the second most educated residents with the highest income. Luxury residential and business towers, along with five-star hotels and an arts center have been constructed on that reclaimed land; the UK's official handover of Hong Kong to China in 1999 was conducted in the Hong Kong Convention and Exhibition Center there.

Is there anything left today to see? Not much. The rebuilt Luk Kwok Hotel has a small display in the lobby acknowledging mostly the movie—Nancy Kwan was an unannounced visitor in 2010—and there is a Suzie Wong bar among the many in the neighborhood, but the young women who work there are mostly from Thailand and the Philippines.

James Clavell

King Rat

In 1966, Western nations had recently fought the Japanese and the North Koreans, and now the Americans and their allies had followed the French in battling the North Vietnamese. The West's view of Asia was not positive. Then along came James Clavell and six novels that reintroduced the continent, giving it adventure, grandeur, and scope. All put Europeans in Asia, exploring the meeting of those two civilizations, from both sides of the cultural fence.

What made Clavell different from other writers associated with Asia was his long historical reach, beginning what came to be called his "Asian Saga" with *Shogun*, a novel set in seventeenth century feudal Japan, moving to Hong Kong (and a fictionalized version of the start-up of Jardine-Matheson) in 1841 in *Tai-Pan*, returning to Japan in the same century in *Gai-Jin*, then jumping ahead to 1945 for a prisoner-of-war story based on his own internment by the Japanese in Singapore, *King Rat*. Another Hong Kong story, *Noble House*, and a novel set in Iran in 1979, *Whirlwind*, concluded the sextet. All were enormous bestsellers and all but the last was adapted by Hollywood or turned into a television mini-series.

James Dumaresq Clavell was born in Sydney, Australia, October 10, 1924, the son of a British Royal Navy officer. He was educated in England, fought in World War Two (spending three years in Japanese prisoner-of-war camps), and afterward married an actress and emigrated to the United States. There, he became a writer and director of the science fiction/horror classic *The Fly* (starring Vincent Price), *Watusi* (Michael Caine), won a Writers Guild Best Screenplay Award for *The Great Escape* (another POW story, this one placed in Germany and starring James Garner and Steve McQueen), and had his biggest hit with the Sidney Poitier film, *To Sir With Love*. He also became an American citizen.

To the public, he was best known for thousand-page novels and their cinematic and television adaptations. The books sold in the multiple millions and in 1980, when *Shogun* was made into a five-part television series starring Richard Chamberlain and Toshiro Mifune, one hundred and twenty million people tuned in, the largest audience for a mini-series since *Roots*.

He died at his home in Vevey, Switzerland, September 6, 1994. His wife of forty years, April, said he had long been battling cancer and died of a stroke. He was sixty-nine.

The Asian Saga

The titles were foreign but not difficult to pronounce—*Tai-Pan*, *Shogun*, and *Gai-Jin*—and the number of pages in the books may have intimidated some readers, but the dramatic stories and vivid characters were compelling. Webster Schott wrote in the *New York Times*, "It's almost impossible not to continue to read *Shogun* once having opened it. Yet it's not only something that you read—you live it."

Critical acceptance frequently fails to accompany great market success—and *Shogun* sold more than fifteen million copies worldwide—yet in Clavell's case the reviews were decidedly flattering. It seemed Clavell could do no wrong. Big sales *and* good reviews, with Hollywood pounding at the door? It didn't happen to everyone.

What made this acceptance all the more unusual was the author's own history in Asia. After being wounded while fighting in Malaya (today's Malaysia) and spending three years in grim Japanese POW camps in Indonesia and Singapore, most would expect him to be anything other than flattering to the Japanese. But both in *Shogun* and *Gai-Jin*, he gave the history and culture of his former captors his full respect, whatever anger he might have felt apparently purged when, in 1962, he wrote *King Rat*, the novel inspired by that experience. Although he put himself in many of his novels, this was the most personal.

Clavell called his sextet a "saga" because characters from one book reappeared in others and the descendants of characters from one novel continued the conflicts and goals of their ancestors in another one. The books were not created chronologically, but in an attempt to make things easier, I'll consider them in the order in which they were written and published, in the context of Clavell's own life and career—showing how his own thoughts about Asia were formed, and changed, and how they were reflected in his novels, which in turn helped introduce the West to the East.

Clavell called his years in the Japanese POW camp his "university...a school for survival," and the "rat" in the novel's title was both a reference to an American enlisted man and a two-pound rat they'd caught and planned to breed to provide protein for the prisoners.

Clavell had intended to follow in his father's footsteps and make the military a career when a motorcycle accident left him with a permanent limp, so after resuming his education at a British university, he met and married an aspiring actress and after fathering two children, took the family to America, first to New York where he worked in television distribution and then to California, quickly finding work as a screenwriter.

Clavell was established in Hollywood before writing *King Rat* (at his wife's urging), having created screenplays for *The Fly* and *Watusi*. *King Rat*, he later said, provided the "catharsis" that allowed him to look at Asia with new eyes. The book became a bestseller and with the earnings from the movie sale—$25,000 a year for five years—he moved his wife and daughters to Hong Kong, where he had spent part of his childhood, to research what became the multi-generational epic titled *Tai-Pan*, which roughly translates to trading company "top gun."

This told the story of two such companies from the period starting at the end of Britain's first "opium war" with China, in 1840. Simplifying, the opium from poppy fields in British India was traded for Chinese silk, tea and other goods, simultaneously creating millions of Chinese addicts and leaving China in debt to the empire. This is how Jardine-Matheson, a large Scottish-owned company of the time and still one of the largest trading firms in Hong Kong, actually got its start, a fact that certainly didn't hurt sales of the novel; although the names of individuals and firms were changed, the author's camouflage was as transparent as the juicy secrets and story lines were close to true.

Some said the novel was over-long and its characters were called stereotypes. It didn't matter. Orville Prescott wrote in the *New York Times* that Clavell "holds attention with a relentless grip. *Tai-Pan* frequently is crude. It is grossly exaggerated much of the time. But seldom does a novel appear so stuffed with imaginative invention, so packed with melodramatic action, so gaudy and flamboyant with blood and treachery and conspiracy, sex and murder." So, of course, it was a bestseller, but it would be twenty years before the movie was made, when (in 1986) it was roundly panned.

Again it didn't matter. By then, Clavell was an institution and a multi-millionaire with three more blockbusters—the first of them, *Shogun*, published in 1975. Clavell's inspiration for this book was twofold. After reading (in a daughter's school book) of a French sailor who became a samurai, he remembered something that happened in the Singapore POW camp, a story he included in *King Rat*. The camp's commandant offered the book's hero a sword with which he was expected to commit honorable *seppuku* by slitting his stomach, after which another Japanese officer would cut off his head. Where the Japanese felt shame at being captured, Westerners believed it wiser to live to fight another day, so the blade was refused, infuriating the commandant. Now, as Clavell reconsidered this cultural divide and doing some reading on Japan's samurai past, he started researching a novel that would, among other things, try to make that difference make sense.

In *Shogun*, Clavell based his story loosely on that of William Adams and the Shogun Tokugawa Ieyasu, who in the early seventeenth century proclaimed the English sailor dead, renaming him Miura Anjin. Add conflicts between competing Western missionaries, the usual Japanese district rivalries, a beautiful woman who believes she must die for her lord, and what the *New Yorker* called "flashy Hollywood dialog and derring-do that haven't been around much since the heyday of the Errol Flynn movie."

Most critics praised the book. Cynthia Gorney hyperbolically described *Shogun* in the *Washington Post* as "one of those books that blots up vacations and imperils marriages, because it simply will not let the reader go" and *Library Journal* said it consisted of "a wonderful churning brew of adventure, intrigue, love, philosophy, and history." While the *New York Review of Books* called it a tribute to an "immense amount of historical and cultural research…a tourist guide to medieval Japan" and the *New York Times* reviewer wrote, "James Clavell does more than entertain. He transports us into worlds we've not known, stimulating, educating, questioning almost simultaneously."

Not everyone loved the book without reservation. Columbia University's Henry Smith edited a book of essays called *Learning from Shogun: Japanese History and Western Fantasy* (1980), its title conveying his and his colleagues' doubts: "…uneasy over the depiction of the Japanese samurai as sadistic and uncaring of life, I was initially unable to read past the first two hundred pages of *Shogun*. Only when pressed by inquisitive students did I read the entire novel and come to understand that the initial image of the Japanese as 'barbarians' was a foil for the hero's eventual understanding that Japan is not only civilized, but maybe even more civilized than the West. In short, the central theme of the novel itself turned out to be exactly our business: learning about Japan.

"For educators, it is useful to understand *Shogun* if only because so many people have read it. Based on our own experience, anywhere from one-fifth to one-half of all students who currently enroll in college-level courses about Japan have already read *Shogun*, and not a few of these have become interested in Japan because of it. With over six million copies of *Shogun* in print (and more sure to follow after the television series), it would appear that the American consciousness of Japan has grown by a quantum leap because of this one book. In sheer quantity *Shogun* has probably conveyed more information about Japan to more people than all the combined writings of scholars, journalists, and novelists since the Pacific war. At the very least, an understanding of *Shogun* may help those of us involved in education about Japan to better understand our audience."

Faint praise, but praise nonetheless, compared to what Smith felt about the TV adaptation, which showed "a tacit conviction that the American television public in 1980 is so xenophobic that it cannot tolerate an image of the Japanese (or presumably other such non-white, non-Christian cultures) as anything more than incomprehensible 'aliens.'" There was a look of authenticity, he added, but it was "a largely cosmetic effect which presented the uncomfortable contradiction of skilled Japanese actors, finely costumed, who often behaved in the most un-Japanese ways."

This became Clavell's most enduring work, nonetheless. Twenty years following publication, in 1995, the *Writer's Digest* listed it as one of the seventy-five books every writer must read. By then, some fifteen million copies had been sold worldwide and several adaptations were made, including the highly success- ful five-part, twelve-hour mini-series on NBC that was watched by some seventy-five million per episode. Japanese restaurants added "Shogun Specials" to their menus and trendy types' starting using the Japanese words for thank you (*arigato*) and "I under- stand" (*wakarimasu*) in their conversation. *Newsweek* published an article about the fad, calling it "Samurai Night Fever."

(Clavell was not, however, the first to bring the samurai to Western audiences. The famed Japanese director Akira Kurosawa released his classic *Seven Samurai* nearly thirty years before *Sho- gun* hit the bookshelves, in 1954, starring Toshiro Mifune. But once Japan's traditional warrior class was part of Western con- sciousness, it kept reappearing, inspiring John Ford to take the samurai film's similarity to the American western and make *The Magnificent Seven* in 1960. The Jedi knights and Darth Vader's helmet in *Star Wars* were direct descendant images as well and in 2003 Tom Cruise took the title role in *The Last Samurai*.)

There was another factor contributing to the novel's success. The United States may have defeated the Empire of the Sun in World War Two, but in little more than three decades, Japan be- came a design and manufacturing powerhouse, its cars and elec- tronics kicking the hell out of US and other foreign competitors. American businessmen, sent to Japan to learn why, discovered that an American, Ed Deming, was partially responsible, having taught the Japanese what came to be called "quality control." NBC broadcast a documentary called "If Japan Can, Why Can't We?" And sales of *Shogun* kept going up, up, up. Who were these peo- ple? Western nations wanted to know and Clavell was one of those who benefited.

Noble House was next, taking the saga back to Hong Kong, where, in a story set in 1963 (and published in 1981), the trading company based on Jardine-Matheson in *Tai-Pan* is updated against a background of European businessmen and police, Chinese communists, Taiwanese nationalists, and spies from a handful of nations, including the Soviet Union. (Peter Marlowe, the British POW from *King Rat* and based on Clavell himself, also reappears, now working in the British colony as a journalist.) Once again, the novel was more than a thousand pages long with a cast of hundreds and overlapping and entangled plots. It further became the predictable bestseller and Pierce Brosnan starred in a four-part, six and a half-hour mini-series, again for NBC.

In the last two novels in the saga, *Whirlwind* and *Gai-Jin*, Clavell remained true to form, casting members of the Hong Kong Struan family in leading roles. In *Whirlwind*, the plot was moved to what generally was now called the Middle East, to Iran in the 1960s, when the Shah was deposed and succeeded by the Ayatollah Khomeini. Because this is a book that focuses on the more commonly defined "Middle East," that's all I'll say about the book, except that it was more than a thousand pages long and another bestseller. It was published in 1986.

In *Gai-Jin*—the Japanese word for "foreigner"—which was the author's last novel (he died a year following its publication in 1993), he returned to Japan and the 1860s and Japan's hostility shown to Westerners. Many of the characters in *Tai-Pan* reappear and as in that earlier novel, much of the action and many of the characters were based on real people and events.

Although both *Whirlwind* and *Gai-Jin* sold well, neither was as well received by critics as earlier novels. "Reviewing James Clavell's most recent work poses an interesting ethical question," said Peter Andrew in the *New York Times*. "When you have been engaged by a responsible journal to report on a 1,147 page novel that bores you bandylegged, how many pages do you have to read before you can bail out and still fulfill your professional obligations? I handed in my dinner pail on page 851 when a character got his throat slit and I couldn't remember who he was."

It didn't matter. Clavell had joined the jumbo book titans—Arthur Hailey (*Airport, Hotel, Roots*), Colleen McCullough (*The Masters of Rome series, The Thorn Birds*), James Michener (pick any spot on the world map), and Mario Puzo (the *Godfather* series)—and for a time claimed Asia as his own patch. He also made his feelings about the continent clear. He believed East and West could meet and obviously did, but for such a partnership to work, it would take generations and compromise.

Politically he was conservative—a fan of Ayn Rand's and William Buckley was a friend—who believed, in the words of a biographer, Gina Macdonald, that "by valuing group over the individual and by theoretically reducing all to the same common denominator, communism denies the value of human difference and restricts human potential, while capitalism, in turn, though subject to the excesses of greed and human selfishness, ultimately encourages individualism and differences and, through free enterprise allows class differences to be negated and society to prosper." In addition, Macdonald wrote in *James Clavell: A Critical Companion*, "survival of the fittest means survival of the most flexible, adaptable, and resilient."

Clavell certainly was that, working successfully as a writer, director and producer in Hollywood (a committee town and industry), not on just his own projects but the scripts of others, and in surprising ways, he delivered more than a little class with his blood and guts—for instance, using Orson Welles as the narrator of the *Shogun* mini-series and when that book was compressed to two and a half hours for the big screen, Japanese characters spoke Japanese *without* subtitles, a daring device that left viewers to figure out what was being said from the context and other actors' response.

Clavell's narrative may have been flamboyant and frequently over-the-top in its plotting and characterization, and he surely took liberties with historical fact when it suited him, but there always, always was a well-researched cultural tapestry hanging on the back wall and along with all the wars, back-stabbings, and slit stomachs and throats came a sympathetic examination of the manners, values, and lifestyles of both East and West.

Clavell may have been mistreated in those Japanese POW camps, but he got over it.

Anthony Burgess
The Devil of a State

Anthony Burgess was one of the most prolific and diverse writers of the twentieth century, best known for *A Clockwork Orange*, but also greatly praised for his first three novels, collectively called *The Long Day Wanes* or *The Malayan Trilogy*. Somerset Maugham's stories placed in the same colonial setting are more widely acknowledged, but critics and historians credit Burgess—who actually lived in what is now Malaysia, as Maugham did not—with greater skill and accuracy, his fluency in Malay and choice of local drinking partners giving him a deeper understanding of the native Malays, Indians, and Chinese.

The books titled *Time for a Tiger, The Enemy in the Blanket*, and *Beds in the East*, published in 1956, 1958, and 1959, followed the experiences of history teacher Victor Crabbe working, as did Burgess, for the British Colonial Service during the British empire's waning days. As recently as 2006, the novels were banned in Malaysia and until recently were sold only in a few city shops. A fourth early novel, *Devil of a State*, followed another teaching assignment in Brunei, whose identity was flimsily masked to discourage a lawsuit. It still isn't available there.

Burgess began writing in his forties and won fame in his fifties when Stanley Kubrick focused on the ultra-violence of *A Clockwork Orange*, making the book an enormous bestseller. Earnings from the film, won only by suing Kubrick for what he thought was a fair share of the profits, also made Burgess rich enough to send him and his second wife into tax exile, thereafter buying and occupying numerous homes in her native Italy, Switzerland, and Monaco.

All that, plus a roistering, somewhat fictionalized pair of autobiographies, and numerous ego-driven television interviews, made Burgess at times seem less serious than he was. Yet, in addition to some thirty novels, his versatility and stamina produced guides to literature, translations and linguistic studies, screenplays, operatic libretti, symphonies, concertos and film scores, as well as what one critic termed "an embarrassment" of journalism, book reviews, and essays, published regularly in England, France, Italy, and the United States, where he also spent four years as a university lecturer and writer-in-residence.

He was born John Burgess Wilson, son of a tobacconist and sometime pub pianist, February 25, 1917, in Manchester, England—the "Anthony" was added at his Christening—and died November 22,1993, of lung cancer, in a London hospital. His ashes were interred in Monaco.

The Sun Finally Sets

When Anthony Burgess, still known as Jack Wilson, accepted a teaching position in 1954 in what was then called Malaya and he and his wife Lynne set forth, the sun that never sets on Britain's empire was inches from the horizon and soon would slip beneath the waves. He would be the last of the great imperial novelists, following Conrad, Kipling, Forster, Orwell, Maugham, and Greene. His wife dreaded Malaya and he rollicked in hearty anticipation.

"As we entered a zone of heat more furious than anything I had known in Gibraltar, I felt I was approaching a world I could live in," he wrote in the first volume of his autobiography, *Little Wilson and Big God*. "I sweated and was happy to sweat. Where there ain't no ten commandments and a man can raise a thirst."

The last unattributed sentence was from "On the Road to Mandalay"—the Kipling classic that Burgess said he recited from memory from the bow of the ship en route—and it set the tone of much of the teacher's life that followed. As his wife lay exhausted in a bed in the Raffles Hotel upon arriving in Singapore, then a part of the Federated Malay States, Burgess went to that city's notorious Bugis Street and picked up a Chinese prostitute, taking her to "a filthy *hotel de passe* full of the noise of hawking and spitting, termed by the cynical the call of the east. I entered her and entered the territory."

Such territory as Great Britain could still call its own in 1954 was not so great. Hong Kong aside, Malaya comprised the last major geography to achieve total independence from British control and it was, in fact, never a distinct colony but three port settlements—Penang, Malacca, and Singapore—situated amidst a number of Islamic sultanates, each with its ruling monarch, who was given a British adviser. To assist in this stumbling move toward self-determination, Britain's Colonial Service sent educators. Burgess was given a three-year contract to teach English at a Malay college in the state of Perak. In his first novel, *Time for a Tiger*—its title inspired by a slogan for the Singapore-brewed Tiger beer[1]—Victor Crabbe taught history at a multi-racial school in Lanchap, Malay.

---

1. Burgess wrote the brewers of Tiger beer about his intention to advertise their product in the title of a book and asked for one of the wooden clocks bearing the slogan then displayed throughout Malaya. Executives said they wanted to read his manuscript first. Stung, he inserted in the text a line of dialogue that read, "Not Tiger, not Anchor. Make it Carlsberg. It costs a bit more, but it's a better beer.")

Almost inevitably, the author's characters were drawn as racial stereotypes—and, often, comic caricatures—but never without what the *New Statesman* called "an impartial generosity." The Chinese, when they weren't "hoiking and spitting," were making money; the Indians (mainly Punjabi Sikhs and Hindu Tamils) drank and fought and spouted English pompously; the Europeans complained about the heat, slept with the local women and failed to understand *anything*; and the Malays cried aloud their loyalty to Islamic stricture then ate and drank what they liked, while (in Burgess's words) they "watched the coconuts fall" and no more, because they knew that it was they who'd inherit the Malayan earth. That said, aside from the protagonist's falling out with his headmaster and getting shifted to another part of the country (just in time for the second novel), all ended well; the Malay divorcée who had been Victor's mistress and then cast off was caught on a bounce by a rich local rajah and the most outrageous drunk (and the amount of alcohol consumed by just about everyone more than justified the book's title) won the national lottery and shared it with his friends.

When published, in 1956, *Time for a Tiger* sold well, going into several printings. By that time, Burgess and his wife were living on Malaya's east coast near the Thai border, in Kota Bharu in Kelantan, where he now taught at a teachers' training college. Here, in the fictionalized Dahaga, again Victor, promoted to headmaster of a school, in a novel titled *The Enemy in the Blanket*— a Malay expression applied seriously to a traitor and jokingly to one's wife—collided with the usual "wickedness, drunkenness, perfidy," this time climbing into bed with a white woman (a colleague's wife), then separated from his wife, who returned to England with a smitten Islamic millionaire. Again all ended well; Victor lost his job because he hadn't the right skin color and ethnic heritage, but a legion of Chinese terrorists surrendered to him, making him a sort of hero anyway.

In the final novel, *Beds in the East*—taking its title from a line in *Antony and Cleopatra* that warned, "The beds in the East are soft"—Victor is the Chief Education Officer for a third fictitious Malay state—this one Burgess said was not inspired by especially anywhere—and his countrymen are leaving in growing numbers. Racial tension is also increasing as independence approaches, and in an effort to forge racial harmony (literally) Victor defends a young Chinese man's symphony as uniquely Malayan music, suggesting it serve as a symbol of collective nationhood. The composer falls under the influence of American pop music played in a newly acquired jukebox in his father's coffee-shop, however, and the work is rejected as sounding too Western. Victor's accidental death by drowning seems an apt metaphor for the end of empire

Repatriated to England following a cancer scare, Burgess wrote four novels in a single year to provide for his falsely assumed widow-to-be—including *Devil of a State* and a novel about his alleged illness, *The Doctor Is Sick*. When cerebral tests showed there was, in fact, no tumor, the misdiagnosis was explained in various ways. Burgess himself later blamed his wife for cursing the Duke of Edinburgh, then himself for speaking openly in support of opposition to the dominant Malayan political party. Still another time he said he was bored and merely lay down on the classroom floor to see what might happen, leaving his biographers shaking their heads and pointing to his acknowledged delight in building personal myth.

Although the four novels set in Southeast Asia sold well, it would be his next book, published in 1962, which changed his life. This was *A Clockwork Orange*, a book about a gang of ultra-violent street toughs for whom he invented an original language, the plot inspired, he said, by an assault on his wife during World War Two by a group of inebriated American GI's, the damage done preventing her from bearing children. When Stanley Kubrick's

movie version of this novel was released in 1971, it was blamed
for real-life violence and banned in the UK. (Where it is still
banned today, both in theaters and on videocassette and disc,
assuring an ongoing run in a Paris theater where it still draws a
fair British crowd.)

Burgess's wife died of cirrhosis in 1968 and he promptly married an Italian translator, Lianna Johnson, who, as his mistress, had
quietly borne their child, a son. They married the same year and
she pretty much took control of his career, suing Kubrick and winning more than $1 million, sending the Burgesses into permanent
tax exile. For a time, she drove a live-in van around Europe while
he wrote in the back, but then they began acquiring homes—
there were ten when he died—in Italy, France, and Switzerland.

Despite the film's notoriety, Burgess managed to construct a
reputation for both originality and versatility, composing numerous film and television scripts (whose subjects included Jesus,
Moses, Shakespeare and Sherlock Holmes, while for another he
concocted a Stone Age language); a symphony inspired by Napoleon; two books, a screenplay, a musical and a ballet suite in Shakespeare's name, three books and a musical in James Joyce's name
(his two major influences); full-length critical studies of D.H.
Lawrence and Ernest Hemingway; a translation of *Cyrano de
Bergerac* that ran at the Guthrie Theatre in Minneapolis in 1971
and on Broadway in 1984; guides to literature; translations; and
hundreds of essays and book reviews, all while cranking out some
thirty novels, several of them little more than hack work but many
taking on such themes as good and evil, original sin, reality, chaos,
authoritarian institutions, materialism, and corruption, nearly all
his works displaying a vocabulary that verged on braggadocio.

(Burgess's overuse of Malay words and phrases without translation throughout the text of his trilogy is equally maddening;
local color is one thing, lapsing continually into a foreign language
in what is intended to be a popular novel is not only misguided,
it is bewildering.)

No wonder he once expressed surprise about his reputation as a prolific writer of comic novels. "One writes in grim earnest," he said, "only to discover that when my work is published that Burgess has done it again, another funny farce. My God, I had to write *Clockwork Orange* in a state of near drunkenness in order to deal with material that upset me very much."

There was no denying his comic style, however. His characters in *The Malayan Trilogy* as well as in many of the novels that followed *were* outsized, their relationships and adventures, if not merely messy, quirky, and surreal, often reminiscent of Hollywood's early slapstick comedies—as if Stan Laurel and Oliver Hardy and perhaps Harold Lloyd and Charlie Chaplin, too, got drunk on Tiger beer, soon to be joined by Groucho and Harpo Marx, who at the sight of the East's most exotic female forms, wore out their eyebrows and horn in joyous response. Inspired by Joyce's fascination with wordplay, Burgess's works also were leavened with puns and literary jokes, some of them secret and somewhat smutty, like those in the Malayan novels, lost in the translation he failed to provide. The overall effect was a softening of his pessimism and for many readers, a failure to take him entirely seriously.

Fueling the same fire, Burgess actually *became* Burgess, leaving the more modest Jack Wilson behind as he created in himself a colorful character, as if he were carrying on his father's piano performances in cinema houses and pubs. On his visits to the UK (when permitted entrance by the taxman) and during his stints as a visiting professor and writer-in-residence in the United States (at Princeton, City College of New York, Columbia, and universities in upstate New York, North Carolina and Iowa), a television studio was never far away. Always erudite and scholarly, there was, nonetheless, a bit of the imp in him, as if he might suddenly produce and play a kazoo.

It was inevitable, of course, that his Southeast Asian stories were compared to Maugham's. Certainly, he invited that by having his protagonist talk about Maugham in *The Malayan Trilogy*, chiding him for his simplicity, simultaneously re-enacting the adulterous plots. In *Little Wilson and Big God*, Burgess took another swipe at the older writer and Conrad as well, writing, "The book was sometimes compared unfavorably with the Eastern stories of Somerset Maugham, who was considered, and still is [considered], the true fictional expert on Malaya. The fact is that Maugham knew little of the country outside the very bourgeois lives of the planters and administrators. He certainly knew none of the languages. Nor did Joseph Conrad. When I stated, as a matter of plain fact, that I knew more Malay than Conrad, I was accused of conceit. Whether *Time for a Tiger* is a good or bad novel, its details of Malayan life are authentic. After Henri Fauconnier's *Malaisie* (which won the Prix Goncourt but is now forgotten in France), it remains the first novel to state what the life was really like. If it sold moderately well, and still sells a little, it was, is, because of the authenticity."

Burgess had a further point to make abut the trilogy when he wrote a brief introduction to it for a British publisher following the conclusion of America's war in Vietnam: "We have to understand the nature of the East, and also of Islam: we can no longer, since Vietnam, regard those far regions as material for mere fairy tales… The Americans understood neither their friends nor their enemies. To many, the Far East hardly exists, except as material for televisual diversion. It is hoped that this novel, which has its own elements of diversion, may, through tears and laughter, educate."

In that, it is unlikely, although the trilogy is now sold openly in Malaysia, making possible some small enlightenment in the country upon which it was based. Up to about 2006, all three novels were banned, an act that was, if nothing else, an indication of their authenticity. *Devil of a State* is now out of print everywhere, but never was available in Brunei. No one ever believed it was about Africa.

There are, of course, numerous places to visit in both Brunei and Malaysia that featured prominently in the author's years there, as well as in the novels. Most important are the schools at which Burgess taught—Malay College in Kuala Kangsar in the state of Perak, and the Malay Teachers' Training College in Kota Bharu in the state of Kelantan, and in Brunei, the Sultan Omar Ali Saifuddin College, so named for the sultan then perched atop the tiny protectorate's throne—and the mosques in the same cities and in Brunei's capital, Bandar Seri Beawan, the Sultan Omar Ali Saifuddin Mosque, under construction when Burgess arrived and now dwarfed by others and made tiny by the current sultan's mansion, with its one thousand, seven hundred and eighty-eight rooms.

Generally speaking, a visit to the schools would be more instructive than to the mosques; Islam and its worshippers played a key role in all the novels, but so, too, did the resident Sikhs and Chinese and, most importantly, the British expatriates who watched their empire's sun finally set.

Marguerite Duras

The Lover

Few individuals and perhaps no other woman in her time earned
a position of such stature and acclaim in both literature and film
as did France's Marguerite Duras. Nor have so many experienced
so much personal drama, much of it to serve as inspiration for
the thirty-four books and thirty-eight films that bore her name
in a career that spanned more than fifty years.

She is best known for her Oscar-nominated screenplay for
Hiroshima Mon Amour (1959), the story of a wartime love affair
between a French nurse and a Japanese architect, and the semi-
autobiographical novel *The Lover* (1984) that sold more than a
million copies in France in the first year and ultimately was published in forty-three languages. The plots were similar but the
latter cut nearer to the bone, revealing a secret affair she had as
a fifteen-year-old girl from a poor French family in what was
then called Indochine (today Vietnam) with an older, wealthy
Chinese man.

Leaving her native Saigon when she was seventeen to study
math and then law at the Sorbonne, drama came to her again as
she worked for the puppet Vichy government during Nazi Germany's occupation of France and simultaneously for the French

underground with a resistance group led by François Mitterrand, a future French prime minister. After her husband was released from a Nazi concentration camp and she spent years nursing him back to health, she had a child by a mutual friend. She also joined and was expelled from the Communist Party and chose journalism as a post-war career—so no one should have been surprised when she began writing books and screenplays, becoming a key figure in the French "New Wave," as a director and actor as well as a scenarist.

However, it was not until she neared seventy that she started *The Lover*, by which time she also was consuming up to nine liters of cheap Bordeaux a day, managing to produce as little as one sentence a day. Not until she sobered up in 1982 at a Paris hospital was the slender book finished, taking her to the top again.

She was born Marguerite Donnadieu, April 4, 1914, in Gia-Dinh, outside Saigon, the daughter of schoolteachers working in the French colony. Her father died when she was five and her mother chose to stay. She died of throat cancer in Paris March 3, 1996, having taken the pseudonym "Duras" from the name of the village where her father was born. She was eighty-one.

"The (Vietnam) Lover"

In the early 1990s, soon after the Vietnamese government initiated a policy called *doi moi*, welcoming foreign visitors to the country still recovering from forty years of war (with first the French and then the Americans and Chinese), I became a regular visitor. At that time, the growing number of tourists included many American veterans, returning in an attempt to find peace within themselves. Although I had been on the other side of the barricades, demonstrating against the war in the 1960s, I was there for much the same reason.

The thing that made the most impact, for me, was how forgiving the Vietnamese were; everywhere I went, I not only felt safe,

I felt welcome. Obviously, it is easier to "forgive" those whose asses you have so soundly beaten than those who have beaten you.

Of course, I was also the target of the swarms of kids on the street selling maps, post cards, day old foreign newspapers, fake Vietnam era Zippo lighters, and dog tags, helicopter and jet fighter models fashioned from beer and soda cans, and badly produced counterfeit copies of Graham Greene's *The Quiet American* and a novel that recently had become the first foreign film produced in post-war Vietnam, Marguerite Duras's remembrance *The Lover.*

Duras was only fifteen in the story she told about her affair with an older man, so I couldn't help thinking about her when I saw young Vietnamese women of her age riding bicycles to and from school in the national dress, the *ao dai,* a sort of shimmery pantsuit fitted to the budding pubescent forms, revealing nothing and at the same time, everything. I purchased a copy of the book. I wanted to be a lover, too.

Saigon had changed significantly since the young Marguerite Donnadieu had walked its streets in the 1920s, when her parents taught the children of French immigrants like themselves. But it also had changed only a little. When the French movie company acquired all the permits to film *The Lover,* all that was required to go back more than fifty years in time—visually—was to cover the paved streets with dirt outside shophouses that hadn't changed at all and needed only a little paint.

I knew nothing about Marguerite Duras at that time, although when she and I were much younger I had seen *Hiroshima Mon Amour,* for which her script was nominated for an Academy Award. In 1959 when it was released in the US, I was studying at Columbia University and lived near what was then called an "art theater," where foreign films attracted an avid student audience. I confess I didn't give the film or its scenarist another thought until I was in Vietnam in 1993. I didn't even know she wrote novels. I had missed a lot of history, film, and literature.

So it can be said for almost everyone else outside France, (as is probably still true today). The woman who called herself Marguerite Duras was one of the great talents as well as one of the most unforgettable "characters" of postwar France, yet elsewhere she was relatively unknown and she now goes largely unremembered. In 1975, she won France's highest cinematic honor, the Cinema Academy Grand Prix for her film *India Song* and *The Lover* received the nation's most prestigious literary prize, the Prix Goncourt, honors that, like the Pulitzer and Booker prizes in the United States and Britain, generally go unnoticed outside national boundaries.

There were times when her "character" and tempestuous history nearly overwhelmed her talent and awards. Whose side was she on during World War Two, for example, when she served on a government committee that decided on a book-by-book basis whether a publisher got the paper on which to print a given title? Books by D.H. Lawrence, Freud, Zola and Colette were turned away, but Goebbels's memoirs and other anti-Semite manuscripts were approved.

Of course, as a de facto censor for the Nazis, she was doing what she felt necessary to survive. Yet, at the same time, she joined the Communist party and clandestinely answered to the leader of a resistance group led by the future French prime minister, François Mitterrand. If any doubt remained about her loyalty, her husband, Robert Antelme, also a writer, was held at Bergen-Belsen, one of the nastier Nazi concentration camps, and when liberated weighed eighty-four pounds and could barely walk.

Duras was not blind to opportunity. At the same time she said no paper would be allocated for *Lady Chatterley's Lover*, she approved it for the publication of her own first novel, *Les Impudents*, a manuscript that had been rejected by several publishers and now was reviewed favorably by someone who served on the same de facto censorship committee and whose wife was the novelist's best friend. Years later, Duras would admit to this deception and say her novel was without merit.

As France's war recovery was long and slow, so, too, that of Duras's husband. While tending him, she worked as a journalist for several magazines, including the *Observateur*, leaving him to have a child, a son (Jean) by Dionys Mascolo, a mutual friend. She also was expelled from the Communist Party for her outspoken opinions and attempts to change the organization. Concurrently, she continued to write novels, in 1950 publishing *Un Barrage Contree Le Pacifique* (*The Sea Wall*), which told the story of a poor French family in Vietnam, thus she became a literary connection to France's colonial past, a role she would play off and on for the rest of her life. This novel became a film twice, in France in 1958 and fifty years later by a French-Cambodian-Belgian production team.

Finding herself among other young filmmakers who came to be called by the French press *Nouvelle Vague*, literally "New Wave," she collaborated with the director Alain Resnais in an inter-racial love story titled *Hiroshima Mon Amour*, so named for the setting in that post-apocalyptic city where a French nurse fell in love with a Japanese man whose entire family was killed in the blast. Leonard Maltin called the film "the New Wave's *Birth of a Nation*" and Jean-Luc Godard described the innovative cinematic techniques as "Faulkner plus Stravinsky." Duras was also recognized for her script at the Cannes Film Festival, although the film was not shown for fear of disturbing the US government. Oddly, it did poor business in Japan, where it was released as *Twenty-four Hour Love Affair*.

The impact of these young filmmakers—at its loose center were François Truffaut, Jean-Luc Goddard, Eric Rohmer, Louis Malle, Jacques Rivette, and Claude Chabrol—lasted only a few years, but thrust France into the forefront of the cinema world. Here, Duras skillfully changed hats, working as an actor, screenwriter, director and sometimes two or three at once. In the 1950s, she published eight novels, in the 1960s, six novels, four plays, and two scripts, with another two films produced. In the 1970s, her name appeared on thirteen films, five in 1979 alone. In the next decade, she continued her prolific output, producing eleven novels, six plays, one movie script, and four films, becoming recognized as not only an intellectual diva and cultural icon but also a one-woman industry.

There was a tendency to pontificate. "Men like women who write," she said. "Even though they don't say so. A writer is a foreign country."

"It was the men I deceived the most that I loved the most," she said.

"When a woman drinks, it's as if an animal were drinking, or a child. Alcoholism is scandalous in a woman, and a female alcoholic is rare, a serious matter. It's a slur on the divine in our nature."

By now, likely as surprised as she was exhausted, Duras was in her seventies and living with Yann Andréa, a man thirty-eight years her junior who became obsessed by her writing, then served as her secretary, acted in her films, and ultimately became her biographer, chronicling her alcoholism and eventual cure. Edmund White later wrote in *The New York Review of Books*, "Before her cure, she was holed up in her chateau dictating one much-worked-on line a day to Andréa, who would type it up. Then they would start uncorking cheap Bordeaux and she'd drink two glasses, vomit, then continue on till she'd drunk as many as nine liters and would pass out. She could no longer walk, or scarcely. She said she drank because she knew God did not exist. Her very sympathetic doctor would visit her almost daily and offer to take her to the hospital, but only if she wanted to live. She seemed undecided for a long time, but at last she opted for life since she was determined to finish a book that she'd already started and was very keen about."

This was *L'Amant (The Lover)*, a short novel in which Duras returned again to her childhood, upsetting literary stereotypes: it was the pubescent girl who seduced the older man, controlling the relationship, refusing to return his love, rather than the other way around. The book seemed to be a faithful retelling of her life at fifteen, without any hurtful truth held back. She described her mother as uncaring, an older brother as cruel, a younger brother as spineless, her dalliance with the Chinese man a way for her to escape, a few sensual hours at a time.

It was classic story of love enjoyed by both lovers for different reasons in the short time, unrequited later, but in this instance it was the man left only with memories—in Duras's words, the lover becoming "so accustomed to the adolescence of the white girl, he's lost. The pleasure he takes in her every evening has absorbed all his time, all his life." Time passed, the "white girl" left, and the Chinese man entered a traditional, arranged marriage. But still, "It was as before…he still loved her, he could never stop loving her…he'd love her unto death."

The brooding, reluctantly regretful moodiness continued when Duras recalled perhaps her own thoughts, writing, "The burst of Chopin under a sky lit up with brilliancies…There wasn't a breath of wind and the music spread all over the dark boat, like a heavenly injunction whose import was unknown, like an order from God whose meaning was inscrutable…and afterwards, she wept because she thought of the man from Cholon and suddenly she wasn't sure she hadn't loved him with a love she hadn't seen because it had lost itself in the affair like water in sand and she rediscovered it only now, through this moment of music flung across the sea."

There were two versions of the story published—first the slim novel in 1984, told in the first person, and then, when the film appeared in 1992, a longer, weaker version written in the third person and retitled *L'Amant De La Chine du Nord (The North*

China Lover). This shift in point of view reflected that taken in the film, much of the script being narrated by Jeanne Moreau, an older woman looking back. (The on-screen Duras role was played by Jean March.) The longer version sold well, but only because of the film and it was the original that became a classic.

Two versions of the film were released as well, a somewhat sexier one for European markets, which surely encouraged sales of both books—although when the film was shown in Vietnam's half dozen or so theaters, the steamier scenes were cut out.

Edmund White wrote in *The New York Review of Books*, "When she was feeling well enough, she surrounded herself with courtiers, laughed very loudly, told jokes, and had opinions about everything. She was an egomaniac and talked about herself constantly. She loved herself, she quoted herself, she took a childlike delight in reading her own work and seeing her old films, all of which she declared magnificent.

"When toward the end of her life she ran into Mitterrand in a fish restaurant, she asked him how she had become better known to people around the world than he was. Very politely, he assured her he'd never doubted for a moment that her fame would someday eclipse his."

In the end, her greatest creation was herself and from that came her art, sometimes with a glass of cheap Bordeaux, a single sentence at a time. Mitterrand knew that.

The Indochine of Marguerite Duras's young life remained unchanged for decades, even after the French were defeated in 1954 and the Americans in 1975, as for half a century the nation was mired in war and extreme deprivation, unable to progress, starved in every way. The first time I visited Hanoi, in 1992, I noticed that there were no birds and asked the woman who served as my government minder why.

"We ate them," she said.

When *doi moi* was introduced and the whole world was invited, Vietnam experienced one of the biggest, unbridled

Southeast Asian development booms in the second half of the twentieth century and much of the past was wiped out. The Mekong River ferryboat on which the young Duras and her lover met was replaced by the mile-long My Thuan Bridge constructed by Australia in 2000. Nearby, the onetime provincial capital of Sa Dec is where Duras's mom taught and it was here that some of the film's scenes were shot, but if you ask where the school was located, several people today will send you in different directions with equal conviction, some to what is now a police drugs unit headquarters. (Sa Dec is now known for its nurseries cultivating flowers and bonsai trees.) Back in Saigon, the movie theater, where her mother once played the piano, has been replaced by a strip of tourist shops and galleries selling copies of paintings by French impressionists that are so realistic, by law they must be slightly smaller than the originals, to avoid confusion.

Yet the feel of old Indochine remains in the surviving and restored architecture in central Saigon, a district called Quarter 1. Here, the wide boulevards and spreading tamarind trees are more than a century old and the main shopping and entertainment avenue, then called Rue Catinat and now Dong Khoi Street, still includes the French wedding cake called the Continental Hotel and the National Theatre next door, both fairly new when Duras was born.

Young pigs are still roasted on spits on the street and ducks hang by their necks in restaurant display cases in Cholon, which is Saigon's Chinatown, where the Chinese lover took his young friend and her siblings, who got drunk and insulted their host and he paid for their drinks and meals without complaint.

Cholon was also where the massive restaurants were matched in size by dance halls where as many as five hundred taxi girls hired themselves out by the dance, another scene from the book. When I visited Saigon in the early 1990s and I was reading *The Lover*, they were still there, probably little changed from Duras's time. Friends tell me now that they've been closed.

Today the calm has become the clamorous. What is now called Ho Chi Minh City instead of Saigon is a wannabe Bangkok. In the late 1980s the most popular mode of transportation was the bicycle. Five years later it was the Honda motorbike. Now, four-wheeled vehicles clog the city and the air is bad.

Still, if you stand in the right place, on the bank of the Mekong at dawn or outside one of those French buildings in Saigon at dusk and close your eyes and breathe deeply the damp, fishy smell of the boats and the sweet scent of frangipani blossoms, for a moment you may think nothing at all has changed.

Pierre Boulle

The Bridge Over the River Kwai

Pierre Boulle was a bestselling French writer known mainly for two novels, both of them reaching huge audiences after getting the Hollywood spin, *The Bridge Over the River Kwai* and *Planet of the Apes*. The first of these was a wildly fictionalized telling of a true story about the construction of the Burma-Siam railway during World War Two by allied prisoners-of-war. The science fiction tale about astronauts landing on a planet populated by intelligent apes eventually became the better known of the two works—inspiring a remake of the original film, four sequels, two television series (one animated), and countless Halloween costumes—but it was the struggle between POWs and their Japanese captors that has the distinction of inspiring one of Thailand's most popular tourist attractions.

Following a mundane start in life as an electrical engineer in Paris, Boulle took a job on a rubber plantation in Malaya in 1938 and a year later when Germany invaded France, he joined the French army in Saigon and served as a secret agent assigned to the resistance movement in Singapore, China, Burma, and back in Indochine. In 1943, he was captured and imprisoned in Saigon, escaping a year later to finish the war with the British special forces in Calcutta.

Thus it was no surprise when he used this background in several of his two-dozen novels and a book of memoirs, *My Own River Kwai. Planet of the Apes* may also be seen not only as an ironical story about the relationship between humans and animals, but also a retelling of the classic prisoner-captor subject so popular during the post-war years.

Boulle's works all were published first in French, the translations becoming bestsellers worldwide—often exploring violence and survival, master and slave, human frailty and absurdity, themes sourced from the same well of wartime experience. The novels were favorably reviewed and *Le Pont de la riviere Kwai* won the French "Prix Sainte-Beauve." He was also an officer de la Legion d'Honneur and a recipient of the Croix de Guerre and the Medaille de la Resistance.

Despite his adventurous early life and subsequent great success, he was a quiet, solitary man who never married and spent the end of his life sharing a large apartment with a sister in Paris.

Pierre-Francois-Marie-Louis Boulle was a lawyer's son, born February 20, 1912, in Avignon, France. He died in Paris on January 30, 1994, aged eighty-one.

Wrong Bridge, Wrong River

It shouldn't really matter—it was a work of fiction, after all—but it is nonetheless interesting that *The Bridge Over the River Kwai*, a bestselling novel based on true events and published in 1952 and subsequently one of the most popular films in movie history, was not on the river Kwai. And for those who saw only the movie, it wasn't destroyed at the end of the book, either.

You can blame the novel's author, Pierre Boulle, for both distortions and it's interesting to know that although he was awarded an Oscar for best script, he didn't write a word of it—

the two blacklisted authors Carl Foreman and Michael Wilson being posthumously recognized at a special Academy ceremony in 1984. Nonetheless, it made Boulle a millionaire.

There were, in all, three versions of the now classic World War Two tale, as invariably there are when facts are first changed and shaped by a writer of fiction and then again by imaginative actors, screenwriters, directors, special effects artists and the rest of that Hollywood gang. Still, when both the novel and film became so popular, what happened in the wake of that success was probably unique.

One of the most surprising things that occurred concerned the river itself. Part of the explanation for the mix-up in name was that Boulle never visited the actual site. He knew the "Death Railway"—so called after some thirteen thousand prisoners of war died in its construction, along with an estimated eighty to one hundred thousand civilians—ran alongside the River Kwai for many miles. So he assumed that that was the river it crossed near the western Thai city of Kanchanaburi. He was wrong. It actually crossed the Mae Khlong.

"*Mai pen rai* (never mind)," said the Thais predictably when David McLean's blockbuster film was released and the potential for a new tourist attraction was seen. "We'll change the river's name."

And so they did. The Mae Khlong is now the Kwae Yai, meaning "big tributary") for several miles north of the confluence with the Kwae Noi (*noi* being Thai for "little"), including the stretch that runs under the bridge.

More disturbing to some reviewers and readers—especially those who hate it when a movie is at great variance with the book—was what really happened to the bridge and the men building it has almost been erased by the popularity of the movie. All of this was the work of the author, who may not have written the script but who suggested the bridge be destroyed at the film's conclusion, rather than suffer minor damage. (While in reality, two bridges were finished—one of wood, the other steel plundered by the Japanese from Java—and used by Japanese forces for two years before being severely damaged by Allied bombers in 1944.)

At the time of the book's publication, little of this was known and the novel, Boulle's third, was modestly received, selling only six thousand copies the first year. (It was published in France in 1952, two years later in England and America.) All that changed when the movie went into theaters worldwide, becoming the highest grossing film of 1958, earning $28.5 million at the box-office, a small figure today but without much precedent then. It also won seven Oscars (picture, actor, director, adapted screenplay, soundtrack, editing and cinematography) and numerous other American and British film awards and drew what was described as the largest television audience up to that time when it was broadcast for the first time (in 1966), the Ford Motor Company reportedly paying $2 million to be the sole sponsor.

When the American Film Institute selected America's 100 Greatest Movies in 1998, *The Bridge On the River Kwai* ("On" was substituted for "Over") was ranked thirteenth, two places ahead of *Star Wars*, and on the British Film Institute list, it was ranked eleventh. (On a tenth anniversary list in 2008, the AFI ranked it thirty-sixth.) The novel, meantime, sold six million copies in the United States alone and was translated into twenty-two languages. It remains in print today and is a steady seller in Thailand bookshops, along with several non-fiction works about the railway.

The story takes place in a Japanese prison camp in a mountainous, disease-infested jungle in western Thailand in 1942-1943 where British, Australian, and Dutch prisoners of war, along with thousands of Malays and Thais, were brutally driven as slaves to construct a wooden bridge that was part of a four-hundred-and-fifteen-kilometer-long section of a railway through the jungle connecting Burma and Siam to supply Japanese troops in Burma without the danger of transport by sea.

A survey by Japanese engineers estimated it would take five years to build the railway line, but prisoners were forced to complete it in sixteen months—the novel's camp commandant, Colonel Saito, being told that if he failed to meet the Japanese emperor's objective on time, he would be compelled to commit *seppuku*, ritual suicide.

Saito's opposite in the camp is Colonel Nicholson, a by-the-book prig who refuses an order to share the labor with his men because the Geneva Accords say officers cannot be made to do hard labor. Consequently, he and his fellow officers are tortured to the edge of death. He also must choose between allowing his troops to sabotage the bridge as they work, thus preventing its completion, and succumbing to pride and ordering them to finish the structure on time. An egotist and perfectionist, he chooses the latter and when he discovers that the Japanese engineer in charge is incompetent, he takes over the project himself, increases his men's daily work quotas, and tells the medical officer if the hospitalized men can stand up unassisted, fresh air and something to occupy their hands will be good for them—all in an attempt to meet the enemy's deadline. Meanwhile in Calcutta, India, another group of Brits is planning to blow up the bridge, the inaugural supply train with it. They are dropped into the jungle, make their way to and into the river and lay the charges, then wait in hiding for the train. In the last hours, the level of the river drops and Colonel Nicholson makes a final inspection to satisfy his "Anglo-Saxon sense of perfection." He spots the sabotage. What happens next will be for readers to learn on their own, save to say that the bridge does escape serious damage.

The film strayed even further from the book when a member of the book's demolition team was transformed into an American prisoner in the camp (played by William Holden) who escapes and then returns to blow the bridge, and again when both the bridge and the train are destroyed in a manner that is so absurd it caused audiences to laugh as well as cheer. And if those viewers failed to grasp the insanity displayed by the opposing officers, another character from time to time muttered, "Madness! Madness!" recalling the final words in Conrad's *Heart of Darkness*, "The horror! The horror!" and making clear that this is another anti-war story and readers shouldn't try any of this at home. There also was an infectious march added to the score, its melody line whistled by the brutalized but never-say-die prisoners, the "Colonel Bogey March," which became a hit recording for Mitch Miller.

All this fictionalizing—in both the book and the movie—was not taken lightly, especially that which led to the punches that were pulled in describing the prisoners' deprivation and torture, under the surmise that reality was too strong for sensitive readers. Ronald Searle, writing in *To the Kwai—and Back*," said Boulle's novel existed "only in the imagination of the author, his ideas of British behavior under the Japanese was equally bizarre." The British military historian, R.P.W. Havens said the story did much "to shape the picture of the collective memory of POWs of the Japanese, although few POWs would testify to its authenticity."

Many attacked what was perceived as Boulle's anti-British attitude, saying his only first-person knowledge of Britain was from his time working on a Malayan rubber plantation and in reading Conrad, Swift, Wells, Maugham, and Stevenson. Digging himself further into a hole, Boulle himself admitted he had based the Colonel Nicholson character on two French officers.

More easily damned were Boulle's blatantly racist descriptions of the Japanese. "Monkeys dressed up as men!" declared one of his characters. "The way they drag their feet and slouch around, you'd never take them for anything human." (A passage that foreshadowed Boulle's later novel about intelligent apes.) When the first Japanese appear in the book, Boulle notes that they "could not speak a word of any civilized language." Their laughter is "savage," as executioners they are "sadistic," and as a race "they have only just emerged from state of barbarism, and prematurely at that." When he introduces Colonel Saito, we learn that "his uncouth manner of speech and uncontrolled gesture could only be attributed to a legacy of brutish violence." (He's also a mean-spirited drunk.) The Japanese are called "Japs" throughout and although that was acceptable at the time of the book's writing, they also are called savages, brutes, apes, and yellow baboons. And there is a guard who is a "gorilla-like Korean."

Ian Watt, an army officer who survived the "Death Railway" and later became a leading British literary critic, vehemently objected to Boulle's stereotyped portrayal of the Japanese as "comically inept bridge builders." (Even the Japanese complained about that.) Such descriptions, he said, only "gratified the self-flattering myth of white supremacy." He also dismissed Boulle's portraying Colonel Nicholson as a collaborator.

If to some critics, Boulle seemed to be a Frenchman bad-mouthing the British and Japanese, the *Village Voice* went a giant step further, delivering a review headlined "Jerry Tallmer Blows Up 'River Kwai.'" He was writing about the movie, but his comments fit the book as well. "Has no one else found it highly peculiar that damn near everybody's choice for the best movie of (let's say) the decade should be dedicated, inferentially but absolutely, to the proposition that Courage is Madness and Cowardice is Best? For this, absolutely, is what *Bridge on the River Kwai* tells us, and not just once but over and over again…"

If the reader can possibly put all this disapproval aside for a moment and allow a novelist the freedom to do what he does best—write fiction—*The Bridge Over the River Kwai* was a spare, skillfully written novel that explored troublesome moral questions and ethical confrontations and did so quite adequately in just one hundred and eighty-four pages. (You could almost read the book in less time than it took to watch the two-hour-and-forty-minute movie and you didn't have that damned whistling in your head for a week afterwards.) You must, however, get past the author's understandable post-war hatred of the Japanese and laugh at his making his main British character a "perfect example of the military snob, which has gradually emerged after a lengthy process of development dating from the Stone Age, the preservation of the species being guaranteed by tradition." Then the novel can be read as a terrific military adventure with serious themes attached that didn't get in the way and still provided the "serious" reader with something to think about.

Boulle also revealed something of himself when he made a member of the demolition team a draftsman in a big engineering firm who had "a pretty dull career" and felt like "a glorified office-boy." So the war and Southeast Asia for this character represented an escape from boredom, adventure, the same being true for Boulle when he left a job in Paris and started working in Malaya and then joined the French army in Saigon.

How much of the bridge and its environs is left today to see? Much more than anyone could reasonably expect and perhaps even more than is appropriate, for Thailand has taken an ugly chapter from a war and, as time passed, turned what once was a modest yet respectful pilgrimage site for "Death Railway" survivors and history buffs into a sort of theme park.

At the end of the war, the British army dismantled the last stretch of track at the Thai-Burma border—thus severing the link between Bangkok and Rangoon—and the Thai Railway upgraded what remained, along with the steel bridge, allowing visitors to take one of three daily passenger trains to the end of the line at Nam Tok, where they can picnic beside a waterfall. Beer and cold drinks are sold on the trains from Bangkok and from Kanchanaburi town to Nam Tok, as well as in dozens of restaurants, bars, hotels and floating guesthouses equipped with massive sound systems, giving the area a distinct party atmosphere.

In addition, there are two beautifully kept cemeteries that may be visited, along with a World War Two Museum that could easily be mistaken for a Chinese temple, a recreation of a bamboo POW hut that is maintained by a local Buddhist temple, a section of abandoned track called "Hellfire Pass" cut through solid rock (so named by the POWs for the way the worksite looked at night by torchlight), and a memorial light-and-sound program in December that for a moment makes you think you are at Universal Studios. Also, there are ten golf courses in the area. So far, there are no statues of Alec Guinness or William Holden.

Besides becoming one of Thailand's tourism cash cows, the Kanchanaburi area also periodically has been a lure for gold hunters seeking Japanese war booty believed still hidden in the region's numerous caves. On the basis of no more than rumor and wishful thinking, earth-moving equipment and dynamite have been employed illegally on national forest land, damaging the environment, and resulting in the death of several participants— supporting for more than half a century the equally mythical "Treasure of the River Kwai" and the "Curse of the River Kwai."

Other popular World War Two visitor sites—such as the American cemetery at Normandy, Auschwitz Camp in Poland, London's Cabinet War Room and the Churchill Museum, Pearl Harbor in Honolulu, and the Hiroshima Peace Memorial—take their inspiration more soberly.

For those for whom such things matter, it might also be interesting to know that the movie was not made in Thailand, but in what today is called Sri Lanka, where, when I visited, there wasn't even a sign marking the spot.

Paul Theroux

American Pimp in Singapore

What's the first word you think of when you hear the name "Paul Theroux"? Chances are it's "grumpy," the adjective usually attached to his name when other writers critique his travel books. (Misanthropic and cynical are often mentioned, as well.) This surely must be one of his greatest irritations, the larger one being that those same books are more highly regarded than his fiction.

His early books were novels set in Africa, but it was *The Great Railway Bazaar*, a chronicle of his journey by train from London to Tokyo and back that gave him his first success. This book, published in 1975, not only set a new standard for travel writing—nobody kisses ass—but also helped turn overland Asia trips into a rite of passage.

Five novels and a play have been placed in Asia, as well, the first of these, *Saint Jack* (published in 1973), telling the story of an affable American pimp who helped American GI's find companionship while on R&R in Singapore during the Vietnam war. Both the book and a film version starring Ben Gazzara were banned in Singapore for twenty years. Other Asian fiction included *The Consul's File*, linked short stores placed in Malaysia

(1977); *Kowloon Tong* (2007); *The Elephanta Suite* (2007) and *A Dead Hand* (2009), the later two set in India; and a play about Rudyard Kipling's life and hard times in America, *The White Man's Burden* (1987).

Self-described as a compulsive traveler with "the disposition of a hobbit," Theroux took trains from Boston to Argentina, across China, and from Egypt to South Africa; walked around the United Kingdom; traversed the southern Mediterranean coastline by various means; traveled the length of the Yangtze River by boat; and kayaked the South Pacific, writing books about each journey. His novel *Mosquito Coast* (1981) was adapted for a film starring Harrison Ford. He also broke off a thirty-year friendship with V.S. Naipaul and penned a bitter account of it.

Paul Edward Theroux was born April 10, 1941, in Medford, Massachusetts, the third of seven children, his Catholic father a French-Canadian shoe salesman, his mother of Italian ancestry. He joined the Peace Corps to avoid military service in Vietnam, participating in a failed *coup d'etat* that got him bounced from both the Peace Corps and Malawi. He then taught English in Uganda and Singapore before beginning to write fulltime. By 2012, he had published nearly fifty books, including various collections of his articles and essays and repacked anthologies.

He has married twice and lives in Hawaii.

Traveling Man

"Singapore thinks of itself as an island of modernity in a backward part of Asia, and many people who visit confirm this by snapping pictures of new hotels and apartment houses, which look like juke boxes and filing cabinets respectively. Politically, Singapore is as primitive as Burundi, with repressive laws, paid informers, a dictatorial government, and jails full of political prisoners. Socially, it is like rural India, with households dependent on washerwomen, amahs, cooks, and lackeys. At the factory, workers—who, like everyone else in Singapore, are forbidden to strike—are paid low wages. The media are dull beyond belief because of heavy censorship…"

It was 1973 when Paul Theroux wrote those words, part of a rant included in *The Great Railway Bazaar*, his groundbreaking description of a train journey from London to Tokyo and return. Most of that epic trip was through territory he'd never seen before, but Singapore had been his home for three years, from 1968 to 1971. It was where he and the British wife he married in Africa both taught in universities and where their second son was born. It was also the setting for his first Asian novel, *Saint Jack*, published later that same year. It was a good thing he was back on the rails and elsewhere when it appeared, because Singapore's government didn't like the novel or its author any more than he liked the government.

Saint Jack was titled for its primary character, a middle-aged American drifter named Jack Flowers, who considered being poor "the promise of success." He worked for a Chinese ship's chandler as a "water clerk," servicing vessels visiting Singapore's busy port. (The occupation once held by the man who was the model for Conrad's Lord Jim.) Paid little, he used the contacts he made to conduct his real business, providing customers for his "girls" from among sailors, tourists, other expatriates, and American soldiers on R&R from Vietnam. Flowers realized his dream, opened not one but two establishments, only to watch everything unravel as he dealt with the local secret societies and the puritanical forces of Harry Lee, soon to use his real name, Lee Kuan Yew, soon to become prime minister. As the war in Vietnam wound down and the US Army excluded Singapore from the approved R&R list, his attempts to blackmail the general in charge were a failure when he decided it wasn't a nice thing to do, proving that he, too, had a heart of gold. Theroux has never said he knew any such individuals, but his years of residence in Singapore, teaching English at the University of Singapore during the years of Lee's rise to power, provided the backdrop for his story and gave the novel a ring of truth.

The book sold moderately, until Peter Bogdanovich turned it into one of his best movies, a low budget effort that was shot on location and produced by Roger Corman and Hugh Hefner, starring Ben Gazzara. A phony script for a film called *Jack of Hearts* was submitted to obtain official approval and this is what the Singaporeans on the cast and crew were told they were shooting as the cameras recorded the true grit of the waterfront, street markets, and notorious Bugis Street. The film, of course, was banned in Singapore when it was released in 1979, and from that point on so was Theroux's novel.

By now, Theroux was well on his way to becoming a literary star, living in England, where he had written *Saint Jack* on a custom-made table he ordered near Singapore's Orchard Road. It would be on that table, which was collapsible for easy transport—a table he still writes on today—that he thereafter determinedly produced at least one book a year. Most were novels, many with foreign settings, and upon completion of a first or final draft, frequently he rewarded himself with another journey and made a book out of that. The global span of those books, and his novels, led a reviewer in the *New York Times Sunday Book Review* to call him "the thinking person's James Michener."

"Theroux delivers richer prose than Michener, subtler insights and slyer dilemmas, but he resembles the late mass-market master of narrative geography by treating societies as his true protagonists while giving his characters (in his novels, at least) the auxiliary role of inciting, observing or acting out the conflicts latent in their surrounding cultures."

That appraisal appeared in a critique of *The Elephanta Suite*, three novellas that might have taken their inspiration from Kipling and Forster and their exploration of what happened when East met West in early and late imperial India. Theroux's post-Colonial encounters, involving somewhat ugly Americans, echoed the same struggle. In each, the protagonists met what Theroux called in one of the tales something "you never expected. The Indian extra. The Indian surprise."

In the first story, a middle-aged couple visits an expensive Ayurvedic spa to be cleansed and are drawn to their young therapists in ways distant from anything spiritual, their world collapsing around them as a consequence. Lust drives the second novella as well when a rich businessman starts screwing underaged females he meets on Bombay streets; this one ends with the man being tricked by an Indian friend into taking a cure, for which he is grateful. In the last, the lust was shared by an elephant when a young woman seeking enlightenment in Sai Baba's ashram in Bangalore and simultaneously teaching American colloquialisms and intonation at a call-center firm got raped by one of her students; getting no satisfaction from Indian authorities, she lured the young man to where a tethered adult male elephant was in musth and as he approached, she released the animal.

An earlier book, *The Consul's File*, a collection of short stories published in 1977, recounted the small adventures of a young American sent to close an unnecessary consulate in an unimportant town during the time of the British empire's final gasp. Theroux takes a poke at Somerset Maugham for glamorizing the dull colonial ciphers in his gossipy Malay tales and as if it were a consequence, makes the consul/narrator of his tales as dull as a sullen Malay afternoon.

"I felt a need to stake a claim," the youthful diplomat said in one of the stories, "so I might carry away a bit of that town undistorted. In a different age, I might have taken a Malay mistress, but in my restless mood…I decided to write."

The reader can judge the worthiness of that choice. He later wrote a sort of sequel called *The London Embassy*. Both were reviewed positively and sold moderately.

The pattern seemed set. Theroux stayed on the road (or on a train or in a boat and so on), producing novels that were received respectfully but without unusual sales success and, between the novels, publishing his quirky—and, yes, sometimes grumpy—travelogues, most of which made a bigger splash. Again and again, he was praised for his charming craftsmanship in his fiction—compared to a wide range of authors, from Graham Greene (too often to be comfortable) to Edgar Allen Poe—and greeted with hoots and whoops about how he never seemed to like the real people he met while traveling.

Theroux defended his view in an interview with Joe Cummings in Bangkok in 2009: "Happy, fulfilled, balanced characters are not going to become writers. They get married and have children and work a normal job. If you feel happy and fulfilled you have no need to puzzle things out or look for order, because you naturally feel a sense of order. You know your place in the world, so you don't need to go out and find it. A writer, even more than a painter or composer perhaps, is looking for some kind of connection with the world that he lacks.

"I noticed very early on that most travel writing was like a postcard saying, 'Everything is fine. Wish you were here.' But a lot of travel is misery and delay. It's what makes a good read. Do you really want to read about someone having a great time?"

Again and again he returned to the Orient, to make a speech (he was the only person to be asked twice to preside over the Southeast Asian Writers Awards in Bangkok), or to research another book, or to promote one. Twenty years after *The Consul's File* came Theroux's final blow to the empire in *Kowloon Tong*, a novel about mother-and-son ugly Brits set in pre-China-turnover Hong Kong.

After forty-five years in the British colony, not once has either Betty Mullard or her son Neville, nicknamed "Bunt," ever made the one-hour train ride to Shenzhen and she has never eaten Chinese food; she is aging now, her husband dead and the Chinese are still termed "Chinky-Chonks" and food eaten with chopsticks is called "muck." He said China regarded the world as its personal "spittoon."

Someone who said he represented the People's Liberation Army made a take-it-or-leave-it offer to buy the textile company they inherited after George Mullard died under mysterious circumstances. Bunt, who has an obsession with short-time Chinese whores and a serious affair with one of the factory employees, is surprised to learn his mother has accepted. Ensuing events made Bunt take his mama's side and the literary history of China as perceived by the West had gained another Fu Manchu.

Kowloon Tong was an unrestrained attack on China and its plans for Hong Kong. *New York Times* columnist, Richard Bernstein, said Theroux offered a prognosis for the colony that was "worse than the most pessimistic nonfiction predictions." In it, and in an article he wrote for the *New Yorker*, Theroux imagined the Chinese might even use the Happy Valley racetrack as an arena for public execution of criminals.

A Dead Hand: A Crime in Calcutta, published in 2009, is another moody almost-thriller—rather short on plot and suspense, long on biting evocations of India, very long on opinion of just about everything and everyone (most pithily the British and the Indians)—and a walk-on-the-wild-side that takes his burnt-out travel writer protagonist into the ecstasy of tantric massage and the grim reality of child abuse. Along the way he also takes dead-eye shots at a wide range of familiar names, from Hunter Thompson to Mother Teresa, and, most remarkably, Theroux suddenly appears himself as a character, permitting the fictional writer to skewer him like a picador in a bullfight with his darts

"Theroux didn't want me to know him," the burnout mused, "didn't want anyone to know him, which was why he did nothing but pretend to write about himself, never quite coming clean, offering all these versions of himself until he disappeared into a thicket of half-truths he hoped was art.

"Later, what I remembered most clearly were his eyes, search-ing, inquisitive, evasive, probing, a bit sad and unsatisfied, trying to see beneath the surface and inevitably misremembering or faulty, because he can't know everything. He was like someone trying to see in the dark."

In the same thirteen-page-long dialogue, Theroux puts even more damning words in his own mouth, saying, "I'm just one of those people Kipling described who spend a few weeks in India, walk around this great Sphinx of the Plains and write books about it, denouncing it or praising it as their ignorance prompts."

If scorecards about literary cause and effect were kept, how would Theroux rank? On the one hand, he helped make travel in China popular, but he didn't much like the Chinese and loathed the communist government. As for Malaysia and India, he probably had no impact on opinion at all.

There's not much left in Singapore that looks like what was described in *Saint Jack*. Bugis Street has not only been laundered but hung out to dry and even the food vendors have been moved off the streets. Singapore has become a robotic city without a soul. Theroux told an interviewer, "If Jack went there today, he would probably be running a place in Geylang." That's Singa-pore's sanctioned red light district; prostitution is legal in Lee's fiefdom now and whores carry I.D. cards that are yellow so that if they're ever stopped and questioned for something, the cops know the level of respect to show.

Hong Kong, Bombay, and Calcutta (now called Mumbai and Kolkotta, respectively) are little changed. It's unlikely when vis-iting them, however, that anyone would think about grumpy Paul Theroux.

Ian Fleming

You Only Live Twice

Few novelists have experienced the level of success that greeted
Ian Fleming during the 1960s and 1970s, nor have readers and
moviegoers embraced many other fictional characters so warmly
as James Bond, the fabulous—and preposterous—Agent 007.

Due to the cartoonish nature of Bond and his foes, it was no
surprise when Fleming made Asia a setting and source of his
stereotyped villains, reprising the "Yellow Peril" of fifty years
earlier—first in the evil Dr. No in a book that took his name as its
title and then in a Korean named Odd Job, whose steel-brimmed
derby hat was a deadly weapon in *Goldfinger*. So, too, in the one
novel of the eleven completed by Fleming that was set in Asia
(before his death and Hollywood took the bond franchise and
ran away with it), he dressed Bond's archenemy Ernst Stavro
Blofeld in the costume of a Samurai warrior.

He was born May 28, 1908, in London of a privileged class,
worked briefly in journalism and finance before serving in British Naval Intelligence during World War Two. Returning to journalism after the war, he was forty-five when he published his first
novel, *Casino Royale*. Still, it wasn't until he wrote *From Russia
With Love* and attracted US President John Kennedy's praise in

1961 that he became a worldwide bestseller—selling thirty million copies of his books during his lifetime, more than double that figure since.

Much of that popularity came from the Hollywood films and the first cinema Bond, Sean Connery, who starred in six of the first seven adaptations. Six other actors followed in movies made after Fleming's death and by 2012, the series had grossed more than five billion dollars at the box office worldwide, more than any other series except *Harry Potter*. Fleming also wrote the children's book, *Chitty Chitty, Bang Bang*.

He lived a comfortable and, for the time, scandalous life. He had a holiday home in Jamaica called Goldeneye, where he wrote several of his novels in three-month sprints, and had an astonishing range of literary, entertainment, and political celebrities among his friends. He loved rich food and drank and smoked heavily, dying of a heart attack in London August 12, 1964. He was fifty-six.

The Return of the Yellow Peril?

"I was full of reservations about Japan," said Ian Fleming, the creator of literature's best-known fictional secret agent, James Bond. "Before and during the war [World War Two] they had been bad enemies and many of my friends had suffered at their hands."

Fleming openly admitted this bias on his first visit to Japan in 1959, a member of a journalistic junket, representing *The Times*, which was owned by the syndicate he served as an editor.

"I decided to be totally ruthless," he said, a reference to planned journalistic reports. "No politicians, museums, imperial palaces or tea ceremonies. I wanted to see a Sumo wrestling match, explore Ginza, have the most luxurious bath, spend an evening with geishas, take a day trip into the country, eat large quantities of raw fish, for which I have a weakness, and ascertain whether sake was truly alcoholic or not."

Fleming had published six novels by now, but he was not yet a big success. His works had drawn a mostly flattering critical reception but sales were such that he kept his "day job," escaping to a vacation home in Jamaica from January through March each year, when he wrote another book. It wasn't until 1961, when *Life* magazine included the fifth novel, *From Russia With Love*, on a list of US President John Kennedy's ten favorite books that the author's world began to tilt. When Kennedy, an extraordinarily popular figure in the US, also praised Fleming as his favorite writer during a press conference, sales for all the Bond books revived and started appearing on bestseller lists.

The grandson of a wealthy Scottish banker and the son of a member of Parliament killed in the "Great War" (Winston Churchill penned his obituary for *The Times*), Fleming was born in London's fashionable Mayfair district and studied briefly at Eton and the military academy at Sandhurst as well as in Austria, where he demonstrated an affinity for languages and young women.

Returning to London, he followed his brother into journalism, joining Reuters, covering a spy trial in Moscow. He then tried banking, living in another of London's best neighborhoods, Belgravia, where he formed a coterie of drinkers and gastronomes. Sent back to Moscow ostensibly for Reuters but in fact for the Foreign Office, Fleming found a calling in espionage and in 1939 joined British Naval Intelligence, participating in what later were regarded as some of the most imaginative and daring capers of the war. One of them was the famed Operation Mincemeat, an elaborate plot involving false documents planted on a corpse that washed up where the Nazis would find it, diverting attention for the invasion of Sicily. From London, he also commanded a unit of commandos sent behind the lines In Spain.

Attending a Naval conference in Jamaica, where there was no war, no rationing, and food fell ripe from the trees, he bought property and designed a house he called Goldeneye, naming it for one of his military operations. It was here he spent his long postwar holidays and had an affair with Lady Anne Rothermere, whom he married after getting her pregnant and she first got divorced. Realizing he never would get rich in journalism, he decided at age forty-three to write a novel. Known for his good and expensive tastes, arrogance, an acid wit, and charm, it was no great shock when the hero he created was very much like himself.

The novels appeared one a year, *Casino Royale* succeeded by *Live and Let Die, Moonraker, Diamonds Are Forever, From Russia With Love, Dr. No, Goldfinger, For Your Eyes Only,* and *Thunderball.* He also published short stories in *Cosmopolitan* and *Playboy* and in a collection titled *For Your Eyes Only.*

So far, he'd paid close to zero attention to Asia. *Dr. No* may have taken its title for an evil half-Chinese (the other half German, another nationality easy for Fleming to dislike), a former member of a Chinese Tong whose hands were cut off after he stole a lot of money, and Oddjob was a killer Korean with a steel-brimmed bowler hat, but their Oriental heritage was incidental to the plots. And if *From Russia With Love* ended with Bond at death's door, poisoned, we learn in the next novel, by the Japanese fugu, a deadly blowfish, the source of the poison was irrelevant.

Then came Fleming's second visit to the land of his wartime foe, Japan, in 1962. This time he was accompanied by *The Sunday Times*'s Far East correspondent, Richard Hughes, an Australian and part-time spy for MI6 who enlisted the services of Japanese journalist Toreo (Tiger) Saito, both of whom became characters in *You Only Live Twice* (called Dikko Henderson and Tiger Tanaka, respectively). The visit lasted two weeks, during which time Fleming had a high, fine time while cementing his dislike of Japan, describing it in the novel as "a country with the highest suicide rate in the world…a country with an unquenchable thirst for the bizarre, the cruel, and the terrible."

That said, sometimes the novel read like a tourist guide, the author going on for pages about the architecture and landscape and how the Japanese culture preached behaving honorably, even if you had to kill yourself. The book seemed a bit of a mess, as if unfinished, as it may have been. The manuscript was not much more than a hundred pages long and was still in the editing process when Fleming died.

The novel was quite different from preceding ones as well—more a character study than a story suitable for an action film and gloomier, preoccupied with death. It opened with Bond despondent and drinking heavily following the murder of his wife by his old nemesis, Ernst Stavro Blofeld. Bond's boss, the ineffable M, considered firing him but gave him final chance, sending him to Japan to convince that country's chief of intelligence (Tanaka) to turn against the CIA and share information intercepted from the Soviet.

Tanaka finally agreed but only if Bond agreed to kill a man who was operating a politically embarrassing "Garden of Death," a place filled with snakes, piranha, and poisonous plants that caused pain, shock, seizures, delirium and death, a popular site for Japanese wanting to commit suicide and lacking the nerve to do it themselves. What a great and wonderful coincidence it was for Bond when he discovered that the garden's proprietor—all dressed up in an elaborate Samurai suit—was none other than the man who murdered his wife. With cosmetic assistance and training to appear Japanese, and with the help of former film star Kissy Suzuki, he infiltrated Blofeld's castle to seek his personal revenge.

All of which sounded like pure comic book Bond. But for most of the book there was no action, until Bond was discovered and he and Blofeld fought to the death (Blofeld's, of course). This was followed by a peculiar ending, leaving some to argue that Fleming intended it to be the last in the series. A head injury sustained while escaping from the castle left Bond an amnesiac and living with Kissy. She got pregnant and before she could screw up the courage to tell him, he wandered off to Vladivostok, thinking that's where he might regain his memory.

Reviews were mixed, but it was serialized in both the *Daily Express* newspaper and *Playboy*, then adapted as a comic strip and syndicated worldwide and in 1967 in a much changed film starring Connery. In 1990, it was adapted as a radio play for the BBC with Michael Jayston playing Bond.

Fleming lived to see only a little of this. A heart attack in 1961 did nothing to slow his heavy cigarette and alcohol habits. There were stressful lawsuits and when his mother died in March, 1964, he was so ill, doctors told him not to go to the funeral. He went anyway and five months later had his second heart attack, dying in London on his son Casper's twelfth birthday.

It is difficult to assess the impact of Fleming's take on Asia on his (mostly Western) reading public, but it is impossible to dismiss the clichés. When an author was truly familiar with the East—think Kipling, Burgess, Orwell, Conrad, Buck—chances were good that however narrow (or focused) the view, at least what was written was usually reported relatively accurately. Novelists who parachuted into an alien place, spent a few days and then went home to write the story, like many journalists and travel writers too often do—and this group included Fleming in Asia—often they got it wrong or at the least, were drawn to stereotype.

The Bond character continued to live on, of course, with a changing cast of actors playing 007 in more than a dozen post-Fleming films and several well-known writers commissioned to write the screenplays or new books, Roald Dahl, Kingsley Amis, John Gardner, and Jeffrey Deaver among them. Gardner alone wrote fourteen Bond novels and two of the screenplays.

Many of those books and movies were set in Asia, at least in part. In Thailand, a tall limestone karst known as "James Bond Island" has become a tourist attraction merely because it appeared in *The Man With the Golden Gun*.

William J. Lederer & Eugene Burdick
The Ugly American

William J. Lederer and Eugene Burdick, both Navy officers during World War Two, met at the Bread Loaf Writer's Conference in Vermont in the late 1940s. At the time, Lederer was still in the Navy and writing amusing stories for magazines about life at sea and Burdick, a political science professor at the University of California, Berkeley, was unpublished.

When they discovered they shared both shame and anger over the way the American government bungled its foreign policies in Asia, and seemed not to care about the local cultures, they wrote what became a runaway bestseller in 1958, *The Ugly American*, which was turned into a film starring Marlon Brando. They further collaborated on three other books, including a novel, *Sarkhan*, named for the fictitious Southeast Asian country in *The Ugly American*.

Both had individually successful careers as well. Lederer was a high school dropout who enlisted in the Navy in 1930, eventually passing the entrance exam for the US Naval Academy, serving as an officer on a river gunboat in China during World War Two. He ended his long military career as a public information officer in Hawaii (where he opened a bar on Honolulu's notorious Hotel Street). He also wrote *A Nation of Sheep*, a serious critique of American intelligence in Asia; two humorous books about Navy life, *All the Ships at Sea* and *Ensign O'Toole and Me,* the latter of which became a television series in the 1960s; and a number of books about skiing and creating happy relationships.

Burdick wrote *The Ninth Wave*, an award-winning political novel placed in California; *The Blue of Capricorn*, a collection of short stories and non-fiction sketches about the Pacific; and, most famously, the 1962 bestseller, *Fail Safe*, a novel co-authored by another political scientist, John Harvey Wheeler, that told of a military communications disaster that led to an American nuclear attack on the Soviet Union.

Eugene Leonard Burdick was born December 12, 1918, in Iowa and died of a heart attack following a tennis game in Berkeley July 26, 1965, at age forty-six. William Julius Lederer Jr. was born March 31, 1912 in New York City and died in Baltimore December 5, 2009 at ninety-seven.

The Ugly American

Several other authors in this book contributed to the contemporary lexicon, most remarkably George Orwell with such terms as "Big Brother," "Cold War," and "Orwellian." Others include James Hilton's "Shangri-La" and Richard Mason's "Suzie Wong," two vastly different but lasting synonyms for "paradise." All bring specific images immediately to mind, many decades after their invention.

But it is arguable that no other phrase has been so frequently used, worldwide, than the title of the collaboration of William J. Lederer and Eugene Burdick in their 1958 novel, *The Ugly American*. It is also likely that no other contribution to the language was been employed so mistakenly. (Some say ironically.)

The term "Ugly American" became a catchphrase to describe what *The Washington Post* (in Lederer's obituary) called "boorish, self-interested Americans who cared little about other countries." Whereas in the novel, the so-called "ugly American," a man named Homer Atkins who thought of himself as *physically* ugly, actually was one of the book's heroes. And not only one of the good guys in the novel, but, as history proved, an inspiration to John F. Kennedy, who later changed history with what he learned from the books. That story, in a moment. A few words about the work's origins first.

Originally, it was supposed to be non-fiction, but when an editor at W.W. Norton, the New York publishing house, suggested that it could be more effective (and perhaps less vulnerable to government criticism and legal action) if it were a novel, the authors went along. In fact, the CIA tried unsuccessfully to suppress the book because part of its storyline closely resembled an ongoing operation in Southeast Asia. The authors insisted they made the whole story up.

That wasn't exactly true. "What we have written is not just an angry dream," they admitted in the book's introduction, "but rather the rendering of fact into fiction." Nearly all the incidents actually happened and many of the characters were based on real people—the names and details of the stories changed to protect the guilty as well as the innocent, and perhaps the authors and publisher from further harassment as well.

The story was placed in a fictitious country in Southeast Asia called Sarkhan, a small nation that was accepting aid from both the United States and the Soviet Union, while wishing to remain independent of both. This was true of most nations in the region during the Cold War 1950s and it was the authors' observation that while the Americans were doing everything the wrong way, the communists were doing everything correctly. Where the US ambassador, a political appointee, knew nothing about the Sarkhan culture and could not speak the language, his Soviet counterpart not only was fluent and could read and write Sarkhanese, he also could play the nose flute, a beloved local musical instrument.

The US aid policy came under more attack for seeming to favor the construction of questionable infrastructure projects that benefited American contractors (who then built the dams and roads) rather than assist the poor population in daily life.

The point Lederer and Burdick wished to make was that unless the US State Department changed directions, it was going to lose the "war."

Several other American characters in the novel—a chicken farmer in Cambodia, a soldier in the Philippines, a Jesuit priest in Burma, a retired engineer in Vietnam—on the other hand, were individuals who knew how to win friends by using their expertise to help improve the living conditions of those who so desperately needed it, without asking for anything in return. The engineer, the man who thought himself physically ugly, for example, was a hard-working engineer who had become rich and now lived with his wife in a rural hut with a dirt floor as they showed farmers how bicycle-powered pumps could be used to improve irrigation.

Such efforts were played out against a background of ambassadorial screw-ups and self-importance in Sarkhan. Sometimes it took the form of simple espionage, as when a shipment of rice from the US was intercepted by the communists and every bag was stenciled in Sarkhanese to indicate the donor was the USSR. In another instance, the American ambassador derailed the dairy farmer's efforts to introduce dairy farming to the economy.

"The American ambassador is a jewel," his Soviet counterpart said in a cable to Moscow. "He keeps his people tied up with meetings, social events, and greeting and briefing the scores of senators, congressmen, generals, admirals, under secretaries of state and defense, and so on, who come pouring through here to 'look for themselves.'"

A journalist from Burma further observed, "For some reason, the [American] people I meet in my country are not the same ones I knew in the United States. A mysterious change seems to come over Americans when they go to a foreign land. They isolate themselves socially. They live pretentiously. They're loud and ostentatious. Perhaps they're frightened and defensive, or maybe they're not properly trained and make mistakes out of ignorance."

All in all, the book's message was a strong condemnation of US foreign policy makers, a righteous boot up the American government's arse. "Our aim is not to embarrass individuals," Lederer and Burdick insisted in the introduction, "but to stimulate thought—and, we hope, action."

The novel was a roaring success, spending seventy-six weeks on the *New York Times* bestseller list and selling about five million copies, winning unanimously positive reviews. Robert Trumbull, a longtime correspondent in the region, called it a "devastating indictment of American policy" and a "source of insight into the actual, day-by-day byplay of present titanic political struggle for Asia." (It would be five years before the movie version starring Marlon Brando was released. Although the original storyline was ignored and much else was changed as well, the message remained: the US in Asia was screwing up.)

The initial impact on Washington was nil. Although President Eisenhower admitted in memoirs published several years later that his administration screwed up in Iran, Guatemala and Vietnam, that was a retrospective view, published in 1961 as *The White House Years: Mandate for Change*. In a paper examining Eisenhower's foreign policy and *The Ugly American*, presented at the International Congress of Historical Science in Sydney in 2005, historian Keith P. Dyrud claimed that "Lederer and Burdick missed several important points in their analysis: The French War in Viet Nam was a war by the French to hold on to a colony in which they were fighting against a nationalist independence movement which was incidentally Communist. And most of the one and a half million Americans working overseas were working for private companies whose objective was to make profits for the American shareholders of those companies, not to benefit the poor people in the developing countries. Lederer and Burdick also did not seem to realize that the big projects—dams, highways, irrigation systems—paid for by American foreign aid were meant to build the infrastructure necessary for those American companies to do business profitably. It was not the concern of American policy makers that these projects did not help the poor in those countries."

Which was the authors' point, however they may have misinterpreted the foreign policy they wanted changed. Homer Atkins was no less a hero.

Change came the same year Eisenhower's memoirs were published, with the inauguration of President John F. Kennedy. When *The Ugly American* was published three years earlier, the junior senator from Massachusetts was so impressed, he had copies delivered to every one of his senatorial colleagues and during his presidential campaign in 1960 in a speech at the University of Michigan he proposed what came to be called the Peace Corps (a notion that his opponent, Richard Nixon, said would be nothing but a haven for draft dodgers).

In fact, the idea had been suggested for several years, going back to 1952 when another senator proposed sending an "army" of young Americans to act as "missionaries of democracy." In 1957, a bill to create the Peace Corps was introduced by still another senator, Hubert Humphrey. But it wasn't until Kennedy picked up the torch that it caught the public fancy and since 1961, some two hundred thousand Americans have served in one hundred and thirty-nine countries, their duties modeled on the original "Ugly American."

However erroneously the phrase has been used in the years since, as the authors learned, it is not often that public perception changes, no matter how much you protest. Thus it was the epithet used at the 2000 Olympics in Sydney when a winning American relay team lorded it over the losers, as well as through much of his career whenever tennis champion John McEnroe threw tantrums during matches and insulted his hosts overseas.

The term also has been applied to George W. Bush and members of his administration, as well as for the country itself for being just one of three in the world refusing to adopt the metric system. (Liberia and Burma were the other two.) At this writing, there is also an English comedy troupe that calls itself the Ugly Americans and as a resident of Bangkok, I hear the term all the time when American male tourists compete with the lads from the United Kingdom for the worst (often alcoholic) behavior in public and most embarrassing sartorial taste. Still loud and boorish, after all these years.

More foreboding is an observation made by Michael Meyer, writing in the *New York Times* in 2009, marking (roughly) a half-century since the book was published. He said, grimly, that "the book's enraging resonance may say less about its literary merits than about its failure to change American attitudes. Today, as the battle for hearts and minds has shifted to the Middle East, we still can't speak Sarkhanese."

Although the locations for the various tales told in *The Ugly American* were based on true events and characters, there aren't many specific sites to visit today. Although the Vietnamese village in the film actually was created on Universal's studio lot, a visit to any Southeast Asian rural hamlet today is suggested; in Thailand, where part of the film was made, the water buffalo have largely been replaced by small hand-operated tractors, but much too little else has changed.

In Bangkok, a visitor might also visit the home of the late Kukrit Pramoj, who portrayed the Sarkhanese prime minister in the film. He was a respected novelist who later became the Thai premier as well and information about tours of his home can be found in most guidebooks.

Unfortunately, Bill Lederer's Bar—"the busiest little bar in Honolulu, where old friends meet and good fellows get together"—is long gone, replaced in the 1990s by a police substation and now the site of an art gallery.

Dominique Lapierre

The City of Joy

Dominique Lapierre already was a literary success, co-author with Larry Collins of five international best-sellers, before striking out on his own to find his richest vein of gold in a Calcutta slum. Published in 1985, *The City of Joy* was made into a movie starring Patrick Swayze, inspired a charitable foundation, and its title became what the Indian city (renamed Kokata) now calls itself.

Poverty doesn't want for story-tellers—Charles Dickens wrote about London's poor magnificently, Pearl Buck's name will forever be linked to the rural poor in China, and Erskine Caldwell depicted the Tobacco Roads of the American South—but few writers have had the impact of this French journalist. His reputation has not eclipsed that of another foreigner who made her name in the slums of the capital of Bengal, Mother Teresa, but he not only brought direct aid to the poorest of the poor about whom he wrote, by making that one particular slum "famous" he was accused of exploiting the wretched of the earth, simultaneously helping create what is known today as "slum tourism," a growing worldwide phenomenon.

Lapierre was born July 30, 1931, in Chatelaillon, Charenté-Maritime, France, his father a diplomat, his mother a journalist.

At thirteen, he accompanied his father to the United States, where as a teenager he drove cross-country, painting mailboxes to pay for the gas, writing his first book, *A Dollar for a Thousand Kilometers*.

While serving as an interpreter in the French army, he met an American GI named Larry Collins and upon their return to civilian life, both became journalists, Lapierre for *Paris Match*. The two collaborated on five bestselling books: *Is Paris Burning?* (how Hitler planned to burn the French capital if it fell into Allied hands), *Or I'll Dress You in Mourning* (a biography of Spanish matador "El Cordobes"), *O Jerusalem!* (the birth of Israel) and *Freedom at Midnight* (the birth of independent India). There followed a novel, *The Fifth Horseman* (describing a terrorist attack on New York), but it was his next book that gave him a spotlight of his own.

The City of Joy told the story of an American doctor, a Polish Catholic priest and an Indian rickshaw puller in the Calcutta slums and became one of the biggest books of 1985. Half the royalties were dedicated to the people of the City of Joy and in 2008, Lapierre was awarded the Padma Bhushan, one of India's highest civilian honors.

Slumming

Walter Besant is now forgotten, but in England's late Victorian period he was an influential critic and writer who published, in 1892, a popular novel called *All Sorts and Conditions of Men*—a romance between two wealthy "do-gooders" who decided to live for a time in London's poor East End, in disguise. Thus, was born a genre called "slum fiction" and, when fashionable Londoners who had read the book started taking midnight tours of East London, the practice of "slumming."

Other novelists in the genre included Rudyard Kipling, Jack London, and the young Somerset Maugham, whose first novel, *Liza of Lambeth*, was inspired by people he met as an intern in a hospital near Lambeth, a London slum. At the same time, in the

United States, Edgar Allan Poe and Stephen Crane placed some of their early writing in the slums of Baltimore and New York City. All depicted the poorest of the poor and their squalid environments sympathetically, but also romanticizing and exploiting them. Simply put, while some of those who then went slumming did so to fix the problems there, others went to enjoy them.

It was not until late in the twentieth century that popular novelists recognized the slums of Asia. This seemed odd because Asia had the largest share of the world's slum population—in 2005, more than half, or nearly six-hundred million people, most of them in China and India. And in India, a disturbing fifty-six percent of its urban residents lived in slum conditions, meaning by the usual measuring sticks that their income was below the poverty line and they lived in substandard housing and squalor, lacking in tenure security.

The author who then stepped to the center ring—wanting to make a difference—was the Frenchman Dominique Lapierre, who in 1980 was a fifty-year-old former journalist with five bestselling books behind him, all co-written with the American Larry Collins. One of them, *Freedom at Midnight*, was a factual account of India's bloody transition from a British colony to an independent nation. Although a collaborative novel followed, Lapierre then spent two years in the slums of Calcutta, mainly in one called Pilkhana, renaming it Anand Nagar (the name of a real city in India many miles away) that translates to "City of Joy."

"This story concerns men, women and children who have been uprooted from their homes by implacable nature and hostile circumstances, and thrown into a city whose capacity for hospitality has been pushed beyond imagining," Lapierre said in an understated note introducing the book. "This is a story about how people learn, despite incredibly difficult odds, to survive, to share, and to love."

There were three protagonists: Stephan Kovalski, a Polish Catholic priest; an American doctor, Max Loeb, who abandoned his upper-class heritage and a lucrative practice to find greater meaning in life; and Hansari Pal, a rickshaw puller from the countryside with a family to support. Add a cast of thousands—the destitute and diseased in one scene after another from Dante or Hieronymus Bosch.

During two years of research, Lapierre said (in an afterward in the paperback edition), "I learned how people could live with rats, scorpions, and insects, survive on a few spoons of rice and one or two bananas a day, queue up for hours for the latrines, wash with less than a pint of water, light a match in the monsoon, share their living quarters with a group of eunuchs…"

The praise for the book was effusive. Reviewers called the book "a triumph of the spirit" and "a positive uplifting experience lending hope and joy to us all." It won the 1986 Christopher Award, established by Father James Keller to "encourage men, women and children to pursue excellence in creative arenas that have the potential to influence a mass audience positively." Mother Teresa, herself appearing briefly in the book, said it was "a magnificent homage to the courage of the poorest of the poor." Pope John Paul II called it "a lesson of hope and faith for the world."

Sales in the first years topped six million as it was translated into more than thirty languages. Lapierre said he received over twenty thousand letters containing contributions—"a check, sometimes a small package with a piece of jewelry, a gold ingot, or a stack of stock exchange shares." A woman appeared at his home in southern France to say she wanted to make his heroes of *The City of Joy* the beneficiaries in her will. One couple sent their wedding rings, saying "they will be more useful in the City of Joy than around our fingers." Lapierre himself dedicated half of his royalties, starting a City of Joy Foundation, and in the first six years he said they, along with reader contributions, totaled nearly two million dollars.

The film adaptation was the joint effort of British director Roland Joffé, whose previous credits included *The Killing Fields*, the Canadian producer Jake Eberts, who had been involved in the production of *Gandhi*, and screenwriter Mark Medoff, who scripted *Children of a Lesser God*. The character of the American doctor was played by Patrick Swayze.

Not all of the reaction was positive. Many in Calcutta, even in the slums, felt that Lapierre exploited them. There were protests in the streets, in newspapers and on television, calling the book an invasive and degrading account written to harm the image of the proud city and India in general. When Lapierre tried to give $400,000 to one of the slums, initially it was rejected. As foreigners arrived by the thousands carrying copies of the book, asking to be taken on rickshaw tours of the slums, merchants from outside opened shops to sell souvenirs. And when the film company moved in for location shooting, in 1991, bombs were thrown onto the set.

In the end, Lapierre was victorious. The protests died as his foundation continued to send money to India's poor. He wrote another book, *Beyond Love* (1990), about AIDS and with Javier Moro penned *Five Past Midnight in Bhopal* (2001), telling the story of the Union Carbide chemical plant disaster. He founded an agency called Action Aid for Lepers' Children of Calcutta, treating nine thousand. He dug wells in rural villages and converted old ferry boats into floating clinics to serve poor fishing communities on the islands of the Ganges delta. By 1999, he told the *New York Times* he and his wife, also named Dominique, spent five million dollars on his projects.

"He has been less successful in dealing with India's pervasive corruption," the *Times* reported. "His clinics, all run by Indians, are entitled to free medicine from the government for three-hundred thousand tuberculosis patients. 'We never—never—get more than ten percent. The rest is stolen on the way.'"

Most telling, and wreaking somewhat in irony, was action taken by the city of Calcutta, now renamed Kolkata, when it adopted *The City of Joy*'s title as its own. When landing at the airport today, the first thing arrivals see is those words emblazoned across the terminal building.

On the other side of India, in what once was called Bombay and now Mumbai, in that city's largest slum, Dharavi, another story emerged in a novel by Indian author and diplomat Vikas Swarup. Titled *Q&A* and so named because it concerned a slum boy who won a million rupees by answering questions on a television program, when the novel was made into a film called *Slumdog Millionaire*, the slum tourism that had its roots in Victorian England and reappeared in Calcutta a hundred years later now became efficiently organized and marketed. Once the movie, released in 2009, won eight Oscars, it was inevitable.

That both films, *The City of Joy* and *Slumdog Millionaire*, were little more than Disney versions of the books merely heightened the appeal. And India was not alone. Even without novels and films to kick-start the phenomenon, in the 1980s and 1990s there were Shantytown Tours in post-apartheid South Africa and Namibia, Favela Tourism in the slums of Rio De Janeiro, Hutong Trips in Beijing, Hilltribe Village Treks in Southeast Asia, Aboriginal Tours in Australia. In 2010, the first international conference on slum tourism was held in Bristol, England.

Proponents said poverty tourism—sometimes called "poorism"—provided jobs for slum dwellers as guides and offered residents opportunities to sell locally produced craft items, as well as educated outsiders. How different was it, they said, from taking a bus tour of the star's homes in Beverly Hills? And wasn't it in fact impossible to travel anywhere in the world without seeing how "the other half lives"?

This activity was not welcomed universally. Many critics described it as voyeurism, without any lasting socially redeeming effect. A Kenyan writer in the *New York Times* said, "They get photos; we lose a piece of our dignity." A columnist in the *London Times* termed *Slumdog Millionaire* "poverty porn" and many called the Long-necked Karen women in Thailand residents of a "human zoo."

Richard Condon

The Manchurian Candidate

The Manchurian Candidate may have been Richard Condon's
only novel that even mentioned anything Asian, but the title became a part of the language and the book and the movie made
from it played a role in China's becoming perceived as a major
Cold War threat.

The USSR remained the greater bogeyman, of course, but
with the war that recently had ended in Korea (the book was
published in 1959) and American troops already being sent to
Vietnam, Asia and the Communists there became a contemporary "Yellow Peril." And if only one chapter of Condon's book
actually was set in Asia, the novel nonetheless made "brainwashing" a sinister reality in the West and the evil mastermind in the
novel, Yen Lo, a modern day Fu Manchu.

The novel also played an interesting role in the American
Cold War psyche when John F. Kennedy was assassinated. Because the novel was about an American GI programmed psychologically by the Red Chinese to become a "sleeper" who when
cued would assassinate a US politician running for President, an
immediate link to Lee Harvey Oswald was made and along with

the movie starring Laurence Harvey and Frank Sinatra it was hastily withdrawn from the marketplace.

Condon was forty-three when he published his first novel, after a long career as a publicist for a number of Hollywood studios. In all, he wrote twenty-five (along with a memoir and a Mexican cookbook, the latter penned with his daughter), and although four others were made into films, including *Prizzi's Honor* (starring Jack Nicholson), it was his second book *The Manchurian Candidate*, that put him and his title in the history books.

In all his work, he said America was hopelessly corrupt, dedicated to power, money, and violence. This dark message was made palatable by Condon's unusual literary style, featuring long lists, diverting trivia, what playwright George Axelrod (who shared screenplay credit with the author for *The Manchurian Candidate*) called "mad similes and lunatic metaphors," obscure literary and classical references, words you can't find in your dictionary, and an off-the-wall sense of the absurd that that *Time* magazine called "a riot in a satire factory."

Richard Thomas Condon was born March 18, 1915, in New York City. He died, ironically, in Dallas, Texas, on April 9, 1996.

Brainwashing

Conspiracy freaks looooooved *The Manchurian Candidate* because it told them how John and Bobby Kennedy were killed: Lee Harvey Oswald and Sirhan Sirhan were programmed/brainwashed/hypnotized by the brothers' hated enemies, the Mafia/Teamsters/CIA/Russia/China/Castro/et cetera.

There are a lot of people today who still think this is what happened: an American was in some way brainwashed as unwitting assassin as part of a political scheme to escalate the Cold War. There are many other theories, but this is the most popular. And because President Kennedy's assassination in 1963 came so soon after the distribution of Richard Condon's novel (in 1959) and the movie based on it, starring Laurence Harvey and Frank Sinatra (in 1962), and because Oswald had lived for a short time in Russia and so on, et cetera, et cetera, et cetera, well, of course the little sonofabitch was robotically trained into doing it.

And so, too, again when the president's younger brother was gunned down in 1968 and the guy who did it, Sirhan Sirhan, was hypnotized.

In this fashion, the term "Manchurian Candidate" entered the English language in the same way that the title of the novel by William J. Lederer and Eugene Burdick, *The Ugly American*, did a year earlier, making Americans in Asia merely boorish but communists evil and insidious.

The novel's plot was preposterous. An American Army platoon is captured during the Korean war and spirited off to Manchuria in the far north of China, where everyone is programmed by a team from the Pavlov Institute in Moscow to believe they were ambushed and their sergeant, Raymond Shaw, saved them, killing an entire company of enemy soldiers, with only two men in the platoon dead. In fact, Shaw had killed them both as part of the training to disprove the old saw about people not being able to do anything while under hypnosis that was morally repellant to them.

The rest of the platoon was programmed to think Shaw was a hero and into believing that they were not in Manchuria but at a ladies horticulture club meeting in New Jersey. As for the two dead, the men now believed they were killed not by Shaw but by the enemy before the sergeant could reach them—this, despite the fact they had watched Shaw strangle one and shoot the other in the head.

All this was accomplished in just four days and the platoon was returned to Korea and released near where they were taken prisoner. Shaw was then returned to the US a hero, recommended by his commanding officer, Captain Marco, for a Congressional Medal of Honor. Photographs were taken at the White House with the President, Shaw's stepfather—an alcoholic, Red-baiting US senator (think Joe McCarthy)—and his conniving mother who had choreographed the event, standing by, counting in their heads the votes this would win the Senator in his upcoming re-election campaign.

Later it was revealed that when it came time for Shaw to kill, his action is triggered by the words, "Why don't you pass the time by playing a game of solitaire?" When Shaw sees the queen of diamonds, he does what he's told to do and immediately forgets everything.

However big a reach this premise was, the story fit perfectly the Cold War paranoia and a widespread fascination with behaviorist psychology so popular in the US in the 1950s. This was a time when American children were taught to get under their school desks in the event of a nuclear attack, as their parents built shelters beneath their lawns. The same year *The Manchurian Candidate* debuted, Castro grabbed control in Cuba and China invaded Tibet, while Nikita Khrushchev banged his shoe on a kitchen countertop in a debate with Richard Nixon. It was a time when satirists and black humorists had to stretch, just to come up to reality.

Condon was primed for the challenge, inventing and describing characters and events that had to have been influenced by his decades as a Hollywood studio publicist. While working for Disney, he said he watched *Fantasia* forty-three times—more than adequate exposure to what might be called the first truly "psychedelic" film to warp anyone's mind—and then while based in New York, his job was to "babysit" stars in town to promote their latest movies, as bizarre a trade as it is possible to imagine. "It was the publicist's responsibility to see that they were entertained, a euphemism for pimping," he said. At age forty-three, he bailed out and decided to write fulltime.

His first novel, *The Oldest Confession*, was intended to be a screenplay, became a novel instead, becoming a movie in 1962, starring Rex Harrison and Rita Hayworth, where it appeared to be little more than a fast-moving "caper" tale about a thief who stole paintings and replaced them with undetectable forgeries. It was on the printed page that Condon revealed himself—the anarchic comedic style and gloomy theme of greed that would characterize everything that followed.

The second novel was *The Manchurian Candidate*, an even whackier view of reality despite the fact that Shaw's stepfather was closely modeled on a real Senator, the demagogic Joe McCarthy, famed in the 1950s for his drunken public rants that said a wildly changing number of card-carrying Communists were influencing government policy.

"Satire can only survive," Condon said, "by holding a very slippery thin edge of reality. You have to try to make people believe in what you're writing about, even if you're mocking what they have accepted."

As the novel's plot twists and turns, Shaw jumps into a Central Park lake when by chance he heard a triggering remark by a stranger and finally the assassin is unleashed when at a costume party someone is dressed as the queen of hearts.

The movie co-written by Condon and George Axelrod (who previously wrote *The Seven Year Itch* and *Will Success Spoil Rock Hunter?* for Broadway) and directed by John Frankenheimer, performed poorly at the box-office, despite critical agreement that it was brilliantly crafted, even more chilling than the book. Unsurprisingly, it was banned behind the Iron Curtain due to its anti-Communist message and less than a year after its release when President Kennedy was shot, it was withdrawn from the US market as well.

Initially it was believed this was done to pay respects to the tragic death of the President, but in fact Frank Sinatra—who not only was closely linked to JFK, raising funds and providing girls for him, and also starred in the film—bought all rights because he believed the studio, United Artists, was cheating him on his profit sharing. (A scenario so bizarre it must have made Condon laugh.) It would be nearly a quarter century before the movie was rereleased, when it was then proclaimed a classic

In 2004, the film was remade by director Jonathan Demme (and, oddly, co-producer Tina Sinatra) and starred Denzel Washington, Liv Schreiber, and Meryl Streep. This time, the conspiracy was set in the Middle East and Washington's programming involved not only brainwashing—a somewhat archaic concept by now—but also the implantation of a microchip that would help him assassinate the presidential candidate. And the bad guys behind the plot were capitalists called Manchurian Global—inspired, Demme said, by Bechtel, Halliburton, and the Carlyle Group, rather than communists.

Condon continued to publish novels at the rate of about one a year, in 1982 moving his attention away from politics to the Mafia with *Prizzi's Honor*, a story about a hit-man who fell in love with a hit-woman. It was made into a film directed by John Huston and starring Jack Nicholson, Kathleen Turner and Angelica Huston, inspiring Condon to write three more novels about the Prizzi family.

But it was *The Manchurian Candidate* that put Condon's face on the literary map and it was with the profits from that book that he left the United States, to live in exile in Mexico City and later in Switzerland and Ireland. He returned to the US after more than twenty years as an expatriate, settling in Dallas in the late 1980s to be close to his granddaughters, children of Evelyn Hunt Condon, his wife of fifty-eight years. He said Dallas was the most foreign of his homes.

Amy Tan

The Joy Luck Club

Amy Tan's mother wanted her to be a concert pianist or a brain surgeon, preferably both. When Tan announced her wish to be a writer of fiction, mom opposed the idea and when the first novel, *The Joy Luck Club*, became a runaway bestseller, mom took all the credit.

With this sort of relationship, it is not surprising that Amy Tan, the child of Chinese immigrants to the United States, made her mother, and other Chinese-Americans of her and her mother's generations, a primary inspiration for her writing. Or that she became a welcome voice in the demystifying (and humanizing) of the Asian at a time when East and West were clashing again. While others were Japan-bashing and recasting the "new" China into an old Yellow Peril, Tan's characters were making it clear that "they" were just like "us."

Amy Tan was born February 19, 1952, in Oakland, California, her father an engineer trained in Beijing, her mother an abused housewife in Shanghai, both fleeing China just ahead of the 1949 Communist takeover. In full conflict with her mother by the time her father died (she was fifteen), Tan earned degrees in English and linguistics, married an Italian lawyer, and was writing speeches and brochures for businessmen when a creative writing workshop changed everything.

Her first short story was published and attracted an agent who took it and some related stories to G.P. Putnam's who offered a large advance to weave the tales into novel form. She quit business writing and *The Joy Luck Club* became one of the biggest books of 1989, followed two years later by *The Kitchen God's Wife*, a novel inspired by a journey she made to Shanghai with her mother to meet the secret children that mom left behind.

A third novel, *A Hundred Secret Senses*, and two children's books were published but then Tan was unable to write for five years as she battled a chronic bacterial infection. Recovering finally, she published two more novels, *The Bonesetter's Daughter* and *Saving Fish from Drowning*, and to celebrate her return to life joined a literary garage band, the Rock Bottom Remainders, whose members included Stephen King, Dave Barry, Barbara Kingsolver, Matt Groening, and Scott Turow.

She is still married to her attorney, who now creates programs for orphanages in China. A sixth novel, *The Valley of Amazement*, was set for publication in 2012.

The Immigrants

When Amy Tan was born in 1952, Asian immigrants were denied the right to become naturalized citizens—a right granted all other immigrants to the United States. At that time, immigration from Asia averaged about fifteen thousand people per year.

But the numbers surged with the passage of a new immigration act in 1965 that relaxed restrictions on immigration from Asia by eliminating national origin, race, or ancestry as a basis for admission. There were forty-three thousand Asian immigrants per year during the 1960s, one hundred and sixty thousand a year during the 1970s, and two hundred and seventy-four thousand during the 1980s. Put another way, during the 1950s, about five percent of immigrants were from Asian countries and by the 1980s and early 1990s, the percentage had risen to thirty-nine percent.

Some of the largest numbers came from Vietnam and Laos at the end of America's war—mainly Vietnamese "boat people" and Hmong hill tribe members fleeing the Communists. And where most immigrants from Asia in the past had settled in coastal cities like Los Angeles, New York and San Francisco, now they were moving into the South and Midwest and in West Coast cities in numbers that stirred the legendary melting pot in new and disturbing ways.

So many Vietnamese settled in Westminster, in conservative Orange Country, California, it became known as "Little Saigon" and there were turf wars between immigrant Vietnamese shrimp fishermen and locally established shrimp fleets in Louisiana and Mississippi. Soon after the first Hmong arrived in San Francisco, all the ducks disappeared in Golden Gate Park and then stray dogs went missing from the streets. Almost overnight, it seemed, there were thirty thousand Hmong living in Fresno, California, even more in Minnesota.

Most of these new arrivals spoke no English, adding pressure to school districts already dealing with other non-English speaking immigrants, mainly Hispanics. At the same time police reported the presence of new Asian gangs, still more Asians—largely Chinese and Korean—were winning university admission in such huge numbers because of their exceptional test scores, they were accused of taking seats from non-Asians.

Add the popular sport of "Japan-bashing" that followed a perceived economic threat in the electronic and automotive markets and a consequent loss of jobs in Detroit and elsewhere, and the reception given these new immigrants was in many quarters less than welcoming.

By 1989, when Tan's first novel, *The Joy Luck Club*, was published, the time was right for some corrective measures. Surely it wasn't the writer's intent to become a voice of reason. She just wanted to be a writer of good fiction and she only did what all good writers have done and that was write about that which she knew: Chinese immigrants battling it out with their Chinese-American kids. Starting with her own childhood, remembered as being so unhappy she has had no children with her husband of forty years for fear she might repeat her mother's mistakes.

She rejected her mother's choice of university and assigned pre-med curriculum to attend five different colleges before earning bachelor's and master's degrees in English and linguistics from San Jose State University. She married and was working as a freelance business writer for telecommunications firms when in 1985 she attended a fiction workshop where she met another writer named Mary Giles. Giles gave her some advice and encouraged her to write more.

From the start her material was autobiographical, taking a social group to which her family belonged when she was a child as the first stories' structure. The mah jong-playing group was called, and became the novel, *The Joy Luck Club* (1989), sixteen interlocking stories about Chinese immigrant moms and their anxious-to-be-all-American daughters. Her agent obtained a $50,000 advance for the book, which then spent eight months on the *New York Times* bestseller list. There followed a $1.3 million advance for the paperback rights and a movie directed by Wayne Wang.

Amy Tan was now fiction's bright new star and millions of non-Asian readers were introduced to immigrants who didn't seem so different after all. Yes, there were cultural differences, but wasn't this, after all, a story about the "generation gap" that was for virtually everyone as unavoidable as breathing? Wasn't this novel, like those that followed, also about the search for female identity, another timely theme?

Tan and her mother were long reunited by now and when mom was sick, the author promised herself to take her to China to find the two daughters she recently learned her mom had left behind. This led to *The Kitchen God's Wife* (1991), a thinly fictionalized biography of her mother. Although the book mainly recalled events in pre-World War Two and wartime China, the story was told as a long flashback with brief returns to the present.

In one of these, mom's best friend, her partner in a flower shop in San Francisco's Chinatown, recreates a gimmick that the American television personality Art Linkletter used on his popular program in the 1960s: walking into the audience to examine what was in the purses of some of the women in his audience. Mom observes, "She pulled out an orange and put that on the table, then two bags of airline peanuts, restaurant toothpicks, her extra wallet for tricking robbers. She turned the purse sideways and spilled out all sort of other junk in case a war breaks out and we have to run away like the old days: two short candles, her American naturalization papers in a plastic pouch, her Chinese passport from forty years ago, one small motel soap, one washcloth, one pair each of knee-high stockings and nylon panties, still brand-new. And then she pulled out more things: her *pochai* stomach pills, her potion for coughs, her tiger-bone pads for aches, her good-luck Goddess of Mercy charm if her other remedies do not work."

Thus with a wave of her authorial wand, Amy Tan helped bridge the culture gap. The purse's inventory may have been "different," but mom's friend was not unlike anyone else Art Linkletter might have approached in his audience, eliciting laughter not at the woman with the purse but at themselves.

And did not everyone—white, black, brown, yellow or green— not have someone in the family who made mountains from molehills, as shown in this dialog that followed a daughter's long-distance call to her mom, who said to her friend, "This time she said she was calling for no reason. No reason! This is not a reason to call. Of course, it wasn't her idea, not entirely. She saw a TV commercial for a phone company, a daughter calling a mother for no reason. I said to my daughter, 'Now you're calling long-distance, for no reason? Don't talk too long, then, too expensive.'

And she said, 'It's okay. After eight o'clock, it's cheaper.' So I told her, 'Don't be fooled. They say all kinds of lies on television. Maybe it's only cheaper if you talk faster. Who knows what their meaning is.' She said, 'Oh, Mommy, the cost doesn't matter.' I said, 'Wah! Doesn't matter? How can you say cost doesn't matter? You want to waste ten dollars? Don't give it to the phone company, then. Send it to me instead.'"

With the great success that greeted both novels behind her, she wrote two children's books and went on tour with a band whose other members were bestselling authors, too. If she'd been Elvis Presley, she'd have had to dedicate a room in her condo to hold all the awards, including finalist positions for *The Joy Luck Club* for the National Book Award and the National Book Critics Circle Award.

In her third novel, *The Hundred Secret Senses* (1995), Tan strayed from her mother-daughter theme to explore the relationship between half-sisters—the older China-born Kwan who talks to ghosts and believes in reincarnation, the younger Olivia born in America who does not. Once again, it is the ordinariness of the characters that counts. It is not the Chineseness of Kwan that is so memorable as her geekiness. Not everyone has a sibling who's so out-and-out strange, but we all know someone who does and the country and culture of origin is irrelevant, the common response universal.

"...when I can't bear it any longer," says Olivia, "I lash out and tell her she's crazy. Before I can retract the sharp words, she pats my arm, smiles, and laughs. And the wound she bears heals instantly. Whereas I feel guilty forever."

There followed instead of more books a long fight with Lyme's disease, an infection that came from a tick bite that made it impossible to work. Once recovered, she returned, in 2001, with *The Bonesetter's Daughter*, another story about an overbearing Chinese mom and her guilt-ridden Chinese-American daughter, and *Saving Fish from Drowning*, in 2005, what appears on the surface to be a story about a group of American tourists who disappear in Burma.

The supernatural plays a key role in both novels—the first telling of bones found in an ancient Chinese cave that may include the teeth of the Peking Man, the second narrated by the ghost of the tour leader, who died mysteriously as the trek began and because she is in the spirit world, has access to all the characters' thoughts. The overall effect of both novels is somewhat akin to walking past a Chinese graveyard and not being permitted to whistle.

The awards continued to pour in. *The Opposite of Fate: A Book of Musings* was published in 2003. *The Bonesetters Daughter* was adapted as an opera, the children's story *The Moon Lady and Sagwa* became a television series, and her work was republished in dozens of anthologies and textbooks, assigned as required reading in high schools and universities.

Through such exposure of exceptional storytelling, she helped her alien characters become ordinary citizens. E.D. Huntley wrote in *Amy Tan: A Critical Companion*, "It seems fair to predict Tan will have a place in American literary history, not as an ethnic writer, but as an American writer who illuminates brilliantly and sensitively a distinctive and colorful aspect of the American experience."

Because Amy Tan is a contemporary writer, walking in her long shadow is easy. Go to San Francisco's Chinatown and get off the beaten track. When you hear the sound of mah jong tiles, you're there.

Michael Crichton
Rising Sun

Michael Crichton was a literary colossus, one of the most popular writers in the world, selling more than two hundred million books during his lifetime and seeing twenty-two of them made into films, several of which he wrote, directed and/or produced.

His first bestseller and the first written under his own name, *The Andromeda Strain*, was published when he was still at Harvard Medical School, training that later led him to create the television hit series *ER*, which won him an Emmy, a Peabody, and a Writers Guild of America Award. His film *Westworld*, an original screenplay that he also directed, was the first to employ computer-generated special effects. His best-known novel, Jurassic Park, brought dinosaurs back to life in a movie by Steven Spielberg and spawned a sequel book and film.

Only one of his books (and films) was related to Asia and it, like many others, was a thriller keyed to a popular theme—one of America's favorite sports in the 1980s and 1990s, "Japanbashing." Many regarded the novel called *Rising Sun* as no more than another fast-moving, literate mystery. Others called it an embarrassing polemic written to exploit the supposed threat Japanese imports were thought to pose to the US economy.

Taking a conservative stance that would become more pronounced in later novels, Crichton challenged the wisdom of inviting foreigners to invest in American high technology. Although all Japanese characters were portrayed negatively in the tale, leading some to call the author a racist, he said he intended *Rising Sun* to be a warning to US industry, insisting that he was more critical of America than Japan.

John Michael Crichton was born October 23, 1942, in Chicago but grew up in New York and Colorado, and following graduation from Harvard, worked with the Salk Institute before turning to writing fulltime. Over the years, he insisted he was no more than an entertainer, but the controversial stands he sometimes took—disputing the validity of global warming in *State of Fear,* for instance—made him more than that. He also was known among his friends as an eccentric for his belief in auras, astral projection, clairvoyance, and despite his medical training that all disease, including heart failure and cancer, was brought on by the victim's state of mind.

Crichton died of throat cancer, in Los Angeles on November 4, 2008. He was sixty-six.

Japan-Bashing

It was like Pearl Harbor revisited. The Big Three automakers in Detroit were in big trouble and it was all Japan's fault. Detroit's Big Three auto companies were closing plants and hundreds of thousands of workers suddenly were unemployed, as Japanese carmakers designed smaller, more dependable, and fuel-efficient vehicles.

Japan already had captured much of the consumer electronics market in America and with its vast, new wealth it was buying up high profile properties that included Rockefeller Center, Universal Studios, Columbia Pictures, every private golf course in Hawaii, and the prestigious Pebble Beach Golf Club in northern California. In 1985, on the fortieth anniversary of the end of

World War Two, US Senator Howard Baker said, "First, we're still at war with Japan. Second, we're losing." One by one, American markets fell to names like Toyota, Honda, Sony, Mitsubishi (the company that had manufactured Japan's fighter plane, the Zero), JVC, and Panasonic. The United Auto Workers took hammers to Japanese-made cars at their events and in Detroit, angry American carmakers beat a man to death with a baseball bat after shouting, "It's because of you little motherfuckers that we're out of work." That the victim, Vincent Chin, was Chinese was additionally tragic but unimportant.

In Washington, Robert Angel, a political scientist at the University of South Carolina and a paid lobbyist for the Japanese government, was looking for a way to reply to Japan's critics "and I hoped to be able to discredit those most effective critics by lumping them together with the people who weren't informed and who as critics were an embarrassment to everybody else."

Angel's model was the Israel lobby's use of "anti-Semitism" to stigmatize opponents of Israel's policies, to link the critics to racism and xenophobia. He decided on "Japan-bashing." With Hiroshima and the Holocaust only a generation in the past and the horrific murder in Detroit, nobody wanted to be known as a Japan-basher. He started using the phrase in speeches and interviews and the media picked it up.

It was the perfect time for Michael Crichton to consider such matters in a novel. The only puzzle was that he didn't tackle it earlier. He had used popular themes before.

Although he had published five novels under pseudonyms before *The Andromeda Strain* (in 1969), that would be the novel that made his name, one of several that would touch on science and technology as a threat. Its plot turned on a mutating microorganism from outer space and was adapted for Hollywood, a pattern that would hold for the rest of his career.

Binary and *The Terminal Man*, both published in 1972, exploited more hot topics—chemical nerve agents and presidential assassination in the first, and the implantation of electrodes in a violent epileptic's brain in the second. Monstrous gorillas and a lost city appeared in *Congo* (1980), an alien spacecraft discovered at the bottom of the sea in *Sphere* (1987), and in 1990 came *Jurassic Park*, whose improbable science involved the recreation of dinosaurs from DNA found in a mosquito trapped in amber. The film version was still in production when *Rising Sun* was published two years later.

Rising Sun seemed to be a simple murder mystery as it opened, with the discovery of a young woman's body in a Japanese-owned high rise in Los Angeles during the building's dedication party, but as the plot unwound it became one of Crichton's more complex and multi-layered: a mystery with a message. A retired cop who had lived in Japan and spoke Japanese fluently was brought in to lend support and as the investigation twisted and turned, blame shifted from a Japanese playboy to a US Senator and finally to an executive of the Japanese corporation that owned the building.

Interwoven with this were subplots involving major characters who had business dealings of their own with Japan. All of which permitted the author, through those characters, to drag in what one reviewer called "every well-known Japanese trade horror story in recent memory." It also allowed one of the large cast, the cop who was supposed to be such an expert on Japan, to keep saying "Japan is" and "the Japanese are" at every opportunity, mouthing every known cliché.

All of which led Christopher Lehmann-Haupt to say in the *New York Times*, "The trouble with *Rising Sun* is obviously that as a serious discourse on why we should begin waging economic war against Japan, the book is far too entertaining. And as an entertainment, it is far too didactic."

The timing of *Rising Sun's* publication was ironic. Japan continued to be a force in the electronics and car industries in the West, but by the early 1990s its economy was entering a downturn that would last for more than a decade. At the same time, as the real estate market in the US reversed, many of its property investments were souring. In 1992, the year of the book's release, the Japanese investor who bought the Pebble Beach Golf Club sold it at a $350 million loss and in Los Angeles, where Japan owned close to forty-five per cent of the premium downtown office space, prices had fallen from twenty to thirty percent.

Japan-bashing was building to a crescendo, nonetheless. As noted by one of the reviewers in www.ew.com, Joseph Nocera, Crichton's work became a part of the controversy and soon had a "life of its own, utterly independent of its literary merits." It was, Nocera said, a "poorly written anti-Japanese polemic thinly disguised as a murder mystery. *Rising Sun* began appearing in bookstores this month [February 1992] just after President [H.W.] Bush returned from his disastrous visit to Japan, and at around the same time a few Japanese officials were publicly calling American workers lazy. The book immediately became part of the heated debate over Japan's economic practices and designs."

Crichton felt it necessary to go on the defensive. He believed that the Japanese threat was real and it was largely America's fault. In a conversation with another popular mystery writer, T. Jefferson Parker, printed in the *Los Angeles Times*, Crichton said, "If Japan-bashing means an unreasoned and intemperate attack based on some irrational motive, then *Rising Sun* is not Japan-bashing. We live in an increasingly small world, and to make divisions based on race is not to anyone's benefit."

Being the number one power in the world after World War Two had led the United States into a "long period of complacency," Crichton said, and at the same time it had "turned away from quality as the principal goal of manufacturing and made cost the principal goal. Japanese, restructuring their companies, made exactly the opposite decision. American quality-control experts who worked in America during the Second World War, became very nearly living treasures in Japan." In addition, institutional investors had replaced individuals in the stock market and new tax laws offered no advantage in terms of long-term as opposed to short-term investment, which made the US stock market "entirely speculative."

Soon after that, in 1993, Hollywood's adaptation of the novel was released—written and directed by Philip Kaufman, with the two lead cops played by Wesley Snipes and Sean Connery—and the debate began anew. Kaufman tried to diffuse the controversy somewhat, softening the criticism of Japan, but it still seemed harsh, almost strident, and while Crichton, who contributed to the script, helped put forward his argument that the tale was a wake-up call for American industry, the film's effect was to do little more than advance the controversy.

Of course, at its root, Japan-bashing was nothing new. Many Americans experienced trouble developing and handling relationships with Asians for more than a hundred years, dating back to when Chinese immigrants were put to work on the early railroads and Chinese, Filipinos and Okinawans were imported to work in the fields in Hawaii. In some ways, Japan-bashing seemed merely to echo the "Yellow Peril" of the same period. Later came anti-Japanese propaganda and the internment of Japanese-Americans in camps during World War Two, and after that anti-Korean and anti-Vietnamese sentiment as war was waged in those countries.

By the time *Rising Sun* was published, such racist feeling had a long history; forgotten, perhaps, by the Japan-bashers was the earlier bias, now faded, toward the Irish and every other ethnic group that formed the legendary melting pot. In an epilogue to his Japanese translation of *Rising Sun*, Sakai Akinobu took it a step further and said Crichton regarded the Japanese as "unknown" and "different" entities that challenged his heroes in the same way the gorillas and cloned dinosaurs did in his earlier fiction. A bit extreme, perhaps, but so was the stance taken by the unusually popular American.

Twenty years have passed and Japan-bashing is still lodged both in lexicon and thought. Only the targets have changed and now the Japanese are being criticized for their continued killing of whales and repeated refusal to apologize to China and other nations for atrocities committed during World War Two and for, of all things, a reluctance to give up child pornography and groping female office workers on the subway trains.

Now there are China-bashers, too, and bashers of just about everything. The word fits nicely into headlines and rolls easily off the tongue.

Arthur Golden
Memoirs of a Geisha

The Japanese geisha is one of the most alluring, enduring, misunderstood, and maligned of Asian stereotypes and Arthur
Golden, an American, was, like countless foreigners before him,
determined to sort fiction from fact. Whatever may be said of his
novel, one thing is clear: by its popularity and notoriety, the myth
of the Asian woman as subservient whore was enhanced. And if
you talk to the Japanologists, you'll hear worse.

Golden, a member of the Ochs-Sulzberger family, owners of
the *New York Times*, wrote *Memoirs of a Geisha* following years
of study in Asian art, language, and history. Published in 1997, it
was on his family's newspaper's bestseller list for more than a
year, sold four million copies in English alone, was translated
into more than thirty additional languages, and made into a film
produced by Steven Spielberg that, true to Hollywood's long
tradition of racial miscasting, put ethnic Chinese in all the leading geisha roles.

It also got caught up in a headline-making slanging match
between China and Japan and perhaps most embarrassing of all,
for Golden, resulted in a lawsuit filed by one of the geishas he

interviewed in Japan while doing his research. She said that he, too, had done her wrong.

Golden was born December 6, 1956 in Chattanooga, Tennessee, majoring in art history at Harvard College, earning a Master's degree in Japanese history at Columbia University, and following a year of study at Peking University (and learning Mandarin), a second M.A., in English, at Boston University.

He now resides in Brookline, Massachusetts.

Does She or Doesn't She?

Is "geisha" just another word for prostitute? That, says Arthur Golden, is the question everyone asks him first. It is not an easy question to answer and it is not, as some may think, irrelevant or impertinent to ask. And like many things Japanese, the answer is not easily understood in the West.

The geisha's roots are in the seventeenth century, during the two hundred and fifty year long period (1600-1850) of peace in Japan, perhaps the only such period recorded in world history. One of the consequences was the astonishing growth of the crafts and arts, as personified by the geisha—*gei* meaning "arts" in Japanese, *sha* meaning "person," a person skilled in the arts.

This required long, rigorous training in musical performance, poetry, the tea ceremony, calligraphy, and even intelligent conversation. Elaborate wardrobe, cosmetic, and hair styling became ritualized, influencing the fashion adopted by Japanese wives. Because they were so highly regarded, both as artists and trendsetters, and could acquire such status that, no matter how low their birth, if they excelled in their study and skill they could become role models. They were the celebrities of the period, along with sumo wrestlers and kubuki actors. Many became wealthy, occupying a luxurious realm called the *karyukai* or "flower and willow world," the walled cities more commonly called "pleasure quarters."

It was the custom to have entertainment in the teahouses while eating. The performers could be geisha, but they might also be jugglers or musicians or dancers. And if the men—and customers at teahouses were always men—wanted sex after the meal, "pleasure quarter women" called *yujo* would be called to the teahouse, perhaps to share the meal. (Confucian code said the elite samurai were not to frequent such places but of course they did.)

Unsurprisingly, many teahouse customers developed an interest in having sex with geisha and, because initially there were twice as many men as women in Edo (today's Tokyo, which was not then Japan's capital), the pressure to acquiesce was high. (So was the incidence of homosexuality.) Although the geisha were held in a kind of indentured servitude in the teahouse—paying off all those years of apprenticeship—their status remained such that they always had the right to say no. For a favored (i.e., generous) customer, the answer was sometimes yes. Customers could also buy a geisha's freedom from the teahouse and pay for her support.

It was against this historical backdrop that Golden wrote an eight-hundred-page draft of a novel about a geisha in pre-World War Two Japan, inspired by a friend he had known while living in Japan whose mother was a geisha. When a friend of Golden's grandmother offered to introduce him to a retired geisha named Mineko Iwasaki, she not only answered all his questions candidly, she took him on an insider's tour of Gion, the present-day geisha quarters in Kyoto, and in doing so, he said, she "took my understanding of a geisha's daily existence and stood it on its head. I had to throw out my entire eight-hundred-page draft and start from scratch."

Still, it was the third draft that was the charm. That's when he changed the narration from third person to first and called his novel *Memoirs of a Geisha*, telling the story of a geisha in Kyoto in the 1930s and 1940s in her own voice. It was not easy, he said, to cross the four "cultural divides"—writing as a man about a woman and as an American about a Japanese, in a time before he was born, while describing "a sub-culture so peculiar" that even a Japanese woman of the period would have been challenged.

Inevitably Golden made mistakes. Most, if not all, writers do. But the response to the book was positive, the story of a poor fisherman's daughter sold into a geisha house ringing tragically yet heartwarmingly true. It was soon after her mother died that the nine-year-old Sakamoto Chiyo and her sister were taken to Kyoto—the sister going to a brothel while Chiyo's unusual blue-gray eyes sent her into an *okiya*, a house for entertainers called *geiko*, the Osaka word for geisha.

There, she encountered the devious Hatsumomo, who saw in the child a future threat to her dominance as the *okiya's* top-earning geisha. Hatsumomo plotted against Chiyo, aiming to destroy her chance to become a geisha, when Chiyo met a prosperous and powerful man known as "the Chairman," who gave her money to buy a sweet. She used the change to offer a prayer at the Gion Shrine.

"I would suffer through any training, bear up under any hardship," she vowed, "for a chance to attract the notice of a man like the Chairman again."

First, she must become a geisha and in that effort not only survive Hatsumomo's devious tricks, but also compete with another young girl in training, a favorite of Hatsumomo's nicknamed "Pumpkin." Eventually, Chiyo was given a new name, Sayuri, as she progressed from novice to apprentice and at last she became a geisha when a bidding war was arranged between wealthy patrons for Sayuri's *mizuage*, a rite of passage that Golden said included her virginity, unambiguously described in the book as "the first time a woman's cave is explored by a man's eel." The unprecedented winning price wiped out all Sayuri's debts and left Matsumomo in the geisha house's second rank.

Although the Chairman remained elusive, with her new patron (a friend of the Chairman's), a successful career as a geisha followed, until World War Two ended luxury entertainment in Japan, sending geisha to work in the factories. Finally, after the war she was reunited with the Chairman, before moving to New York where she opened a teahouse and dictated her life story to a fictitious university professor, whose preface began the book.

Some readers felt deceived by that, believing they had been fooled into thinking the story was true. Golden reasonably shrugged this off: "When I'd written the novel in third person, the narrator had had the freedom to step away from the story for a moment to explain things whenever necessary. But it would never occur to Sayuri to explain things—that is, it wouldn't occur to her unless her audience was not Japanese. This is the role of the translator's preface, to establish that she has come to live in New York and will be telling her story for the benefit of an American audience."

Golden was not the first author to use geisha as essential characters. Vern Sneider preceded him by nearly half a century in a novel that was adapted for Broadway and then Hollywood called *Teahouse of the August Moon*, in 1951. (It depicted US Army military officers in occupied Okinawa following World War Two and in the movie version, Shirley MacLaine and Lucille Ball disguised themselves as geisha to comic effect.) James Clavell included geisha in *Shogun* in 1975, selling fifteen million copies of the book, and turned it into a monster success as a television mini-series. (See "The Asian Saga," page 155.) Anthony Grey made a nineteenth century geisha the love interest in *Tokyo Bay* in 1996. There were others, but no previous Western writer had made the novel the geisha's own; men may have been *why* geisha existed, but in *Memoirs of a Geisha* they had little better than supporting roles.

One thing remained unchanged. However sympathetic Golden's portraits were, geisha were still portrayed as erotic and exotic, epitomizing what Narrelle Morris called "the fetishisation of Japanese women in Western fiction" in an academic paper that opened with a quotation by Lafcadio Hearn, the American often credited with introducing Japanese culture to the West: "For it has been well said that the most wonderful aesthetic products of Japan are not its ivories, nor its bronzes, nor its porcelains, nor its swords, nor any of its marvels in metal or lacquer—but its women." That was published in 1904, nearly a hundred years before *Memoirs of a Geisha*.

Golden's book was a critical success as well as a popular one. "I still can't quite believe that an American male can so seamlessly enter the soul of a Japanese woman, and catch her world, it's textures, its hopes, and its sinuous patter with such perfection," said Pico Iyer, himself then a resident of Kyoto: "*Memoirs of a Geisha* evokes all the delicate steel of Kyoto's geisha culture with such uncanny fidelity that, after you've finished, you feel as if you're entered not just another world, but an extraordinary and foreign heart."

Mineko Iwasaki, the retired geisha who turned Golden's view of the geisha world upside down, did not agree. After having the book read to her—she knew little English; Golden's interviews were conducted in Japanese—she sued him for copyright violations, defamation, and breach of contract for, among other things, printing her name in his acknowledgements after promising her anonymity. "If I had any inkling that Arthur Golden was going to use my name, I would have never allowed him inside my house," she said. "This book has brought shame upon my profession."

He claimed he never agreed to not use her name, nor had she asked to keep her identity secret; in fact, she was "initially delighted in being associated with the book" and had asked him to arrange a publicity tour for her in the US. "Following Mineko's wishes," he said, "was a bit like chasing a leaf."

Iwasaki claimed ninety per cent of the book was based on her life and asked for "the appropriate percentage" of ten million dollars, the sum she said the book earned. The suit was settled out of court in less than a year for an undisclosed but reportedly large amount and her name was removed from the Japanese edition.

Iwasaki never mentioned it publicly, but when she wrote a memoir of her own—published as *Geisha: A Life* in the US, *Geisha of Gion* in the UK—she claimed Golden had turned her story on its head as well, making everything positive negative and everyone who had been kind to her spiteful and mean.

Iwasaki also objected to the implication that the book's heroine had lost her virginity in the *mizuage* ceremony. That had not happened in her case, she said, and, in fact, her housemother matched the winning bid, a sum reported by the *Financial Times* to be as high as US$850,000 (reports vary), plus a mansion and kimonos. Readers may believe her claim or not.

More controversy arose during production of the film when the roles of the three most important geisha went to two Chinese actresses (Zhang Ziyi in the title role and Gong Li) and to an ethnic Chinese from Malaysia (Michelle Yeoh). This was racial stereotyping, an issue dating to the time of Charlie Chan and by now long regarded as "politically incorrect."

Politics on another level added further headlines, when Golden's creation became a football between China and Japan. When the film was released, in 2005, Japan had just published rewritten history textbooks, minimizing its horrific wartime atrocities in China and the prime minister, Junichiro Koizumi, made repeat visits to a shrine honoring its dead, including many convicted of war crimes. China's veto of a Japanese seat on the United Nations Security Council was not considered coincidental.

Still more harsh criticism came from what remained of Japan's rarified geisha community, where discretion is an unbreakable, time-honored rule. Speaking off the record, a number of older and retired geisha told media that Golden placed too great an emphasis on sex. "It's not a racy novel," the author replied. "There's remarkably little sex in it." This was true, from a Western point of view.

The effect of all the controversy was that the movie attracted nearly two hundred million in ticket sales, millions more books were sold (in more than thirty languages), and there appeared in pop culture something called "geisha chic." As had happened in the late 1970s, when *Shogun* was such a blockbuster, both in bookstalls and on TV, again things Japanese became hip. Geisha dolls, long a tourist staple in Japan, appeared in stores in the West; Barbie wore a kimono as early as 1963, but now had a full wardrobe. Madonna wore a red vinyl *obi* and gown with jumbo kimono sleeves to the Grammy awards ceremony and in a music video. Fashion magazines advised readers to "Geisha-ize."

So, is she or isn't she? Does she or doesn't she? Is the geisha a prostitute or not? Let Sayuri have the final word from Golden's book: "Since moving to New York, I've learned what the word 'geisha' really means to most Westerners. From time to time at elegant parties I've been introduced to some young woman or another in a splendid dress and jewelry. When she learns I was once a geisha in Kyoto, she forms her mouth into a smile, although the corners don't quite turn up as they should. ... A moment later she's rescued by her escort, a wealthy man a good thirty or forty years older than she is. Well, I often find myself wondering why she can't sense how much we really have in common. She is a kept woman, you see, and in my day, so was I."

What is Gion like today? Are the geisha still clopping through the streets of the ancient city in their wooden shoes, white makeup, scarlet lips, and bright kimono? Is it possible for visitors to see true geisha in action?

Much has changed over the years. After World War Two, many prostitutes servicing American occupation troops called themselves geisha and styled themselves to look more or less like the real thing. With the Japanese economy wrecked, the number of true geisha never approached pre-war figures, although a revival did occur once the country was rebuilt, the economy boomed, and Japan went onto the world tourist map. In recent years, with Japan's economy back in the slow lane, work for the geisha has fallen again.

Modern geisha still train and reside in *okiya* in areas called *hanamachi* (flower towns) and the focus is still in Kyoto, although they may be found in other major cities, including Tokyo's Shimbashi district. (The ancient Yoshiwara district is no longer home to the geisha, but offers sex in the infamous bathhouses called "soapland."). Many entertain in banquet houses called *ochaya* and usually for Japanese customers only; unless you are accompanied or referred by someone already known to the *ochaya*, you will be greeted with crossed arms at the door, the meaning clear.

However, some of the better inns, hotels, and restaurants may arrange parties at which geisha entertain, the cost set by the number of diners and drinkers, the menu, number of geisha, et cetera, the cost usually starting at US$150 and up per person. A dinner for two with one geisha, tea ceremony and music included, may cost $700 or more.

There are cheaper shows and tours, of course, but it's rather like watching the hula at a commercial *lu'au* in Hawaii, entertaining but lacking authenticity. Tourist shops also offer a selection of geisha dolls in a head-spinning price range. For more information, there are numerous helpful websites, among them http://gojapan.about.com/cs/japanesegeisha/a/geisha3.htm.

Alex Garland

The Beach

Could there be a better book to take when you go on holiday to some remote sun and surf destination than a book actually called *The Beach*? The question was a simple one for a north Londoner named Alex Garland who at age twenty-six in 1997 published a Generation X manifesto about a gang of pot-smoking backpackers who created an island utopia in Thailand and proceeded to screw it up, along with most of their lives.

A worldwide bestseller and in the words of many critics an "instant cult classic," *The Beach* was translated into twenty-five languages and adapted for a film starring Leonardo DiCaprio and directed by Danny Boyle, who already had made the popular cult film *Trainspotting* and soon would plant his personal flag at the top of the cinema mountain with *Slumdog Millionaire*.

Garland attended universities in London and Manchester, majoring in art history and deciding to draw comic strips until, he told one interviewer, it occurred to him that he would "never be as good as my father," a political cartoonist for *The Daily Telegraph*. As a teenager, he had traveled to Asia—first to India, then to the Philippines and Thailand—and just short of his twenty-fourth birthday he started writing a novel he considered more a satire than true reporting of the backpacker style of travel he observed in his journeys.

Without any push from its publisher, *The Beach* benefited from rave reviews and the best promotion of all, word of mouth. Soon the book was seen on buses in India and Mexico, on London's underground, and in dormitories and departure lounges everywhere…while Garland was hailed as the new voice of Generation X and on *Vogue* magazine's most eligible bachelors list.

His second bestseller (1999), *The Tesseract*, a more experimental work placed in Manila that critics compared in style to the films of Quentin Tarantino, was made into a movie as well, starring Jonathan Rhys Meers. In 2003, he wrote the screenplay for Danny Boyle's *28 Days Later*, a zombie flick, and four years later collaborated with Boyle a third time, writing the script for *Sunshine*, an end-of-the world story about what happens when the Sun begins to die. A third, novella-length book, placed in London and called *The Coma*—illustrated with woodcut drawings by his father to give it some missing heft—was published in 2007. It was neither a critical nor a popular success, but by then Garland was living in Southern California and more interested in writing movies than books.

Shangri-La with Palm Trees

The so-called "backpacker trail" was well traveled long before *The Beach* was written, becoming a sort of travel cliché that coalesced in the early 1970s when it was termed "the hippie trail" and Alex Garland was still packing his diapers. In those good old days, when the Love Generation rather than Generation X occupied the media, it roughly followed the dual road to drugs and possible enlightenment, running from America and Europe to Lebanon (for the hashish) and Afghanistan (for the opium), then on to Goa (for the beach and ganja), and into an Indian ashram somewhere to "get your head together" for a fortnight or so, concluding with a visit to the top of the world in Nepal (bunking on the charmingly named "Freak Street") or, less frequently, Tibet.

It was then that the lifestyle was firmly set—the music, the hair, the wardrobe, the drugs, shared and non-committal sex, and traveling on the cheap. By the time Garland joined the throng, going first to India on a school trip and on his own to the Philippines, numerous minor changes had occurred. As the music and drugs became less mellow, more frenetic, the young decorated their bodies with tattoos and bits of shiny metal rather than the oil of patchouli, and the youthful fellow travelers came to be called "backpackers" rather than "hippies," tens of thousands now headed for Khao San Road in Bangkok and islands in Thailand's sunny south, the settings chosen by Garland for his novel.

The book's plot was simple, rooted in the ageless search for the Garden of Eden with the notion that the tropics were where maybe it might exist. Thailand was the perfect place for such a quest. As one unspoiled island after another fell in the go-go 1980s and early 1990s to uncontrolled resort development, the Ecstasy and banana pancake crowd moved on, seeking and then devouring still another piece of paradise and then another and another, etc.

Joe Cummings, who wrote the *Lonely Planet* guide to Thailand for twenty years, told me that a common complaint from young travelers was that he put these new island destinations in print, destroying them. Joe shrugged and said it wasn't his descriptions that changed fishing villages into tourist slums, but backpacker word of mouth.

Garland's premise was this: what if there still remained one pristine, undiscovered place, an island whose location remained a secret? On his first night in Bangkok, Garland's alter ego, a young British vagabond named Richard, stayed in a guesthouse on Khao San Road, where the man in the next room killed himself by cutting his wrists. Before doing that, he gave Richard a map to an island inside a Thai national park closed to tourists.

Richard decided to find the place, accompanied by a young French couple, Francoise and Ettiene.

Numerous, colorful adventures ensued as the trio pay a fisherman to take them most of the way, then they swim a long, perilous distance, finally coming ashore to face a walk through a tropical jungle—barely escaping the notice of AK-47-toting marijuana farmers—and then plunge down a waterfall. Because membership in the commune they finally reach is by invitation only, they are not made to feel welcome, but because they now know the location, and they brought news of a former member's death, they are permitted to join what seems to be an idyllic community.

In the months that follow, a series of mishaps puts the group in jeopardy, as a spoiled squid meal poisons several communards, a shark attacks the fishing team, and a rice-destroying fungus forces an emergency supply run to the tourist island of Samui, where two Americans with whom Richard shared the map then discussed it with two Germans. By now, factions have formed in the group and upon returning, in an effort to patch things up, they plan a party to mark their sixth anniversary of stoned and reportedly self-sufficient bliss.

But Richard, who by now has developed psychotic symptoms and was overheard conversing with the man who killed himself as well as Vietnam war veterans, spikes the stew with marijuana and that, along with homemade hooch (made from fermented coconut), puts the celebrants over the edge, just as the marijuana farmers carry in and dump the dead Americans and Germans, killed when they arrived on the island. The group tears into the bodies in a frenzy and when they discover that it was Richard who gave them a map, they cut him with knives, almost killing him as well.

It was no surprise when several critics compared the book to William Golding's *Lord of the Flies*, a 1954 novel about a group of children on another remote island who turned upon each other violently. Garland insisted that he was, rather, writing about "the breakdown of a society." If *The Beach* was to be compared to another writer's work, he said, he preferred J.G. Ballard's *Empire of the Sun*, an autobiographical novel about a young boy being held in a Japanese prisoner-of-war camp in China during World War Two.

"I don't mind people saying he's just ripped off this writer or that writer," Garland told the *New York Times*, "as long as they get the right writer."

No matter. The damage was done and the same word of mouth that drove Thailand's island tourism development now made *The Beach* an immense bestseller, quickening Thailand's tourism industry pulse and fattening the wallets of guesthouse owners in Bangkok (and elsewhere in Southeast Asia; the whole region benefited) and those who rented cabins on the beach in Thailand's south, as well as bar owners and food vendors and a hundred other business categories. Full moon parties became a monthly occurrence on an island named Koh Pha-ngan, where, following instructions found on the Internet, up to ten thousand backpackers came to worship Dionysius, the ancient Greek god of partying. So successful were these parties, other islands introduced them, too.

When someone pointed out that Buddhists considered the four monthly phases of the moon in much the same way Christians regarded Sunday and thus the "raves" were staged on a religious holiday, they were merely moved ahead one day,

More protests came when Leonardo DiCaprio and Danny Boyle and his crew arrived on Koh Phi Phi and the set designer decided to "improve" the beach selected for filming, bulldozing and landscaping, removing numerous palm trees and shifting tons of sand around to widen the beach to fit Hollywood's image of paradise. Throughout the shooting schedule, environmental protests intensified, but filming never stopped, and afterward, the trees and sand were moved around again to approximate the original look and 20th Century Fox established a fund to maintain the beach, dutifully handing over bags of cash to Thai politicians who promised to save the earth.

Changes were also made in the plot, as usually happens when a book is adapted to the screen—Richard became an American, sub-plots disappeared, and added focus was placed on a fleeting affair between Richard and the French woman—but the overall feeling of paradise (and society) unraveling remained. When the movie premiered in Thailand in 2000, some Thai politicians called for a ban, objecting to the use of drugs in the film and a Buddha image in a bar (even though most of the girlie bars have them), saying such gave the country a bad image. But few seemed to listen and fewer appeared to care.

In 2004, four years after the movie was released—to less acclaim and fuss than greeted the book, but arguably encouraging and increasing the backpacker numbers nonetheless—a tsunami rolled into the region, moving virtually all of Koh Phi Phi around permanently, while destroying virtually every manmade feature at least temporarily.

During the same period, Khao San Road was gentrified. The cheap guesthouses remained (although the nightly rates increased), but now hotels with air conditioning, hot water, and WiFi so their guests could check their email flanked them. The *pad Thai* and banana pancake joints with the latest bootlegged movies running on closed circuit TV were still in abundance, along with shops where backpackers could purchase cheap clothing and fake diplomas and identity papers, but now there were good restaurants, trendies from the Thai middle class formed a substantial customer base, and magazines sent their models and photographers there to add a little "substance" to their fashionista spreads.

Thailand stayed on the backpacker map and if the Tourism Authority of Thailand and others launched campaigns aimed at the five-star hotel crowd, claiming they preferred "quality" visitors, no one dared to do anything to discourage the banana pancakers because, like the sex tourists who formed another untidy but needed foreign revenue source, they spent money, too, stayed longer and kept returning.

Garland told the *Wall Street Journal* that his readers had missed his point. "A lot of the criticism of *The Beach* is that it presents Thais as two-dimensional, as part of the scenery," he said. "They don't see them or the Thai culture. To them, it's all part of a huge theme park, the scenery for their trip. That's the point. This book is anti-traveler in a lot of ways. That was absolutely my intention. *The Beach* was meant to be a criticism of this backpacker culture, not a celebration of it."

The backpackers surely disagree. One of the most Frequently Asked Questions on the Official UK Website for Tourism in Thailand is, "Where was *The Beach* filmed?" Whether he desires the credit or not, Garland arguably is one reason why more visitors go to Thailand from the UK than from any other Western place.

Eric Van Lustbader (and Friends)

The Ninja

Has any group of fictional characters done less to advance aware-
ness and understanding of Asia and Asians than those created in
the name of martial arts?

The most damage done has been in the movies, a medium
better suited than the written word for the complex strikes, grappling and use of weaponry key to the numerous and various
combat systems that originated in East Asia. The novels go back
much further, of course—to fourteenth century China—and as
knowledge of the various combat systems slowly spread to the
West they began appearing in novels in the West, predictably in
the detective and spy genres. Thus, some forms were employed
by Sherlock Holmes in the early twentieth century and James
Bond some fifty years later.

It was following World War Two and the Korean conflict that
a small boom occurred and when discovered by TV and the
movies, it exploded throughout much of the Western world—
becoming so fashionable today that no ordinary thriller seems
to be written without someone delivering a practiced round-
house kick or two or killing someone with a playing card or a
drinking straw.

Surely the most successful modern novel that included martial arts was James Clavell's *Shogun*, the first in his richly detailed Asian trilogy, set in seventeenth century feudal Japan and published in 1975 (see "The Asian Trilogy," page 155.) Other Western writers using martial arts to enliven their plots included Isaac Azimov, one of the giants of science fiction, who combined fight disciplines into one in his *Foundation* series (1988); Dr. Rodney William Whitaker, who wrote a martial arts spoof called *Shibumi* under the name Trevanian (1979); Robert Crais, whose private detective Elvis Cole stays in shape with hatha yoga and tae-kwando; and Barry Eisler, creator of a series of thrillers about a half-Japanese assassin called John Rain (starting in 2002).

Of them all, Eric Van Lustbader may have been the most influential as the man who spawned a martial arts industry when he created a modern "ninja" in his novel of the same name, *The Ninja*, a bestseller in 1980 and the first of six novels about a man called Nicholas Linnear, raised by Anglo-Chinese parents and trained in a variety of Japanese martial arts.

Lustbader was born in New York City January 1, 1946. He has published twenty-five novels, many in the fantasy field, and in 2003 was contracted by the Robert Ludlum estate to continue the series based on Jason Bourne. By 2012, he had written seven and was describing himself on his webpage as a "*New York Times* bestselling sensation."

Wham! Bam! Pow!

When most people think about the systems of codified practices and traditions of combat called "martial arts," the images that come to mind are action scenes in movies featuring Bruce Lee (the master and godfather of all who followed), Jackie Chan, Jet Li, Chow Yun Fat, Michelle Yeoh, and, in Hollywood, Chuck Norris, Jean-Claude Van Damme, and the early Steven Seagal.

Martial arts as depicted in television and the movies made the greatest impact on the West, getting its (uh) kick-start with Bruce Lee and films made in Hong Kong from the late 1960s and a few years later with the television series, *Kung Fu* starring David Carradine. At the same time, Elvis Presley made karate a key part of his Vegas and concert performances. And then in fairly quick succession the books, *Shogun* (1976), *The Ninja* (1980), and the movie *The Karate Kid* (1984) appeared.

As a result, suburban moms from California to Cape Cod put millions of young children into after school classes to learn the deadly arts of ju-jitsu, judo, kendo, karate, aikido, taekwando, and kung fu, the last becoming synonymous with all Chinese martial arts and the world's most popular in number of students.

Still, the written word came first, the earliest novels dating from the Ming (1368-1644) and Qing (1644-1911) dynasties in China. It was during China's Republican era in the twentieth century, however, that the most popular books were written, including those of Wang Dulu, one of whose novels became the basis for the 2000 movie *Crouching Tiger, Hidden Dragon*, and Jin Yong (known in the West as Louis Cha), whose numerous novels originally were serialized in his own Hong Kong newspaper.

The first Western writer to win any attention for the use of martial arts was Arthur Conan Doyle, whose detective hero Sherlock Holmes is described in the first published story, "A Study in Scarlet" (1887), as "an expert singlestick player, boxer, and swordsman." (Singlestick being a method of fencing that simulated the use of a sword using a round wooden rod and may in fact refer to Holmes's walking stick.) Most scholars refer to a later tale, "The Adventure of the Empty House" (1903), and the misspelled mention of *bartitsu*, a method of self-defense influenced by Japanese arts but developed in England at the turn of the twentieth century by a British engineer who had spent three years in Japan.

Holmes described a fight with his nemesis, Professor Moriarty, saying, "He drew no weapon, but he rushed at me and threw his long arms around me. He knew that his own game was up, and was only anxious to revenge himself upon me. We tottered together upon the brink of the fall. I have some knowledge, however, of *baritsu* (sic), or the Japanese system of wrestling, which has more than once been very useful to me. I slipped through his grip, and he with a horrible scream kicked madly for a few seconds and clawed the air with both his hands. But for all his efforts he could not get his balance, and over he went."

This, however, was the extent of Doyle's use of the antagonistic arts and they remained largely unknown in the West even as late as the 1950s when, for example, in 1959 Ian Fleming demonstrated his ignorance in *Goldfinger*. Although this novel featured a Korean martial arts expert named Oddjob, who killed with a metal-rimmed bowler hat—so far, so good—the author's expertise disappeared when he said karate was a branch of judo, when in fact they are so different it might fairly be said that all they have in common is one person's skill and another's pain.

In just over a decade greater authorial scholarship was displayed in James Clavell's samurai blockbuster, *Shogun* (1975). (See "King Rat," page 155.) While the military nobility of pre-industrial Japan were not martial artists in the purist sense, their facile and flashy use of bladed weaponry influenced much that came later—for example, kendo (way of the sword). Although the samurai-themed films of Japan's Akira Kurosawa—notably *Seven Samurai*, released in 1954—pre-dated Clavell, it was the novelist's work and the adaptations for film and television that found the larger audience, introducing the subject to the West most effectively. Clavell's earlier novel, *Tai-Pan*, set in Hong Kong and published in 1966, also included numerous fight scenes noted for their Chinese fighting styles.

A somewhat mysterious American writer who called himself Trevanian took the martial arts a step further and in another direction, writing two spoofs of James Bond that were so sophisticated and skillfully crafted, "it was an open question whether he was being playful with a genre or expanding its limits" (quoting the writer's obituary in the *New York Times*). The second of these was *Shibumi*, so named for a somewhat mystical state of perfection and grace pursued by the novel's anti-hero Nicholai Hel. Born of Russian and German parents in Shanghai and raised in Japan during World War Two, Hel had mastered the ability to escape reality (returning fully refreshed and rested) and to find his way in the dark, as well as sense when any thing or person threatening was approaching, skills helpful in his role as an aging assassin.

A more credible weapon was what he called *Hoda Korosu* or "Naked/Kill," a martial art comprised of nothing more complicated than using whatever ordinary objects were close at hand to kill—a tightly rolled magazine, a plastic cup, a drinking straw, a straight pin (you have to know where to stick it), a credit card.

It was not until he wrote—following his two earlier bestsellers—*The Eiger Sanction* and *The Loo Sanction* that he revealed himself to be Rod Whitaker, married father of four and chairman of the Department of Radio, TV and Film at the University of Texas in Austin, a post he continued to occupy for several years. Years later, he said in an interview, "After the definitive exercise of the genre that was *Shibumi*, there was no point in me writing further in this genre—or anyone else, for that matter."

Of course, many were standing in line. One of these was Eric Van Lustbader, a onetime New York City schoolteacher and low level music business executive who wrote *The Ninja* after running into a childhood friend who was writing Western novels and "because I was fascinated with the idea of having this agent of chaos and ancient secret knowledge set down in the middle of modern-day Manhattan."

Thus was created Nicholas Linnear, whose Anglo-Chinese parents send him to a *dojo* in Japan, where, along with his evil cousin, Saigo, he learns a variety of martial arts. Saigo and Linnear fight. Linnear wins. Time passes, they fight again, and this time Saigo wins, going on to kidnap, rape and murder Linnear's girl-friend. Both then become ninjas, one white, the other black, and Linnear moves to New York. More time passes, the cousins meet again and the fighting resumes.

Lustbader and Clavell heroes were similar, but Lustbader was much shallower when it came to dispensing cultural background, while being more committed to sex and violence. Every twenty pages there seems to be a sex scene, followed by a terrible fight. In *Tai-Pan*, Clavell used a lot of fight scenes, too, and both writers created Sun-Tzu spouting men of action, a genre cliché, but next to him, and Trevanian and others, Lustbader was coarser and more formulaic.

Nonetheless, his novels featuring Linnear were successful, spawning shelves of pulpy clones, helping push the ninja into the forefront of contemporary popular media. Lustbader got his comeuppance when someone created a comic book (in 1984) that morphed into several television series and a decade's worth of action figures and children's clothing, skateboards and breakfast cereal, video games and school supplies, called *Teenaged Mutant Ninja Turtles*. Like Linnear, the turtles came from Manhattan, but in the reptiles' case from the storm sewers, trained in the fictional art of ninjitsu.

Ninjas were not fictitious, but the SAS agents and SEALS of their time (circa fourteenth century Japan), trained in espionage, sabotage, assassination, disguises, and in the use of a panoply of fantastic tools and weaponry, including extending ladders and grappling hooks, collapsible boats, wooden shoes that allowed them to walk on water, extending spears, rocket-propelled arrows, swords and daggers, darts, spikes, and star-shaped discs. Now dress them all in black, a modern invention, and throw in some hocus pocus brotherhood. As bad guys, they were untoppable.

Another writer using a half-American, half-Asian (again Japanese) anti-hero was Barry Eisler, a Cornell University law graduate who held what he describes as a "covert position" with the CIA from 1989 to 1992, before working as an attorney in Silicon Valley and Japan and then in 2002 publishing *Rain Fall*, the first of his six-book series featuring John Rain.

Rain is a cliché in numerous ways: a Vietnam vet, ex-Special Forces and CIA, an aficionado of single malt whiskies and jazz whose history includes, training in martial arts (judo and a Russian system called Sambo), and a spell as a mercenary, who now works as a freelance assassin. Taking him outside this predictable box, the author also had Rain given a Japanese name at birth and undergo plastic surgery to hide his Caucasian features. He also made him what *Entertainment Weekly* called a "contract killer with a conscience." Thus, he rails against despoilers of the environment and, like an old woman with her worry beads, frets about every move he makes and, as if it made a difference, will not kill someone if the collateral damage might include moms and kids.

There was no mystery in why such fighting techniques were welcomed by authors so avidly. Throughout literary history, many fictional characters and the works in which they appeared were practically defined by combat methods and weaponry. What would Alexandre Dumas's *Three Musketeers* have been in 1844 without their swords or Zorro, the creation of pulp writer Johnston McCulley in 1919, without his whip? How important was the "heat ray" in H.G. Wells's *The War of the Worlds* in 1898 and hypnosis in Richard Condon's *The Manchurian Candidate*, published in 1959?

The martial arts offered new and clever choices to writers in crafting their fight scenes, and also a way to depict—and sometimes to caricature—their Asian characters. Like the practitioners, the arts themselves could be seen as devious, perhaps even mysterious, and to those who bought into the Asian myth, inscrutable.

Most writers regarded their incorporation of the martial arts seriously, even when creating fictional arts. Some, however, went in the opposite direction. Robert Rankin, British author of a series of novels called *The Brentford Trilogy*, published in the 1980s and 1990s, invented what he called "the deadliest form of martial art known to mankind," insisting that someone using it could, with no more than a finger's touch, cause his opponent to walk sideways like a crab for the rest of his life. Another Brit, Jonathan Routh, best known for co-hosting the television show *Candid Camera* and writing *The Good Loo Guide: Where to Go in London*, devised something he called *shindai*, the "ancient Japanese art of bed fighting," a ritualized form of pillow fighting practiced between samurai warriors and geisha.

Others chimed in. "Mama Su's Spit-Fu" was defined as a shamanistic Tahitian fighting style that involved spitting betel nuts with extreme force and accuracy." "Upsidazi" was called "a complete waste of bricks." And those who mastered "Deja Fu" could hit opponents before the blows were actually thrown, thereby catching the victims off-guard, resulting in their being left with "the feeling that they've been kicked in the head this way before."

Michel Houellebecq & John Burdett

Thailand's Sex Industry

By the mid-1990s, Thailand had earned a reputation as one of the world's most popular destinations for sex tourists. In a major story, *Rolling Stone* magazine in 1991 headlined a story about AIDS and Bangkok "Death in the Candy Store." Two years later, the British company, Longman, published a *Dictionary of English Language and Culture* that described Bangkok as a city known for its Buddhist temples and as "a place where there are lots of prostitutes." Not long after that, in a story about Thailand's economy *Newsweek* quoted a Western diplomat in Bangkok as saying, "Thailand has two comparative advantages—sex and golf courses."

Thailand's government was not amused, but many writers who had made the Southeast Asian nation their new home or a favorite holiday spot laughed and started writing novels about the place, furthering its already soiled reputation. Novels about Western men rediscovering their penises and reclaiming their adolescence. Westerners became entranced and disappointed by beautiful, young Asian women. Novels became so numerous that they virtually became a genre—a popular and badly written genre. Bookshop shelves in Thailand groaned beneath their weight.

The two writers who found the biggest audiences worldwide were an already controversial French author who used the pen name Michel Houellebecq and a British attorney named John Burdett. Their novels placed in Thailand—Houellebecq writing just one and Burdett writing (so far) four—were among the better crafted of the lot, but none of the others exceeded them in grisly exploitation, creating a Thailand that was not only licentious but also ridiculous.

Houellebecq was born Michel Thomas on the island of La Réunion near Madagascar in 1958 and was a poet and author of a well-regarded biography of H.P. Lovecraft whose third novel, *Plateforme (Platform)*, published in France in 2001, told of a French travel company trying to avoid bankruptcy by converting hotels in the Caribbean and Thailand into sex resorts. Because the Thai resort's opening was marred by a massacre led by turban-wearing men with AK-47s, many regarded the book as little more than a Muslim rant.

Then came John Burdett, the son of a London policeman in 1951, an attorney who created an incorruptible, half-American Thai cop, the bastard son of a GI who fought in Vietnam and a prostitute who now distributes Viagra alongside the drinks in a bar she operates for senior citizens. Burdett also is known for his bizarre ways to die.

The Legacy of Suzie Wong

It has been clearly established by historians that prostitution in Thailand was not invented by foreigners and contemporary surveys show that the sex industry still mainly serves the local population, but the media and fiction writers, unsurprisingly, focus on sex involving foreigners. With some three hundred thousand Japanese troops stationed in Bangkok during World War Two and some thirty thousand British and Indian soldiers arriving as a transition force after it, Thailand had a lively commercial sex infrastructure accustomed to providing for foreigners. Report-edly, there were eighty-five cabarets spread across the capital, along with a nine-story brothel in Chinatown, touted as the world's largest, and in one block elsewhere, some two thousand women ready to become a new best friend.

With the withdrawal of military forces, of course, the number of sex venues fell, until the early 1960s when the US government made Bangkok one of nine approved R&R destinations during the American war in Vietnam and coordinating with the Thai government, oversaw the construction of a five-kilometer-long row of bars, massage parlors, cheap hotels and other facilities distant from the city's downtown. Unsurprisingly, Bangkok was a favorite destination for the 17,000 troops sent on R&R from Vietnam every month (fewer in the early years and later, as the war wound down).

At the peak of what became, at eleven years (1964-1975), America's longest war, there were an additional forty thousand American servicemen actually based in Thailand, most of them Air Force personnel on seven air bases, others what were called REMFs, or "Rear Echelon Motherfuckers," serving in Bangkok offices and port cities.

Thus were created Thailand's first sex tourists, men who came from elsewhere on holiday for what they called "intercourse and inebriation." The loss of revenue that resulted when the war ended and again a military force went home spurred a govern-ment campaign to attract European holidaymakers to take its place and in this fashion, perhaps, make sex tourism a permanent part of the GNP.

Concurrent with this government push was the emergence of a group of foreigners who decided to make Thailand home, largely on the basis of the sexual availability and affordability they encountered during holidays. The first were Vietnam vets who decided not to return to the United States. Others, joined them mainly from Europe and North America, and by the early

1990s they had their Boswell, a Canadian lawyer who called himself Christopher G. Moore.

It was what Moore called "The Land of Smiles Trilogy" that really launched the Bangkok noir as a genre, although in 1991-1993 when *A Killing Smile, A Bewitching Smile* and *A Haunting Smile* were published by a small Bangkok company (with limited distribution) he still had the city's sexpat book scene pretty much to himself. Moore then introduced and over the next fifteen years wrote ten novels about an American private detective, Vincent Calvino, and his saxophone-playing Thai police sidekick, Prachai (Pratt) Chongwatana, thus establishing himself as bar scene's authorial top gun.

By the late 1990s and into the twenty-first century, what *Time* magazine called "the art of titillation" (get it?) had become a runaway publishing craze in Thailand as new books by young foreigners recounting their misfortune in the bars seemed to appear every month—many of them badly written, poorly produced and seldom proofread.

"The farang-bargirl theme has been seized upon by a dreary succession of hacks," wrote Jim Eckardt in *The Nation*. "It's as if there were a whole school of Thai male writers living in New York City who confine their novels to Times Square."

Why were they published? According to David Johnson at Asia Books, Thailand's primary distributor, "They sold better than books that actually had something to say."

Up to the year 2000, none of the authors found a large audience. Then came two who did. The first was Michel Houellebecq, a French poet and author of a well-regarded biography of H.P. Lovecraft. His second novel, *Les Particules élémentaires (The Elementary Particles)* published in 1988, sold 300,000 copies in France alone, was described by *New York Times* as "a deeply repugnant read" and made the author an international star. Some called Houellebecq combative in a Gallic style that went back to the Marquis de Sade.

Three Worth Reading

Of all the Westerners who wrote about Asian prostitutes since Richard Mason met Suzie Wong on the Star Ferry in Hong Kong more than sixty years ago, there are three worth reading, for their factual accuracy as well as for their reasonableness, taking the position that when a relationship between a sex worker and a foreign visitor lasted about as long as a skyrocket, everybody should share the blame.

The first and perhaps best of these is *A Woman of Bangkok*, a novel that went into the bookstores the same year Suzie did (1957) and although it was not adapted by Hollywood, it remains in print today. In it, a hopelessly naive English salesman assigned by his firm to Thailand comes under the spell of a predatory dancehall queen named Vilai and known as the White Leopard. Young Reg—she aptly pronounces his name "Wretch"—becomes obsessed, losing his heart, his composure, his money, and his job. (Minus the drugs, think Charlie Sheen.) At one point, he even considers committing murder for her.

Despite the ordinary plot, and as much of a period piece as the novel is today, it remains one of the most honest and skillfully crafted depictions of the Bangkok sex scene of all time. The novel also is remarkable for its shift of a point of view, from Wretch's to Vilai's, without confusing effect. The author, an English vicar's son writing as Jack Reynolds, knew the women upon whom he based his characters and unlike most writers in the genre since, he understood them. Thus at the end of the story, there was no villain, nor any hero. The world was what it always has been: shades of gray, with splashes of unusually bright color.

The second novel was by Stephen Leather, a journalist born in Manchester, England, in 1951. He was already established as the author of thrillers set in the UK before writing several novels about Southeast Asia, including two Vietnam war-themed stories (*The Tunnel*

Rats, The Vets). His books sold well, but when his London publisher rejected a manuscript inspired by a disappointing experience of his own in the Bangkok bars, Leather made it available in 2000 as a free download through his website. Forty thousand downloads later, over a period of five years, he decided to publish *Private Dancer* himself. By 2012 he had sold close to fifty thousand copies of the paperback and another ten thousand as eBooks. Fans could also purchase a variety of tenuously related products on line, including undergarments and a teddy bear.

Much of *Private Dancer's* storyline is true and was told in an article in *Esquire* magazine some time before the book was written. In it, Leather falls for a bargirl in Bangkok's Nana Plaza, hires a detective who discovers she has a husband, and then plots his revenge. What distinguishes the book—besides the author's writing skill—is that the male is now the principle reason the relationship fails. Leather explained in an interview that he "wanted to write the standard 'ripped-off-by-a-hooker' story, but told in the voices of everyone involved so that you can see that everyone has a different opinion of what is happening, but that no one really understands what is going on…which pretty much sums up Thailand for me."

Timothy Hallinan has not found a mass audience yet but deserves special mention for four novels featuring Poke Rafferty, a travel writer who married a former Bangkok prostitute named Rose and adopted a street urchin called Maiow. It is Rose's story that is told in one of them, *The Queen of Patpong* (2010), and even if a small minority of the young Thai women who go into the bars catering to foreigners were trafficked—as happened to Rose—and most entered the trade quite willingly (sent instead by poverty), her story rings true, told in detail and compassionately.

The follow-up was greeted similarly. This was *Plateforme (Platform)*, published in France in 2001 and in English the following year. This told of a French travel company's plan to convert several hotels in the Caribbean and Thailand into sex resorts, thereby providing work for needy Asian women and satisfaction for the growing number of European sex tourists while solving the travel company's cash flow problem—a win-win-win situation.

"...you have several hundred million Westerners who have everything they could want but no longer manage to obtain sexual satisfaction: they spend their lives looking but they don't find it and they are completely miserable. On the other hand, you have several billion people who have nothing, who are starving, who die young, who live in conditions unfit for human habitation and who have nothing left to sell except their bodies and their unspoiled sexuality. It's simple, really simple to understand: it's an ideal trading opportunity. The money you could make is almost unimaginable: vastly more than from computing or biotechnology, more than the media industry; there isn't a single economic sector that is comparable."

Houellebecq was equally blunt when it came to his opinion of Muslims and following numerous anti-Islamic rants the book ended with a turbaned terrorist attack on one of the Thai resorts, killing more than a hundred whores and their customers.

In part because it seemed to anticipate 9/11 in the US and the Bali nightclub bombings, the book made Houellebecq a superstar. His poetry was admired and recorded by such diverse characters as the wife of the French president Carla Bruni-Sarkozy and Iggy Pop. But it also got him sued for his racist language, both in the novel and during a publicity tour. He won the lawsuit, but moved to Ireland.

Next came John Burdett, an attorney who worked for a dozen years in Hong Kong before quitting the law to become a fulltime writer. Although he had published two earlier novels, *A Personal History of Thirst* (1996) and *The Last Six Million Seconds* (1997), success came when he started writing about a half-American Thai cop named Sonchai Jitpleecheep, whose beat included Bangkok's by-now well established sex bar scene, a milieu that included his own mother's bar.

By 2012, Burdett had written four novels in the series, three of them placed entirely in Bangkok and notable for their shocking deaths. The first, *Bangkok 8*, published in 2003, opened with a man trying unsuccessfully to escape from a car that had been filled with cobras. The sequel, *Bangkok Tattoo* (2005), took its title from men who had had large tattoos removed from their bodies with a knife, and *Bangkok Haunts* (2007) had a murder connected to the production of a snuff film, while another unfortunate soul was placed inside a large wicker ball into which long nails had been hammered; the ball was then kicked around a field by playful elephants. Burdett did not make that up. Such was the punishment in at least one of Thailand's prisons not so long ago. Writers like Burdett dream of such stories and when they show up in real life, of course they are going to include them in their books.

Burdett defends his violence, inferring he saw as much practicing family law in England and criminal law in Hong Kong—an exaggeration, surely. His books, like Houellebecq's, are also peppered with factual and cultural errors, but he's a champion of the bargirls who lectures puritanical Westerners in *Bangkok 8*, saying: "These are all country girls, tough as a water buffalo, wild as swans, who can't believe how much they can make by providing to polite, benevolent, guilt-ridden, rich, condom-conscious *farangs* [foreigners] exactly the same service they would otherwise have to provide free without protection to rough drunken whoremongering husbands in their home villages." This is more hyperbole, although not without some foundation in fact.

In an introductory note in the same novel, Burdett explained that: "Bangkok is one of the world's great cities, all of which own red-light districts that find their way into the pages of novels from time to time. The sex industry in Thailand is smaller per capita than in Taiwan, the Philippines or the United States. That it is more famous is probably because Thais are less coy about it."

Still more hyperbole? Maybe not, this time.

V.S. Naipaul

A Million Mutinies Now

The grandson of indentured laborers sent to the Caribbean in the mid-nineteenth century, Vidiahar Suraiprasad (V.S.) Naipaul was born in rural poverty August 17, 1932, in Chaguanas, Trinidad, and after winning a scholarship to Oxford University declared, "I want to become top of my group. I have got to show these people that I can beat them at their own language." In a career that has spanned more than half a century and seen the publication of twenty-eight novels and non-fiction books, he has inarguably done just that.

Regarded as one of the greatest living writers in English, knighted in 1990 and awarded a long-anticipated Nobel Prize in 2001, his public persona at times has nearly sunk him in the same way misbehavior has overwhelmed the reputation of talented actors and musicians. His friend Paul Theroux in a memoir called him "a grouch, a skinflint, tantrum-prone, with race on the brain," creating an image then topped in his authorized biography by Patrick French, *The World Is What It Is* (2008), who described in wincing detail the forty-year-long abuse of his English wife that included a decades-long affair with an Anglo-Argentine woman (whom he also violently dominated), and an infatuation with prostitutes. This notoriety was furthered by controversial and frequently insensitive opinions that often seemed calculated to provoke—that women writers were inferior to men, that every country he visited and then profiled was corrupt and doomed, and that all non-Arab Muslims were the pawns of Islamic imperialists.

Despite such distraction, in novels set in the Caribbean, Africa, India, and Britain, Naipaul became what critic James Wood called in *The New Statesman* "the greatest living analyst of the colonial and post-colonial dilemma"—most remarkably in *A House for Mr Biswas* (1961), inspired by the life of his sign painter and sometime journalist father, his quasi-autobiographical *The Enigma of Arrival* (1987), and two short novels about an immigrant from India to the UK, *Half a Life* (2001) and *Magic Seeds* (2004), whose protagonist, Willie Chandran was described as "half a person, living a borrowed life."

His non-fiction country investigations on five continents, though generally gloomy, also were highly praised, most notably the book that followed his first visit to his ancestral homeland, *An Area of Darkness* (1964), and subsequently *India: A Million Mutinies Now* (1990) and *India: A Wounded Civilization* (1997), the three showing his perception moving from denunciation to hopefulness.

Dislocation, Oppression, Confusion

"The world is always in movement," said V.S. Naipaul in accepting the Nobel Prize in Literature in 2001. "People have everywhere at some time been dispossessed."

This is not news. Everyone is from somewhere else, given that all of us came from the Rift Valley in East Africa. Yet such words ring true today, with millions living in refugee camps, largely in Asia and Africa, and millions more blurring all cultural boundaries through migration to countries in the once predominantly

Caucasian, Christian West. The numbers of non-whites (Hispanic, African and Asian) now comprise forty-four percent of the population of the United States, headscarves are a hot button in France, and there's a Thai restaurant on every corner nearly everywhere.

As Naipaul said, human movement and subsequent confusion is not new, going back to the Jews wandering for forty years in the desert and far beyond. Yet, in recent times, no historical movement contributed more to the sense of dislocation than the construction and subsequent collapse of empire during the nineteenth and twentieth centuries. It is that era of colonial oppression and post-colonial disarray that Naipaul has made his patch, taking readers for an often uncomfortable tour of the "area of darkness" that the writer also claims is his own.

It began in Trinidad, "a dot on the map...a ridiculous little island," as he described it in his first novel, *The Mystic Masseur*, published when he was twenty-five and living in London. It was here that he grew up in a large, impoverished and dysfunctional family of mixed caste Indian heritage. Claiming his maternal grandfather was a Hindu Brahmin—a dubious claim for someone roped into indentured servitude—Naipaul admits that his father's side was of lower caste, which trumps the higher one in India; no mixed blood allowed. Never mind. Naipaul would transform his accented island patois into mellifluous Oxonian tones once he migrated to England and while working at the BBC he told a mulatto friend from Guiana that he was going to "become English." He further behaved for most of his life as if he were better than everyone else, so if it walks like a Brahmin and it quacks like a Brahmin, a Brahmin it shall be.

However personally disorienting (and satisfying) that metamorphosis must have been, in all his work Naipaul almost always took the underdog's side, insisting they didn't know what they were doing, either, but at least they usually came from innocence or ignorance and always were the most disadvantaged and oppressed. Even in England, he said, where numerous freedoms were guaranteed (religion, speech, etcetera), it meant nothing if there weren't any freedom of opportunity.

Predictably, the author's early works were set in the West Indies. The first, written when he was twenty-three years of age, secretly married to a fellow student from Oxford, and working for the BBC in London, was a linked collection of frequently funny short stories drawn from the Indian community in Port of Spain, called Miguel Street. Depicting a grim and survivalist life from which there seemed no escape, it would be four years before André Deutsch published it, who wanted a novel first.

Thus, not one but two novels, *The Mystic Masseur* and *The Suffrage of Elvira*, preceded the stories, both set in the same milieu and continuing the hard-bitten comic style that got him compared in the *Sunday Times* to Damon Runyon. Miguel Street then appeared, winning the Somerset Maugham Award. His financial situation hadn't changed much and his books had yet to find a readership in the US, but the young writer was winning praise from serious critics not only for his comic view but also his descriptions of how post-colonial politics worked, and didn't work, and what life for the disenfranchised was really like.

In 1961 came Naipaul's first big book, *A House for Mr Biswas*, a novel inspired by his father and his failed attempt to write stories about life in Trinidad and extricate his own family from his unbearable in-laws to live in a house of his own. *The Observer* called it a "Caribbean masterpiece," *London Magazine* said it was "one of the clearest and subtlest illustrations ever shown of the effects of colonialism" and Angus Wilson welcomed Naipaul into "the small group of unquestionably first-class novelists."

Naipaul continued to return to the Caribbean, but always in non-fiction and history, and in following novels the setting shifted to the UK and then to Africa, where he had taught for a year (and met another teacher, the young Paul Theroux, befriending him). It wasn't until 1964 that he made his first visit to India.

He didn't merely dislike his country of origin, he loathed it and the book that resulted, *Area of Darkness*, took its name from how he felt about his own past but also how he saw India, as a shithole, literally, where the people were petty, materialistic, corrupt, hypocritical, and callous to human suffering, and the sanitary habits left everything covered in excrement. It was, quite simply, one of the best crafted and most corrosive rants ever composed and, however much it was criticized in India, it also became a major influence on a generation of Indian writers coming up.

Later, speaking of one of his Africa novels, *In a Free State*, he explained, "I was not responsible for the world I was discovering. I was recording what I had discovered. I had no point of view. I think I just laid out the material, the evidence, and left people to make up their mind." In this fashion, in the 1970s and 1980s, he traveled five continents, writing reports for a variety of newspapers and magazines that left countries and cultures strewn in his wake like bloodied bodies on Armageddon's battlefield.

But he also made two more trips to India, publishing *India: A Wounded Civilization* in 1977 and *India: A Million Mutinies Now* in 1990, the last characterized by a softer, more positive judgment. These were then balanced—if that's the right word—by *Among the Believers: An Islamic Journey* (1981), a blistering attack on Islam that followed a tour of four non-Arab Muslim nations, Iran, Pakistan, Malaysia, and Indonesia.

There were more brilliant novels interspersed, including a second set in Africa, *A Bend in the River* (1979), and the quasi-autobiographical *The Enigma of Arrival* (1987), placed in England but in fact a meditation upon Trinidad. It was not until after he'd become a Nobel laureate in 2001 that he returned to India and the themes of exile and post-colonial confusion. This was in two short novels recounting the life of Willie Chandran, the son of a Brahmin mystic who founded the ashram that W. Somerset Maugham visited while researching his novel *The Razor's Edge* (thus the protagonist is named Willie, for Maugham).

In the first novel, (written, Naipaul said, to satisfy a publishing contract), *Half a Life* (2001), Willie, a wannabe writer, migrates to post-colonial England, then follows a girlfriend to Africa, where he remains for eighteen years as the days of empire wind down. In the sequel (possibly his last novel, Naipaul said), *Magic Seeds* (2004), Willie returns to India and joins one of the "million mutinies," an anti-government guerilla group whose members are as unattractive as they are misguided.

At one point, Willie asks one of his fellow revolutionaries, a veteran of thirty years in the metaphysical trenches, how he spends his time: "Avoiding capture, of course. Apart from that I am intensely bored. But in the middle of this boredom the soul never fails to sit in judgment on the world and never fails to find it worthless. It is not an easy thing to explain to outsiders. But it keeps me going."

Eventually Willie kills someone, surrenders and is jailed, but then is miraculously released to return once more to the UK, where he gets involved with a swish group of Brits who are every bit as hateful as the would-be revolutionaries. Naipaul puts a final thought into Willie's mind: "It is wrong to have an ideal view of the world. That's where the mischief starts. That's where everything starts unraveling."

And that's where the novel ends and perhaps the laureate's fiction career.

When Paul Theroux published a memoir of his onetime mentor, *Sir Vidia's Shadow*, in 1998, it was as if Naipaul was the target of a gigantic mud pie and all of the mud stuck and stank. He called him a "soothsayer who sees only evil" and a "miserable grouch," "a racist and a misogynist" who treated his wife, Pat, with "disdain and cruelty."

Then, in 2008, came Patrick French's authorized biography, *The World is What It Is*, the title taken from the first line of *A Bend in the River*. Theroux wrote a blurb for the cover: "It seems I didn't know half of all the horrors." From Naipaul's closed archives, which included his deceased wife's diaries (still unread by him), and in candid interviews Naipaul fully dropped his pants, admitting his infatuation with prostitutes might have been a factor in hurrying his wife's death and that he beat his Anglo-Argentine girlfriend of more than two decades so brutally his hands hurt and she could not appear in public. The racism, the rudeness, the condescension, the misogyny, the vanity, the sadistic sex, it was all there.

Critics reviewing the biography were appalled and devoted more ink to reviewing the author. Christopher Hitchens' article in *The Atlantic* was headlined "Cruel and Unusual." Elle magazine called him a "brilliant monster." French said in his introduction to the book that he was given no direction in its writing, nor when Naipaul read the finished manuscript did he ask to change a word. French called his willingness to allow such a book to be published in his lifetime "an act of narcissism and humility." The biographer also quoted his subject as saying, "I remain completely indifferent to how people think of me, because I was serving this thing called literature."

Naipaul said in his Nobel lecture, "…everything of value about me is in my books. I will go further now. I will say I am the sum of my books. Each book, intuitively sensed and, in the case of fiction, intuitively worked out, stands on what has gone before, and grows out of it. I feel that at any stage of my literary career it could have been said that the last book contained all the others.

"I am near the end of my work now," he said in conclusion. "I am glad to have done what I have done, glad creatively to have pushed myself as far as I could go."

Acknowledgements & Apologies

Noticeable by his absence from mention so far in this book is Edward Said, the man whose writings about Orientalism set the course for much of what is here. His thesis was simply that the Western perception of the Orient was based largely on prejudice and misconception. He was writing mainly about what is called the Near East, but his theory extended to the Far East, too, and many others have preceded me in exploring this area of thought.

I am further indebted to the glorious Internet—all praise Google!—as any researcher these days must be. I am certain that I've picked up some misstatements of fact because of this. (Trying to correct the many errors that seem to plague Wikipedia is an unending chore.) I apologize for any misinformation that I've here passed on and trust that the errors will not interfere with the point of view.

Many individuals have assisted me in preparing this book. Special thanks go to John Solt, who gave me a fuller and more accurate understanding of the geisha and vetted my chapter on James Clavell; Larry Grobel, who published a book of his interviews with James Michener; Phil Cunningham for years of information and advice about China, Thailand and Japan; John Frederick for keeping me honest on the subject of South Asia (and for suggesting authors who might otherwise have been overlooked); Steve Ross for his insightful comment on Suzie Wong; and Joe Leoni for helping me with Charlie Chan.

Many writers who took Asia as a subject are not in the book. For instance, I made an arbitrary decision to exclude virtually all novels about the West's three most recent Asian wars (with the Japanese, the North Koreans and the Vietnamese). I'm sure there are others I missed and to them (or their memory) and their fans, I extend my apologies.

Finally, I would like to thank all the authors who are included here for improving my reading list over the four years since the book was conceived. Now I shall return to my less challenging reading, enriched by this experience but not yet cured of a life-long addiction to mysteries. A statement that may, in fact, explain why I am so enamored of Asia. It's the mystery.

Thanks again to all.

The Tuttle Story: "Books to Span the East and West"

Most people are surprised to learn that the world's largest publisher of books on Asia had its humble beginnings in the tiny American state of Vermont. The company's founder, Charles Tuttle, came from a New England family steeped in publishing, and his first love was books—especially old and rare editions.

Tuttle's father was a noted antiquarian dealer in Rutland, Vermont. Young Charles honed his knowledge of the trade working in the family bookstore, and later in the rare books section of Columbia University Library. His passion for beautiful books—old and new—never wavered throughout his long career as a bookseller and publisher.

After graduating from Harvard, Tuttle enlisted in the military and in 1945 was sent to Tokyo to work on General Douglas MacArthur's staff. He was tasked with helping to revive the Japanese publishing industry, which had been utterly devastated by the war. When his tour of duty was completed, he left the military, married a talented and beautiful singer, Reiko Chiba, and in 1948 began several successful business ventures.

To his astonishment, Tuttle discovered that postwar Tokyo was actually a book-lover's paradise. He befriended dealers in the Kanda district and began supplying rare Japanese editions to American libraries. He also imported American books to sell to the thousands of GIs stationed in Japan. By 1949, Tuttle's business was thriving, and he opened Tokyo's very first English-language bookstore in the Takashimaya Department Store in Ginza, to great success. Two years later, he began publishing books to fulfill the growing interest of foreigners in all things Asian.

Though a westerner, Tuttle was hugely instrumental in bringing a knowledge of Japan and Asia to a world hungry for information about the East. By the time of his death in 1993, he had published over 6,000 books on Asian culture, history and art—a legacy honored by Emperor Hirohito in 1983 with the "Order of the Sacred Treasure," the highest honor Japan bestows upon non-Japanese.

The Tuttle company today maintains an active backlist of some 1,500 titles, many of which have been continuously in print since the 1950s and 1960s—a great testament to Charles Tuttle's skill as a publisher. More than 60 years after its founding, Tuttle Publishing is more active today than at any time in its history, still inspired by Charles Tuttle's core mission—to publish fine books to span the East and West and provide a greater understanding of each.